Women and Politics

Recent Titles in
Women and Society around the World

Women and Politics

Global Lives in Focus

Malliga Och, Editor

Women and Society around the World

ABC-CLIO®

An Imprint of ABC-CLIO, LLC
Santa Barbara, California • Denver, Colorado

Library of Congress Cataloging-in-Publication Data

Names: Och, Malliga, editor
Title: Women and politics : global lives in focus / Malliga Och, editor.
Description: Santa Barbara, California : ABC-CLIO, LLC, [2023] | Series: Women and society around the world | Includes bibliographical references and index.
Identifiers: LCCN 2022037478 | ISBN 9781440871900 (hardcover) | ISBN 9781440871917 (ebook)
Subjects: LCSH: Women—Political activity. | Women's rights. | Feminism.
Classification: LCC HQ1236 .O324 2023 | DDC 320.082—dc23/eng/20220804
LC record available at https://lccn.loc.gov/2022037478

ISBN: 978-1-4408-7190-0 (print)
 978-1-4408-7191-7 (ebook)

27 26 25 24 23   1 2 3 4 5

This book is also available as an eBook.

ABC-CLIO
An Imprint of ABC-CLIO, LLC

ABC-CLIO, LLC
147 Castilian Drive
Santa Barbara, California 93117
www.abc-clio.com

This book is printed on acid-free paper ∞

Manufactured in the United States of America

Contents

Series Foreword

Women's roles in society and the issues they face differ greatly from those of their male counterparts. In some corners of the world, women may manage households but are deemed unworthy of an education; in other areas, women scientists are pioneers in their fields, juggling family life and their careers. Gender inequality looms in all aspects of life, from employment to education to opportunities in sports and the military. What are the challenges, issues, and achievements women around the world face?

The *Women and Society around the World* series looks at women's lives as they pertain to various issues. The volumes cover topics such as

- Health;
- Violence;
- Religion;
- Sexuality;
- The military;
- Sports;
- Education; and
- Technology, among others.

Each volume begins with an introductory background essay on the volume's topic and is followed by a general chronology of significant world events pertaining to the topic. Eight chapters follow, focusing on the world's regions: United States and Canada, Latin America and the Caribbean, Europe, North Africa and the Middle East, Sub-Saharan Africa, Central and East Asia, South and Southeast Asia, and Oceania. All chapters include a list of further reading resources, and a selected bibliography at the end of each volume provides students with additional print and electronic resources for further research needs.

The chapters examine women in each region with broad brushstrokes, highlighting specific examples of key customs and policies in specific countries that help to illuminate cultural nuances among countries within each region. They can be read alone or be reviewed cumulatively to make cross-cultural comparisons. The volumes are ideal for high school students doing projects, undergraduate students writing research papers, and even general readers interested in learning about women's lives.

The goal of the *Women and Society around the World* series is to depict the roles of women worldwide by exploring the major issues they face and the accomplishments they have made, especially in terms of bridging the gap in gender inequality and fighting for basic human rights. While readers will learn about the challenges that half of the world's population face, they will also discover the empowering ways women succeed and overcome social and cultural barriers in their daily lives.

Acknowledgments

This volume would not have been possible without the support I have received over the years from colleagues and friends. When I embarked on my career as a women and politics scholar, I found a community of wonderful strong women who believe that, as women, we must raise each other up. Many people I met along the way—especially Sarah Childs, Louise Davidson-Schmich, Fiona Mackay, Susan Franceschet, Amy Atchison, Jennifer Piscopo, Christina Xydias, Shauna Shames, Anna Sampaio, Farida Jalalzai, and Karen Beckwith—provided me with encouragement, advice, and a shoulder to cry on. I can never thank them enough. Marie Wilson's book *Closing the Leadership Gap* was fundamental in making me realize the work we still have ahead of us to achieve political parity, setting me on a rewarding career path I could never have foreseen as an undergraduate. I hope that the book you are holding in your hands right now will play a little part in lighting the fire for a new generation to continue to fight toward women's political equality.

Preface

Malliga Och

Have women achieved political parity? To many, the answer is a resounding yes. After all, women can vote in every country in the world, and wherever we look today, we see women in politics: German chancellor Angela Merkel, Liberian president Ellen Sirleaf Johnson, and New Zealand prime minister Jacinda Ardern all invoke images of powerful leaders. In the United States, the 2020 Democratic primary field included six women presidential candidates. Countries as diverse as Canada, France, Rwanda, Ethiopia, Costa Rica, and Finland have gender-balanced cabinets, where the same numbers of women and men are appointed to cabinet positions (IKnowPolitics 2019). Gender-balanced parliaments exist in Rwanda (61.3 percent), Cuba (53.4 percent), the United Arab Emirates (50 percent) and Mexico (50 percent), and in another twenty countries— for example, in Sweden, Namibia, and Argentina—women occupy over 40 percent of parliamentary seats (IPU Parline 2022b).

Yet, when we look a little bit closer, the picture becomes more complicated. When it comes to **universal suffrage**, it took 122 years from the first time women were granted the right to vote in 1893 (New Zealand) until 2015 when Saudi Arabia became the last country to enfranchise women. While women leaders were lavishly praised in 2020 for their handling of the COVID-19 pandemic, women only lead 22 countries, and 119 countries have never elected a woman as president or prime minister (UN Women 2021). While gender-balanced cabinets under Trudeau and Macron made headlines, women only make up 20.1 percent of cabinets globally. Three countries have majority-women parliaments, but the average percentage of women in parliaments worldwide is 26.5 percent (IPU Parline 2022a). And twenty-three countries have fewer than 10 percent of women in their parliaments, including Japan, Lebanon, and Sri Lanka (IPU

Parline 2022b). Further, progress has been uneven and slow across regions and political areas. For example, the average of women in parliament ranges from 32.3 percent in the Americas to 18.6 percent in the Pacific (IPU Parline 2022a). Similarly, Europe has elected the largest number of women leaders, while North America and the Middle East have elected only one woman to executive office (Jalalzai 2019).

Thus, the better answer to the question, *Have women achieved political parity?* is *kind of.* While women in politics have undoubtedly come a long way, women are still far from political parity. At the current rate, political parity will not be achieved until 2051 for the executive (presidents and prime ministers), 2077 for cabinets, and 2063 for parliaments (UN Women 2021).

This book will help readers understand the multitude of barriers women face in politics and the solutions that exist today to address and remove these barriers. The book starts off with an introduction that provides an overview of the three main barriers to politics: institutional structures, socioeconomic conditions, and political culture. The introduction orients the reader to the big issues and questions we ask when studying women in politics. The remainder of the book is divided into eight chapters that discuss the status of women in politics in each world region. Each chapter was written by regional experts and is divided into three main parts: (1) a history of suffrage, (2) an overview of the status of women in politics today, and (3) a discussion of the unique challenges for women in politics, including ways forward to political parity for each region. Throughout the volume, authors will use political science terms that are crucial to understanding the topic but that might be unfamiliar to the reader. For an explanation of these terms (highlighted in **bold**), the reader should consult the glossary.

No discussion about women in politics is complete without asking *why*—why should we care about political parity? At the core of the idea stands the belief that men cannot adequately represent women because women as a group have a distinct identity and lived experiences that differ from the interests and identities of men. Thus, women's interests and ideas will not be adequately represented without women being present in politics (Pitkin 1967; Phillips 1995).

We can differentiate between several arguments in favor of political parity (Hughes and Paxton 2019). The justice argument presents a rights-based claim: because women constitute half of the population in every country, they should constitute half the representatives in government. The democracy argument holds that no country can be considered a fully fledged democracy unless women are equally represented in politics. In contrast, utility arguments emphasize the additional value and usefulness that women bring to politics. For example, the experience argument holds that women bring different perspectives and ideas to politics. There is plenty of research to back up this claim (Piscopo 2011; Swers 2005). Studies have indeed found that women, more often than men, engage in and initiate debates about women's issues, that women are twice as likely as men to support feminist and pro-equality measures, and that women are more likely to cosponsor or sponsor bills addressing women's issues. Another line of argument holds that women represent an untapped resource; by including women in politics, governments will draw on the full range of talents available in society, which in turn will improve policy processes and outcomes. For example, women legislators in the United States have been found to provide better constituency service by delivering more federal money to their districts (Volden, Wiseman, and Wittmer 2013), and greater number of women in parliament have also been linked to lower defense spending globally (Koch and Fulton 2011).

In the end, it does not matter what kind of argument is put forward. Together, they make a powerful case for women's inclusion in politics and the achievement of true and lasting political equality. Without it, women will remain second-class citizens who are unable to decide their own fates.

REFERENCES

Hughes, Melanie M., and Pamela Paxton. 2019. "The Political Representation of Women over Time." In *The Palgrave Handbook of Women's Political Rights*, edited by Susan Franceschet, Mona Lena Krook, and Netina Tan, 33–51. London: Palgrave Macmillan UK.

IKnowPolitics. 2019. "Here Are the Most Gender-Balanced Cabinets in the World Today." October 2, 2019. https://www.iknowpolitics.org/en/learn/knowledge-resources/here-are-most-gender-balanced-cabinets-world-today

IPU (Inter-Parliamentary Union) Parline. 2022a. "Global and Regional Averages of Women in National Parliaments." https://data.ipu.org/women-averages

IPU Parline. 2022b. "Monthly Ranking of Women in National Parliaments." https://data.ipu.org/women-ranking?month=6&year=2021

Jalalzai, Farida. 2019. "Women Leaders in National Politics." In *Oxford Research Encyclopedia of International Studies*, edited by Nukhet Sandal. Oxford University Press.

Koch, Michael T., and Sarah A. Fulton. 2011. "In the Defense of Women: Gender, Office Holding, and National Security Policy in Established Democracies." *Journal of Politics* 73 (1): 1–16.

Phillips, Anne. 1995. *The Politics of Presence*. New York: Oxford University Press.

Piscopo, Jennifer M. 2011. "Rethinking Descriptive Representation: Rendering Women in Legislative Debates." *Parliamentary Affairs* 64 (3): 448–472.

Pitkin, Hanna F. 1967. *The Concept of Representation*. Berkeley: University of California Press.

Swers, Michele L. 2005. "Connecting Descriptive and Substantive Representation: An Analysis of Sex Differences in Cosponsorship Activity." *Legislative Studies Quarterly* 30 (3): 407–433.

UN Women. 2021. "Facts and Figures: Women's Leadership and Political Participation." January 15, 2021. https://www.unwomen.org/en/what-we-do/leadership-and-political-participation/facts-and-figures

Volden, Craig, Alan E. Wiseman, and Dana E. Wittmer. 2013. "When Are Women More Effective Lawmakers Than Men?" *American Journal of Political Science* 57 (2): 326–341.

Introduction

Malliga Och

WOMEN AS VOTERS

The very first step toward equal representation is gaining universal suffrage, that is, the right to vote and stand for election. The struggle for women's suffrage started in the late 1800s and continued until 2015. Women won universal suffrage in three waves centered around World War I, World War II, and the periods of decolonization when colonies achieved independence. Women suffrage in most countries was delivered piecemeal (IPU n.d.): First, countries limited suffrage to the right to vote and only later allowed women to run for office (or vice versa). For example, women in New Zealand could vote in 1893 but had to wait until 1919 to be able to run for office. In the United States, women could stand for elections since 1788 in some territories and states but did not gain the right to vote until 1920. Second, a contested question was whether women should be granted the right to vote under the same conditions as men. At that time, the vote was often restricted to white, educated, and wealthy men. Some suffragettes, particularly those belonging to the international socialist movement, wanted to extend the right to vote to more people, while upper-class, educated, wealthy, and white women, who often were the main leaders of the suffragette movements, preferred to have the vote limited by socioeconomic status and race. As a result, many of the early states who granted women the right to vote limited the vote to a small group of women. For example, in Australia, white women were enfranchised in 1902, while Aboriginal women had to wait until 1962. Similarly, in South Africa, white women were granted the right to vote in 1930; however, Indian and Colored women (mixed race) had to wait until 1984, and Black women had to wait until the apartheid regime ended in 1994.

Opposition to suffrage was particularly strong during the first wave, during which men (and some women) argued that women did not have the mental capabilities and lacked the qualifications to engage in politics, that women's God-given place was in the house, and that women's enfranchisement would lead to the destruction of traditional family values. If these arguments sound familiar, it is because they are still voiced today whenever women demand greater equality and access to public life that takes them away from their domestic responsibilities. The right to vote was not won easily and peacefully either: the early suffragette movements in the United States and the United Kingdom often employed militant tactics and engaged in civil disobedience to be heard and garner support for their cause. Public protests, hunger strikes, and the storming of legislatures were not uncommon. In the United Kingdom, suffragettes chained themselves to the ladies' gallery in Parliament and destroyed the windows of businesses. In the United States, Susan B. Anthony illegally cast a vote in the 1868 election and was arrested for voter fraud and fined $100. She refused to pay the fine and subsequently organized other women to illegally cast their votes in the 1872 election (Hawkesworth 2012). In the end, the early struggles for suffrage paid off. By the 1960s, women suffrage was seen as a sine qua non for a modern state and was adopted without much debate and fanfare during the third wave of suffrage extension.

Women's Political Engagement

Overall, women tend to vote at lower rates than men. Even though we lack reliable data that disaggregates women's and men's voter turnout, there are signs that this trend is slowly changing. At least in industrialized countries, the voting gap is slowly narrowing or, in some cases, has been reversed. In the Global South, the gender gap in voter turnout still favors men (Henderson and Jeydel 2014). The same is true for women's political engagement, where studies have shown that women are less likely to be knowledgeable about, discuss, or be interested in politics (Karp and Banducci 2008). One major reason why women are less likely to vote and participate in politics is a lack of education and knowledge of the political process. Educational discrepancies—particularly in literacy levels—prevent many women from political participation, including voting. A study of seventeen Latin American countries found that the gender gap in political participation closes when we take women's education, employment, and economic resources into account (Desposato and Norrander 2009).

Put differently, once women receive a formal education and enter the workforce, they are more likely to participate in politics. The authors conclude that the closing of the gender gap in political participation in industrialized countries is because women have made important gains in education and entered professional careers. In the United States, several studies have also shown that women become more interested and engaged in politics as the number of women in offices increases (Campbell and Wolbrecht 2006; Reingold and Harrell 2010).

We now know that women's political engagement is different from that of men, but do women also vote for different parties than men? The answer is yes. When it comes to voters' preferences, we can differentiate between a traditional and a modern **gender gap**. A traditional gender gap exists when more women than men support conservative parties. The traditional gender gap was particularly pronounced after women gained suffrage in the first part of the twentieth century, when women and conservative parties shared religious and traditional family values (Norris and Inglehart 2001). The modern gender gap—when more women than men vote for parties on the left—did not emerge until the 1980s. The 1960s–1970s witnessed societal upheaval, including the rise of the women's liberation movement. During this time, women graduated from college and entered the workforce in greater numbers. For the first time, the pill allowed women to limit the number of children that they would bear and space the timing of their children to match with their educational and career aspirations. With increased education levels and independent streams of income, divorce became more common and acceptable, as women were no longer financially dependent on a husband. Young people decided to live together without getting married and postponed having children or had children outside of marriage. At the same time, religious attachment and church membership started to decline, making changes in gender roles and relations more societally acceptable. The women's liberation movement of the 1970s and all accompanying societal changes ultimately expressed themselves in the emergence of a modern gender gap, where women aligned themselves more closely with parties on the left, which support women's equality and progressive gender roles, while rejecting the traditional family and religious values of parties on the right, which women used to support.

The modern gender gap is largely driven by economic development and changes in societal attitudes that have led to more progressive gender roles. Thus, in countries with less advanced economies and a more traditional culture—such as postcommunist countries and those in the Global South—traditional gender gaps are still commonly found (Giger 2009). In contrast, the modern gender gap mostly exists in industrialized countries as diverse as Austria, Sweden, Argentina, and Canada and is especially noticeable among young voters. It is important to note, however, that in some industrialized countries, such as Great Britain, the traditional gender gap still exists, even though it has narrowed significantly over the years (Lopes 2015). In the United States, the modern gender gap is particularly pronounced: in 2020, 16 percent more women voted for Biden compared to Trump, and 13 percent more women voted for Clinton than Trump in 2016 (CAWP 2021). This means that in many countries, women voters are critical to win elections, and as a result, political parties and leaders have started directly catering to women by promising women-friendly policies to win their support.

This overview of the suffragette movement and women as voters has necessarily been brief and serves only to orient the reader. One major challenge is that data on women voter turnout and political engagement is sparse and often does not take a comparative approach (comparing different countries to each other) or a longitudinal perspective (comparing turnout and engagement over time). As a result, the upcoming chapters will only include a discussion on women as voters and women's political engagement where data is available, while most of each chapter focuses on women in parliament and the executive.

WOMEN AS MEMBERS OF PARLIAMENT

Once women secured the right to vote, the focus shifted to getting women elected to parliament. Parliaments differ, whether they are unicameral or **bicameral**. When they are bicameral, the lower house usually has more power than the upper house. In parliamentary democracies specifically, the upper house is often by appointment and only has ceremonial or advising functions. A prominent example is the British Parliament (Westminster); it consists of the popularly elected House of Commons and the House of Lords, which only serves an advisory function. Thus, throughout the book, we will focus on women in the lower chamber if the parliament in question is a bicameral parliament.

Overall, we evaluate women's numerical representation, formally called the descriptive representation of women, based on the percentage of women in parliament. Parliaments are considered gender balanced when

Table I.1   Descriptive Representation of Women—Regional Averages as of September 2022

World Region	Percentage of Women Parliamentarians
Americas	34.4
Europe	31.3
Sub-Saharan Africa	26.4
Asia	21.2
Middle East and North Africa	18.3
Pacific	19.9

Source: Inter-Parliamentary Union (2022a).

women occupy 40–60 percent of parliamentary seats (Dahlerup 2017). Unfortunately, progress has been slow, incremental, and uneven. In 2022, women make up 26.4 percent of elected officials worldwide (IPU 2022a), ranging from 61.3 percent in Rwanda to no women in Yemen (IPU 2022b). Likewise, we also see a variation across regions (see table I.1). The Americas and Europe typically perform the best, while the Middle East and North Africa (MENA) region and the Pacific perform the worst. Against this backdrop, we need to ask ourselves these questions: why are there so few women in political office, and how can we increase the number of women representatives?

Barriers to Political Office

We can identify three major barriers to political office: institutional, socioeconomic, and cultural. Institutional factors are the rules of the (political) game, for example, how votes are allocated, the laws detailing who can run for political office, and any norms that determine how open political actors, such as political parties, are to recruiting women for politics. Socioeconomic factors refer to the resources and capabilities individuals need to run for office, for example, access to education and employment that endow individuals with the ability to mount a political campaign and execute the duties of political office. Cultural factors describe the prevailing cultural norms in society and how likely society sees women as capable political leaders.

Institutional Barriers

While each institutional factor has its own influence on the descriptive representation of women, research has shown that electoral systems have the greatest impact on women's representation. Electoral systems are a set of rules that determine how votes are translated into seats. There are two major electoral systems: proportional and majority. Majority systems are also called first-past-the post systems: whoever wins the most votes is elected. In proportional systems, seats are allocated based on the proportion of the vote a party wins: if a party wins 30 percent of the overall vote, it receives 30 percent of the seats in parliament. Countries with proportional electoral system have more women in parliament on average than countries with majority systems. In a 2006 study that compared the average percentage of women in parliament across electoral systems found that majority systems have on average 10.5 percent women in parliament, whereas proportional systems have an average of 19.6 percent (Norris 2006, 42).

One reason for this difference is that majoritarian systems are typically associated with lower district magnitude while proportional systems have a higher district magnitude. The district magnitude refers to the number of representatives elected in an electoral district. In a single-member district, voters can only elect one representative. In a multimember district, voters elect more than one representative. Single-member districts are negatively correlated with women's representation because single-member districts represent a zero-sum game: the victory of one candidate means the defeat of all other candidates. Thus, parties want to nominate the strongest possible candidate. Unfortunately, party leaders often believe that women are less electable than men—even though research has proven otherwise. In contrast, in multimember districts, parties can expect to win more than just one seat, and thus the nomination of a woman candidate is less risky. Further, parties can signal their progressive nature by nominating a diverse slate of candidates to win over voters who put a premium on diversity. First-past-the-post systems, such as the one used in the United States, are typically paired with single-member districts, while the proportional electoral systems used in much of Europe are combined with multimember districts.

Party ideology plays another important part when it comes to the election of women. Parties on the right emphasize traditional family values, while parties on the left support progressive values that include gender equality. Parties on the right elect fewer women to parliament than parties on the left. This party gender gap is particularly pronounced in the United States, where the Democratic Caucus has more than double the number of women than the Republican Caucus in Congress (see chapter 1 for an in-depth discussion). Why is this the case? First, parties on the right embrace traditional gender roles that see women's rightful place in the home as a wife and mother and are less likely to consider women fit to be political leaders. And vice versa, conservative women might be reluctant to run for office, as conservative family values dictate the priority of the home and the family for women. Second, parties on the right object to the use of affirmative action such as electoral gender quotas, which have proven one of the fastest and most efficient ways to increase the number of women in politics. In contrast, parties on the left, particularly green parties, were first to introduce electoral gender quotas aiming for a gender-balanced caucus where women make up at least 50 percent of the parties' representatives in parliament. Additionally, parties on the left historically have close ties with the women's movement and have a long history of advocating for equality and inclusion of marginalized groups such as women and minorities.

Electoral gender quotas are the most effective institutional tool to improve women's descriptive representation leading to an enduring and often accelerated increase in the number of women elected. Countries with quotas have on average 7 percent more women in parliament than coun-tries without quotas (IPU 2019). The most common argument against quo-tas is that they force parties to nominate unqualified women to meet the quotas. However, plenty of studies have shown that women elected via quotas are equally and often more qualified than their male counterparts and women not elected via quotas (Franceschet, Krook, and Piscopo 2012).

Quotas can be applied to different stages in the electoral process. Most quotas focus on the nomination stage and mandate that a certain number of candidates must be women. Voluntary political party quotas are adopted by individual political parties that promise to appoint a certain percentage of women to their candidate lists. In proportional electoral systems, voters do not vote for a candidate but for a party. Each party nominates a slate of candidates. Voters then vote for the party list rather than individual candi-dates. If a party wins 30 percent of a total of one hundred parliamentary seats (so thirty seats total), the top thirty candidates on the party list are elected to parliament. For example, the German Green Party has a 50 per-cent candidate quota for its party lists, which means that half of the candi-dates on its party list must be women.

In contrast, legislative electoral quotas are mandated by law and equally require that a certain percentage of political candidates are women. When quotas are applied to party lists, it is of utmost importance that women are not just put at the bottom of the party list but receive spots at the top of the list, which increases their chances of becoming elected. For example, if a party nominates one hundred candidates on its list, women must make up 50 percent of these candidates. The party can nominate women for the spots fifty through one hundred and comply with the quota requirement. Then, in the election, if the party wins thirty seats, the top thirty candidates on the list are elected, which means they are all men since the party did not nominate women until spot fifty on the list. Thus, rank-order rules—for example, where men and women are alternated on a candidate list—are important for electoral gender quotas to be effective.

Finally, reserved seats focus on the last stage in the electoral process, the electoral outcome. Reserved seats are legally mandated and require that women occupy at least a certain number of seats in parliament. For example, in Rwanda, 30 percent of parliamentary seats must be reserved for women.

Socioeconomic Barriers

To a certain extent, the presence of women is a question of having a supply of individuals willing and qualified to run for office. The candidate pool is typically made up of managers, academics, lawyers, and journalists (Norris and Lovenduski 1995). What these professions have in common is that they require skill sets like those needed in politics. First, all professions require a university degree. During university studies, individuals acquire skills such as public speaking and a general knowledge about political and legal rules. Second, university studies allow individuals to amass resources necessary for political success: creating professional networks and engaging with professional associations allow individuals to tap into these very connections for fundraising and political support. Finally, these professions come with prestige, flexibility, and financial compensation that allow people to afford the time and money necessary for a political career.

If women are not present in these professions, their chance of being recruited as a candidate is lower than for a man. While women have closed the gap in university education, and in many countries even represent most university graduates, women are still underrepresented in managerial positions, particularly in the highest echelons of business, academia, and the law. Instead, women make up most part-time workers and are more commonly found in feminine professions such as nursing, teaching, or administration, with limited opportunities for career advancement into management positions. Thus, countries where equal numbers of men and women graduate from university and where women have entered professions from which political candidates are traditionally recruited should have more women in parliament. However, the findings have been mixed. While some studies have found links between the socioeconomic status of women and women's descriptive representation, other studies have not. Thus, as with cultural factors, socioeconomic conditions are a possible but not the only explanation for the number of women in parliament.

Political Culture

Another barrier to office is the political culture of a country. Generally, countries with a traditional culture are less likely to elect women than **egalitarian cultures** (Norris and Inglehart 2001). Traditional cultures emphasize women's importance in the home as caring mothers and wives. Consider how women candidates are always asked about who is taking care of their children while they are on the campaign trail; men are very rarely asked the same question, as people assume that the wife will be responsible for childcare. Accordingly, women are seen as less capable political leaders and often elicit negative responses when running for office. These negative responses can go far beyond sexist comments directed toward women on social media or a refusal to vote for women candidates. More recently, scholars and women parliamentarians have called out the problem of physical and sexual violence against women in politics as well as deeply personal and misogynistic attacks by the media and other members of parliament against women in politics (see specifically chapters 2, 4, 5, and 8 for a more in-depth discussion).

Traditional culture affects women's representation in two ways. On the one hand, women are less likely to step forward as candidates because they either do not consider a political career to be appropriate for women or because they fear a backlash against their candidacy. On the other hand, political parties are less willing to recruit and nominate women because they are either outright opposed to women in politics or because they do not believe that voters will support them. Countries in the Middle East typically have traditional cultures (see chapter 4 for a detailed discussion), as do countries with strong Catholic or Orthodox roots (Kenworthy and Malami 1999). But, as the following chapters show, traditional cultures are not confined to these contexts. Aspiring and existing women representatives must contend with traditional cultures and gender attitudes to varying degrees across regions.

In contrast, countries with an **egalitarian culture** are more likely to elect women to political office, as both women and men are seen as capable political leaders. Countries where women won the right to vote early on and countries with strong women's movements typically have a more egalitarian culture. Likewise, societies are more open to gender equality when people are better educated, less religious, and women are part of the workforce. A typical example for egalitarian countries are those in Scandinavia, which traditionally have had a high proportion of women in politics (see chapter 3). While there is a link between political culture and women's descriptive representation, evidence has been mixed and by itself cannot explain the number of women in politics (Henderson and Jeydel 2014).

To summarize, there are three major barriers to women's political representation: institutional, socioeconomic, and cultural. Of these three, institutional factors—most noticeably the electoral system and the presence of electoral gender quotas—have the greatest impact on women's representation, as all the following chapters show. In contrast, socioeconomic and cultural barriers are potential barriers but cannot explain women's absence from politics by themselves. In most cases, it is a combination of barriers that keep women out of politics.

WOMEN AS LEADERS

Women are not only absent from parliament but also from executive office; most countries have never had a woman president or prime minister. It depends on a country's constitution which one is the more powerful position. Often, one position is elected and the other appointed. The elected position usually holds the most executive power. In countries that have both a president and prime minister, the prime minister is the head of government who commands legislative power, sets the political agenda, and appoints cabinet members. The president, if one exists, is largely symbolic and has little political power. For example, in constitutional monarchies, such as the United Kingdom, a queen or king rather than a president is the symbolic head of state, and the prime minister is the political leader of the country. In countries such as the United States, the president is both a symbolic figurehead and has vast executive powers. The exception are **semi-presidential systems** such as France where powers are equally distributed between the president and prime minister.

In 1965, the island country of Sri Lanka became the first country to ever elect a woman prime minister. As of 2022, 121 women have served in executive office, not including interim leaders: 59.5 percent (72 women) served as prime ministers and 40.4 percent (49 women) served as presidents (data courtesy of Farida Jalalzai). The great majority of countries have elected a woman to executive office only once. Notable exemptions are Finland (three women prime ministers and one president), Iceland (one woman president and two women prime ministers), New Zealand (three women prime ministers), Poland (three women prime ministers), and Peru (four women prime ministers). More so than national parliaments, the presidency and premierships have largely remained male domains (table I.2).

Women typically come to power through four different pathways: family ties, surrogacy, as insiders, or as outsiders. The family path is most common in Asia, where women rise to the presidency/premiership because they belong to a prominent political family. For example, the first woman prime minister of Thailand, Yingluck Shinawatra, was the sister of ousted former prime minister Thaksin Shinawatra. The surrogacy path describes a scenario where a woman obtains the presidency/premiership after her

Table I.2   Women in the Executive by Region as of 2020

Region	Women Prime Ministers	Women Presidents
Africa	13	5
Asia	6	10
Caribbean	7	2
Europe	34	22
Latin America	4	9
Micronesia	0	1
Middle East	2	0
North America	1	0
Oceania	5	0

Source: Data courtesy of Farida Jalalzai (excludes interim or appointed leaders).

political spouse or a relative has died. For example, Argentinian president Isabel Martínez de Perón succeeded her late husband, Juan Domingo Perón, when he died in his third presidential term. The familial and surrogacy paths to power remain a common path to office for women, particularly in nondemocratic systems, where name recognition, networks, and economic and political resources of prominent political families aid women's election. Familiarity and trust in those politically prominent families may also help women overcome any gender-based concerns voters might have. In fact, two-thirds of women in executive office in Asia have come to power through either family ties or surrogacy (see chapters 6 and 7 for a detailed discussion).

In contrast, the insider path requires women to slowly climb the political ladder by running for local, state, and federal office as well as serving in party leadership positions prior to becoming a candidate for executive office. German chancellor Angela Merkel and British prime ministers Margaret Thatcher and Theresa May are the most famous examples of the insider path (see sidebars in chapter 3 for profiles of Merkel and Thatcher). An alternative path to office is through being a prominent outsider who wants to challenge the status quo—think of the candidacy of Carly Fiorina in the 2016 Republican presidential primary as an example. Of all the different pathways to office, the outsider path is the least successful.

Even in cases where women have achieved executive office, they are more likely to be elected to the less powerful position. Most notably, in countries where the executive power is divided between a prime minister and president, the woman is typically elected to the less powerful and more ceremonial position (Jalalzai 2019). Women are more likely to be elected in countries with parliamentary systems than those with presidential systems. In parliamentary systems, voters elect the parliament, and the party who wins the most votes then forms the government; the leader of the majority party then becomes the prime minister. In most countries, no single party can command the majority of seats in parliament, and as a result, coalition governments in which several parties form a majority governing coalition are common. In presidential systems, parliament and the president are both directly elected by voters in two different elections.

There are two main reasons why more women leaders are elected in parliamentary systems. First, in parliamentary systems, executive power is subject to parliamentary control, and power is shared between the executive and the legislative branch. This limits the power that leader can wield, and coalition governments, where the government is made up of two or more parties, further constrain their ability to act and require constant negotiation and compromise. Compromise, deliberation, and consensus are traits stereotypically associated with women, which makes women seem to be a better fit for a premiership. In contrast, in countries with strong presidential systems, such as the United States, the president can act with great autonomy and is not subject to parliamentary control. A major reason why the presidency remains more elusive to women is the strong masculine character of the office; the image of commander in chief typically evokes leadership traits stereotypically associated with men: decisive, strong, and unwavering are just a few that come to mind.

Second, parliamentary systems allow for the removal of the prime minister in multiple ways, such as through a vote of no confidence, the dissolution of parliament, or a party vote, which makes the prospect of a woman prime minister seem less risky and maybe even less threatening. In presidential systems, the parliament cannot remove the president from office except for through impeachment, which requires criminal conduct by the president; as a result, presidential impeachments are relatively rare. Brazilian president Dilma Rousseff and South Korean president Park Geunhye are notable exceptions to this rule (see chapters 2 and 6, respectively, for more details).

In contrast to women's descriptive representation in national parliaments, structural and cultural barriers are less important for electing women to executive office. Countries where women have a low socioeconomic status, such as Liberia and Haiti, have had women leaders, while countries where women have a relatively higher socioeconomic status have never elected a woman to executive office, for example, Japan and the United States. The same is true for traditional cultures. Women have been presidents or prime ministers in Poland and Brazil—both heavily Catholic countries—while the Netherlands, a Protestant country with egalitarian values, has not. When it comes to explaining the election of women to the presidency or premiership, then, institutional factors, particularly the power and authority of the office, determine women's likely access to executive office.

Women in Cabinet

Women not only serve in the executive as leaders but also as cabinet **ministers**; in the United States, a member of the cabinet is referred to as *secretary*. As in all other areas, women are grossly underrepresented in cabinets. As of 2021, women made up 21 percent of cabinet ministers worldwide (UN Women 2021). The relative lack of women in cabinet positions explains why French president Emmanuel Macron and Canadian prime minister Justin Trudeau both made headlines when they appointed gender parity cabinets. At the time of writing, a mere fourteen countries have gender parity cabinets, where women make up at least 50 percent of cabinet ministers. However, cabinet ministers are typically assigned to so-called pink portfolios, such as education, health care, and welfare, which are topics stereotypically considered to be women's issues (Atchison and Down 2019). These portfolios are generally less prestigious, carry less influence, and are less likely to serve as stepping stones to the presidency or premiership. The most common portfolios held by women are family affairs (including children, the elderly, the disabled, and youths), social affairs, the environment, employment or labor, and women's affairs or gender equality (UN Women 2021). In contrast, men typically hold traditional masculine domains, such as defense, the interior, foreign affairs, and finance, which are more powerful and influential and are commonly seen as great preparation for the highest executive office.

A WAY FORWARD FOR POLITICAL PARITY

Now that we understand the barriers to office, what are some ideas that could advance political parity? Across all chapters, authors agree that electoral gender quotas are the fastest and most effective way to address women's underrepresentation. There are several benefits to electoral gender quotas when properly designed and implemented. First, they can significantly increase the number of women from one election to the next. Second, once elected to office, women can prove themselves by illustrating that the sky will not fall when women are elected and that they are as good as, if not better than, the male politicians. Over time, quotas help normalize the presence of women in politics and potentially lead to more egalitarian attitudes toward women. Third, when parties are forced to nominate women, the commonly held beliefs that there are not enough women interested or qualified for politics are contested. Quotas force political parties to look beyond their common recruitment pool and strategies and reconsider what it means to be qualified for office.

Another solution common across several chapters is gender-sensitive parliamentary reforms. Among other things, gender-sensitive parliaments allow both men and women to balance work and family life. Recommendations to that end include but are not limited to providing free and on-site childcare for all members of parliament and their staff, limiting parliamentary sessions to school days, scheduling meetings during school hours, and establishing an official permanent oversight body, such as a women caucus, in charge of ensuring gender equality through parliament (see, for example, chapters 3 and 8 for greater detail on this subject).

Finally, as several chapters point out, one major barrier to office is funding. Addressing women's access to funding through special campaign funds for women (see chapter 1 for details on political action committees in the context of the United States) is one immediate and short-term solution. Taking the long view, several chapters emphasize the need to improve equal access to education and the workforce for women so that women can build the resources and networks necessary to raise funds for political campaigns.

CONCLUSION

This introduction serves as a broad orientation on the topic of women in politics and necessarily takes a bird's-eye view, even though the barriers to women in politics as well as the solutions to remedy women's underrepresentation are complex, nuanced, and often region and even country specific. The following chapters pick up on the topics raised in the introduction and discuss them in relation to their respective regions. Each chapter follows the same outline as the introduction: women as voters, women as members of parliament, and women as leaders. Each author then highlights the challenges to women's representation in the region and concludes the chapter with ideas on how to improve women's representation going forward. The reader can read the book front to cover or, after reading the preface and introduction, delve into the regions they are most interested in.

REFERENCES

Atchison, Amy L., and Ian Down. 2019. "The Effects of Women Office-holders on Environmental Policy." *Review of Policy Research* 36 (6): 805–834.

Campbell, David E., and Christina Wolbrecht. 2006. "See Jane Run: Women Politicians as Role Models for Adolescents." *Journal of Politics* 68 (2): 233–247.

CAWP (Center for American Women and Politics). 2021. "Presidential Vote Choice." The Gender Gap, January 22, 2021. https://cawp.rutgers .edu/gender-gap-presvote

Dahlerup, Drude. 2017. *Has Democracy Failed Women?* New York: John Wiley & Sons.

Desposato, Scott, and Barbara Norrander. 2009. "The Gender Gap in Latin America: Contextual and Individual Influences on Gender and Political Participation." *British Journal of Political Science* 39 (1): 141–162.

Franceschet, Susan, Mona Lena Krook, and Jennifer M. Piscopo. 2012. *The Impact of Gender Quotas*. New York: Oxford University Press.

Giger, Nathalie. 2009. "Towards a Modern Gender Gap in Europe? A Comparative Analysis of Voting Behavior in 12 Countries." *Social Science Journal* 46 (3): 474–492.

Hawkesworth, Mary. 2012. *Political Worlds of Women: Activism, Advocacy, and Governance in the Twenty-First Century*. New York: Routledge.

Henderson, Sarah, and Alana S. Jeydel. 2014. *Women and Politics in a Global World*. New York: Oxford University Press.

IPU (Inter-Parliamentary Union). 2019. "New IPU Report Shows Well-Designed Quotas Lead to Significantly More Women MPs." May 3, 2019. https://www.ipu.org/news/press-releases/2019-03/new-ipu -report-shows-well-designed-quotas-lead-significantly-more -women-mps

IPU. 2022a. "Global and Regional Averages of Women in National Parliaments. Averages as of 1st September 2022."

IPU. 2022b. "Monthly Ranking of Women in National Parliaments. Ranking as of 1st September 2022." https://data.ipu.org/women-ranking ?month=9&year=2022

IPU. n.d. "Women's Suffrage. A World Chronology of the Recognition of Women's Rights to Vote and to Stand for Election." Women in Politics. http://archive.ipu.org/wmn-e/suffrage.htm

Jalalzai, Farida. 2019. "Women Leaders in National Politics." In *Oxford Research Encyclopedia of International Studies*, edited by Nukhet Sandal. Oxford University Press.

Karp, Jeffrey A., and Susan A. Banducci. 2008. "When Politics Is Not Just a Man's Game: Women's Representation and Political Engagement." *Electoral Studies* 27 (1): 105–115.

Kenworthy, Lane, and Melissa Malami. 1999. "Gender Inequality in Political Representation: A Worldwide Comparative Analysis." *Social Forces* 78 (1): 235–268. https://doi.org/10.1093/sf/78.1.235

Lopes, Maxine. 2015. "The Sweep of the Modern Gender Gap: Is Britain Next?" *Political Analysis* 17 (4): 57–77.

Norris, Pippa. 2006. "The Impact of Electoral Reform on Women's Representation." *Acta Politica* 41 (2): 197–213.

Norris, Pippa, and Ronald Inglehart. 2001. "Cultural Obstacles to Equal Representation." *Journal of Democracy* 12 (3): 126–140.

Norris, Pippa, and Joni Lovenduski. 1995. *Political Recruitment: Gender, Race and Class in the British Parliament.* Cambridge: Cambridge University Press.

Reingold, Beth, and Jessica Harrell. 2010. "The Impact of Descriptive Representation on Women's Political Engagement: Does Party Matter?" *Political Research Quarterly* 63 (2): 280–294.

UN Women. 2021. "Facts and Figures: Women's Leadership and Political Participation." January 15, 2021. https://www.unwomen.org/en/what-we-do/leadership-and-political-participation/facts-and-figures

Chronology

1893
New Zealand is the first country to grant women the right to vote.

1960
Sirimavo Bandaranaike of Sri Lanka becomes the first elected woman prime minister of Sri Lanka and the world.

1980
Vigdis Finnbogadóttir becomes the first woman to be elected to the presidency in Iceland and the world.

1991
Argentina becomes the first country in the world to adopt a mandatory gender quota for national legislative elections.

2011
Saudi Arabia becomes the last country in the world to grant women universal suffrage.

2012
Bolivia becomes the first country to criminalize violence against women in politics.

2019
Ursula von der Leyen becomes the first woman to be president of the European Commission.

2021
Chile becomes the first country to draft a constitution through a parity convention.

ONE

North America

Sarelle Azuelos, Catherine Wineinger, and Amanda Bittner

In both Canada and the United States, a history of colonialism, racism, and sexism continues to uphold barriers to women's and gender nonconforming people's participation in civic life. This chapter focuses on the status of women's representation in formal politics and what can be done to achieve gender parity in Canadian and American political institutions. We cannot truly conceive of equality unless we consider the multiple ways that identities intersect to inform the daily lives of women, as the experiences of Indigenous and **racialized** women, for example, vary substantially from those of white settler women. Women with disabilities face systemic barriers that others do not, and immigrant women's experiences across both countries vary substantially by class, education level, ethnicity, employment status, and so on. Table 1.1 shows that while Canada and the United States technically expanded suffrage to women in 1918 and 1920, respectively, not all women had access to the ballot until decades later. From childhood to cabinet positions, girls and women face a minefield of systemic opposition to gaining and holding leadership positions. We track some of those challenges in this chapter and propose solutions to these systemic issues within the contexts of the Canadian and American electoral systems.

Table 1.1   Universal Suffrage Achieved

Country	Year
Canada	1960 (1918)
United States	1965 (1920)

Note: Incarcerated people gained the right to vote in federal elections in Canada in 2002, after the Supreme Court case *Sauvé v. The Attorney General of Canada, the Chief Electoral Officer of Canada and the Solicitor General of Canada*. In the United States, felony disenfranchisement differs from state to state. As of 2020, Vermont and Maine were the only states where incarcerated felons could vote. The Voting Rights Act of 1965 was also undermined in the Supreme Court's 2013 decision in *Shelby County v. Holder*. As a result, the United States has seen an increase in state laws that suppress access to the vote.

WOMEN IN CANADIAN POLITICS

Canadian Women as Voters

The plaza across from city hall is a popular spot for marches and protests of all kinds in Calgary, Alberta. It is the site of the now annual wintery Women's March, it was where protestors camped for weeks during Idle No More for environmental protections and Indigenous sovereignty, and it occasionally hosts people in yellow vests holding racist anti-immigration placards. Off to the side of the park is a statue of the Famous Five, a group of women cast in bronze, which commemorates their early work in fighting for women's right to vote and ultimately the recognition of women as persons under the law. Like many movements for women's equity in Canada, the suffrage movement was made up of disparate groups with a variety of goals and motivations. Today, the statue epitomizes the need for honest recognition of the qualified successes of early twentieth-century feminist activism: improving the status of some women while continuing the oppression of others.

The suffrage movement in Canada was not a singular event. While white women in the western Prairie Provinces gained the right to vote relatively early (1916 in Alberta, Manitoba, and Saskatchewan), some of the eastern provinces took much longer. In Quebec, the suffrage movement faced strong opposition from Catholic leaders and anti-Anglophile organizers and initially had limited support from rural women. White women there gained the right to vote in 1940. Racialized women faced even greater challenges; Chinese and South Asian Canadians gained the right to vote in 1947 and Japanese Canadians in 1949. Much of the organizing around enfranchisement for these communities came from **civil rights** groups and prodemocracy political parties, not women's rights organizations (Sangster 2018). Similarly, Indigenous communities had varying levels of enfranchisement until the 1960s. There were mixed levels of support from Indigenous leaders, as enfranchisement was occasionally framed as yet another form of assimilation and possibly a threat to existing treaty rights. Political and public opposition to the extension of voting rights was often incredibly racist, colonialist, and classist, from which women's organizations were not entirely immune.

Members of the Famous Five, like many of suffragists of their time, claimed women had inherent moral superiority that was linked to their maternal instincts and desire to create a better world for future generations. Unfortunately, these instincts were seen as existing in white women and not in racialized women or women with mental health issues. For example, Emily Murphy (one of the Five) was an avid proponent of forced sterilizations of institutionalized women in Alberta, which officially ended the practice in 1972, after 2,800 recorded cases (Moss, Stam, and Kattevilder 2013). Nellie McClung, who toured the country speaking about women's suffrage, took conflicting stances on women's rights throughout her life. She wrote in support of several marginalized groups, including the Métis-led Red River Rebellion and Jewish refugees during World War II; called for the sterilization of women with mental health issues; and believed in the superiority of white Christians (Sangster 2018). The Five were such controversial figures that even the erection of the statue in the late 1990s was met with significant resistance. In many ways, their work foreshadows both the opposition to increasing women's representation in politics and the problems with taking a sexist, racist, and classist view on what women's leadership looks like.

Women's Political Engagement in Canada

Most women are more interested in civic participation (voting, volunteering for political campaigns, fundraising, etc.) over direct involvement in traditional political roles (running for office). Motherhood complicates political involvement in several unique ways. Shifting expectations have changed the way women experience parenthood and the ways that parenthood interacts with other aspects of day-to-day living. Additionally, many

YOUTH, GENDER PRESSURES, AND POLITICAL INEQUALITY

Canadian researcher Leigh-Anne Ingram interviewed groups of Toronto teenagers to explore their thoughts on gender and active citizenship. She found that the girls experienced pressure to conform to traditional gender roles from family and institutions, including their schools and popular media. Girls said their education about women's issues and women's history was limited to the suffrage movement, which made it seem like total equality had been achieved decades ago (Ingram 2014). When it came to their thoughts on leadership in political realms, girls were surprised by the low number of women in office and pointed to the power of stereotypes in shaping their long-term goals. Girls are well aware of the ways that gender can shape and limit their opportunities, but they also understand that gender does not change their inherent ability to be leaders (Ingram 2014). Girls who have traditional leadership qualities are labeled unfeminine, while girls with stereotypically more feminine qualities are considered poor leaders. Girls are being asked to both uphold traditional gender roles and do the work to dismantle them.

As more women enter executive and political leadership positions, the norms around what makes a good leader will continue to expand and shift (Archard 2013). That said, we know that girls' emotional well-being, mental health, and self-confidence dramatically declines with adolescence due to often daily experiences of sexism and racism. Research links girls' participation in civic activism and community projects with better mental health outcomes, but continual cuts to community supports contribute to economic, social, and political inequalities that stymie their participation in all these areas of life (Girls Action Foundation, Glass, and Tunstall 2013). By addressing these inequalities for youth, it is possible to create a more level playing field for political engagement later on in life.

of the long-standing assumptions about how, why, and the degree to which motherhood may impact a person's political engagement do not hold up to continued scrutiny and research.

Women in Canada, like many other parts of the world, continue to spend more hours contributing to unpaid labor in the home, including cooking, cleaning, and childcare. According to the 2015 Time Use survey from Statistics Canada, women are spending more time in paid labor positions outside the home, while men are increasingly contributing to unpaid labor in the home, although these increases are not happening at the same rate (Moyser and Burlock 2018). The trends are promising, but it will take years for equal distribution to take place (and possibly longer due to long-term impacts from COVID-19). Parents are also spending more time primarily focused on caregiving than thirty years ago, but, again, women's time has increased more than men's time. While overall birth rates are on the decline, women are still working a second shift and are also more likely to multitask, combining leisure activities or childcare with domestic errands. It is important to remember that not all women experience these traditional gendered labor roles in the same way; the data suggest that low-income women and women with no postsecondary education tend to spend more time on housework. Of course, ethnicity and immigration status are strongly correlated with income and education, suggesting that gender roles and women's experiences in the home are also highly dependent on race, ethnicity, and immigration, as well as religion.

Does a mother's time commitment to paid and unpaid labor act as a barrier to her civic and political participation? It is complicated. Mothers vote in comparable numbers to women without children. Mothers are similarly inclined to sign petitions and more likely to volunteer when they have children between the ages of five and twelve (O'Neill and Gidengil 2017). Increases in volunteering have been linked to the growing social networks of mothers of young children. Volunteering may also fulfill social and civic desires in place of work; childcare is expensive across the country, hard to find in nontraditional hours, and rarely aligns with part-time shift work. The exception seems to be single mothers, as they are less likely to engage in voting or volunteering. Many mothers can find the time to prioritize and engage in political activities in their communities, but this does not translate into equal numbers when it comes to representation in joining political parties, running for office, or holding political leadership positions.

Canadian Women as Members of Parliament

In 1917, Louise McKinney was the first woman elected to public office in Canada (to the Alberta legislature). In 1921, Agnes MacPhail became the first woman elected to the Canadian House of Commons. In 1972, Rosemary Brown was the first Black woman elected to a legislature in Canada; she was elected in British Columbia. In 1988, Ethel Blondin-Andrew was the first Indigenous woman elected to the Canadian House of Commons. In the most recent Canadian federal election (2019), ninety-eight women won seats in Parliament (see table 1.2). This is 10 more than in the 2015 election but still represents only 29 percent of the 338 seats in

Table 1.2   Women in the Canadian Parliament

Chamber	Percentage of Women
House of Commons	30.5
Senate	48.9

Source: Inter-Parliamentary Union, Percentage of Women in the
Canadian Parliament, October 2022.

the House of Commons. Figure 1.1 shows the percentage of women in the
Canadian House of Commons over time.

Of course, before a woman can win a riding (electoral district), she must
win a nomination within her party. Melanee Thomas and Marc André
Bodet (2013), for example, point to the fact that parties continue to run
women as candidates in ridings where the party has little chance of winning. Women are thus put forward as sacrificial lamb candidates, or as
name-on-ballot (NOB) candidates, adding to the perception that women
are not as successful as men at winning races. Political parties in Canada
have varied approaches to gender and diversity quotas in the nomination
process (Thomas and Bodet 2013). In the lead up to the 2011 federal election, the Conservative Progressive Party had few guidelines in place about
candidate nominations, instead using language focused on "merit." This

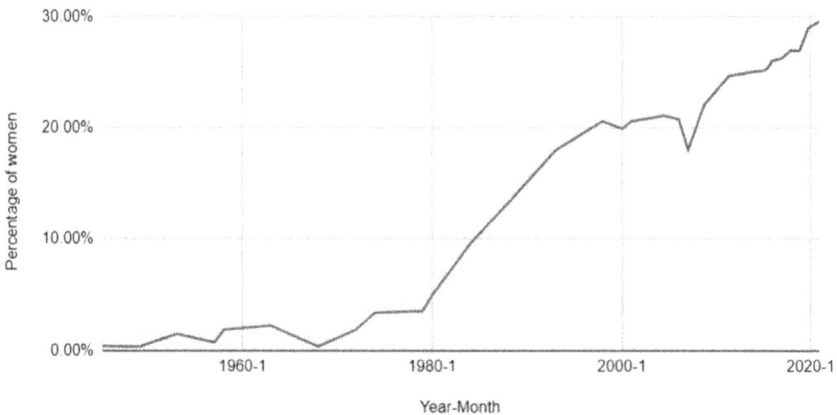

Figure 1.1 Percentage of Women in Canada's House of Commons (Inter-
Parliamentary Union: Parline database on national parliaments, July 31,
2021).

kind of language serves to further claims of color and gender blindness, which continues to default whiteness over other racialized, nonmale candidates. What is deemed worthy of merit is subjective and founded in the same racist and sexist roots as many other Canadian institutions. The left-leaning New Democratic Party (NDP) is the only party with formal rules requiring affirmative action efforts in the nomination process; as a result, they tend to have the largest slate of women candidates. The party is also known historically for being a laggard when it comes to nominating racialized candidates (Tolley 2019), although this was reversed in the most recent 2019 election after a concerted effort to nominate a more diverse slate of candidates (this was also the first year that a racialized candidate was a leader of one of the major parties, with Jagmeet Singh at the helm of the NDP). Of all the major parties, Conservative women candidates were most likely to be sacrificial lambs, nominated in areas with less chance of success, rather than securing nominations in party strongholds (Thomas and Bodet 2013). Unless parties take this seriously and run women in winnable ridings, progress is unlikely to be made.

In rare cases, stereotypes reflect positively on some women candidates. White women are seen as good communicators, compassionate, and considerate of the social good, harkening back to the maternal feminism of the suffrage era. Voters in low-information elections may rely on stereotypes to some degree to inform their choices, but the impact of stereotypes on voting behavior seems to be on the decline (Gidengil, Everitt, and Banducci 2009). Elizabeth Goodyear-Grant (2009) found that women are cognizant of these stereotypes and are able to use them strategically to craft narratives to benefit their political engagement or campaigns with varying degrees of success.

Media coverage of candidates and elected officials varies based on gender, focusing differently on appearance, sexual orientation, and tone in addition to parental status. Media coverage of racialized candidates is more negative than that of white candidates and frames them as exotic or focuses on aspects of their identity more than their policy positions and experience (Tolley 2015). Novelty can lead to a higher-than-average level of coverage in a race, but this additional coverage is usually not flattering or positive. Women of color are doubly impacted by racism and sexism in the media and must navigate a unique set of pressures and scrutiny around femininity. By contrast, the race and gender of white male candidates largely goes unmentioned, as whiteness and maleness are both considered defaults.

The challenges faced by women candidates does not mean that they do not win at the ballot box. The evidence shows that women win in equal proportions to men, and scholars have argued that "when women run, they win" (Sanbonmatsu 2006). However, it is important to note that women's qualifications are usually substantially higher than men's, suggesting that women are only as competitive as men because they are candidates of much higher quality (Fulton 2012).

Canadian Women as Leaders

While seats in legislatures are important and seats in the cabinet are integral to women's representation, who holds the job of prime minister of Canada or **premier** of a province is also a very large indicator of the nature of power holding in Canada. In 1993, Kim Campbell became Canada's first (and still only) woman prime minister for about four months, before losing the 1993 Canadian federal election (table 1.3).

To date, there have been a total of thirteen women who have served as **first ministers** in Canada; twelve women have held the position of premier of their province or territory. In 2013, Kathleen Wynne became the first LGBTQ2+ premier of a province (Ontario). At their height (2013), women held the office of first minister in six provinces or territories. In 2021, Canada had only one woman first minister, Caroline Cochrane, who is the premier of the nonpartisan government of the Northwest Territories. O'Neill, Pruysers, and Stewart (2021) find clear evidence for a phenomenon called the "glass cliff," whereby women's leadership tenures are shorter than those of men's, suggesting that "women's shorter tenures are explained by the harsher set of standards being applied to women party leaders." This glass cliff normally also encompasses a phenomenon where women gain nominations for leadership positions when parties are on a downward trend. Simply put, while women may have formal legal equality in Canada, and while much progress has been made in women's representation, the daily reality in politics is not one of equality (table 1.4).

After the 2015 election, Prime Minister Justin Trudeau drew international attention with Canada's first national parity cabinet, claiming he made this decision "because it's 2015." The 2019 cabinet was no different, and at the time of this writing, there are eighteen women ministers in a thirty-six-person cabinet. Parity in numbers is important, but Trimble and Tremblay (2005) encourage us to consider the type of cabinet portfolio women are assigned to, as historically women have often been allocated

Table 1.3   Women Heads of State

Country	Name	Region	Position	Years Served
Canada	Queen Elizabeth II	United Kingdom and Commonwealth	Head of state	1952–2022
Canada	Kim Campbell	Canada	Head of government	1993

portfolios that are less important or less powerful than those of men. For example, women rarely hold the position of minister of finance, and when they do, as was the case when Minister Chrystia Freeland was recently assigned this position, their qualifications are debated at length.

Jody Wilson-Raybould was sworn in as the minister of justice and Canada's attorney general in 2015. Prior to being the first Indigenous person to act as justice minister, Wilson-Raybould worked as a prosecutor in Vancouver's Downtown Eastside, a neighborhood with disproportionately high rates of homelessness and addiction. She later served as **councilor** of the We Wai Kai First Nation at Cape Mudge, supporting First Nations governance, land rights, education, and health care of over 200 Indigenous bands in British Columbia (Conn 2019). As justice minister, her major accomplishments included introducing medical assistance in dying (MAID) legislation, legalizing recreational marijuana, and adding gender identity and expression to the list of prohibited grounds for discrimination in the Canadian Human Rights Act.

Wilson-Raybould is a longtime outspoken advocate for Indigenous communities and announced a list of ten principles to guide federal government toward reconciliation in July 2017, less than a full sixty years after "registered Indians" gained the right to vote (Department of Justice Canada 2018). Wilson-Raybould's term in office was not without controversy. She was shuffled to the ministry of Veterans Affairs in 2019 and resigned from the cabinet soon afterward. In the following months, she pointed to pressure from the Prime Minister's Office to interfere in a federal case against SNC-Lavalin, a large construction company based out of Quebec, as the reason for her demotion. This scandal is one of the larger "power scandals" in Canadian history, and many applauded Wilson-Raybould's ethics and willingness to stand up to the Prime Minister's Office. Wilson-Raybould successfully ran as an independent candidate in the

Table 1.4   Women First Ministers

Country	Name	Province/Territory	Years in Office	Party Affiliation
Canada	Rita Johnston	British Columbia	1991	British Columbia Social Credit Party
Canada	Nellie Cournoyea	Northwest Territories	1991–1995	NA
Canada	Catherine Callbeck	Prince Edward Island	1993–1996	PEI Liberal Party
Canada	Kim Campbell	Canada	1993	Progressive Conservative Party of Canada
Canada	Pat Duncan	Yukon	2000–2002	Yukon Liberal Party
Canada	Eva Aariak	Nunavut	2008–2013	NA
Canada	Kathy Dunderdale	Newfoundland and Labrador	2010–2014	Progressive Conservative Party of Newfoundland and Labrador
Canada	Christy Clark	British Columbia	2011–2017	British Columbia Liberal Party
Canada	Alison Redford	Alberta	2011–2014	Progressive Conservative Association of Alberta
Canada	Pauline Marois	Quebec	2012–2014	Parti Quebecois
Canada	Kathleen Wynne	Ontario	2013–2018	Ontario Liberal Party
Canada	Rachel Notley	Alberta	2015–2019	Alberta New Democratic Party
Canada	Caroline Cochrane	Northwest Territories	2019–Present	NA

Source: Trimble, Arscott, and Tremblay (2013).

2019 federal election, separate from the Liberal Party and the financial and organizational supports that come with it. She has since announced that she will not be running for office again.

Barriers to Political Parity in Canada

Running for office requires more time than volunteering or signing petitions and is therefore more dependent on the availability of affordable quality childcare, access to social networks and funding, and training and skill development for specific types of careers. Women make up a disproportionate percentage of part-time workers in the service industry, for example, which does not usually provide them with opportunities to develop skills deemed valuable in politics, such as project management, public speaking, or designing budgets, nor access to individuals who have power or money.

Women running for political office face a gauntlet of stereotypes that are depressingly similar in nature to those that girls and teenagers grow up with. Women with children are questioned about balancing life and work, and women without children are questioned on their ability to consider family-friendly policies. The possibility that they may someday have children is complicated by the lack of parental leave policies and infant-friendly infrastructure. In 2016, Member of the Legislative Assembly Stephanie McLean was the first Legislative Assembly member in Alberta's history to deliver a child during her term, nearly two weeks after her appointment as minister of the newly established Status of Women. The event initiated the creation of a committee to examine family-friendly policies in the legislature, from leave, to on-site childcare, to changing tables in the bathrooms in legislature (Huncar 2016). Systemic issues of sexism manifest in incredibly simple and tactile ways, but each overlooked detail creates yet another barrier to parents participating in public life. McLean faced a mixture of community and media backlash and support for taking a short leave and again later for occasionally bringing baby Patrick to the legislature. In 2019, the Canadian House of Commons passed legislation allowing for parental leave of MPs, but the nature of the job of politicians is such that formal leave from the legislature is inadequate and imperfect, as representatives continue to work full-time in their constituency offices, feeling the pressures related to reelection that prevent them from actually taking time off from work, while simultaneously being prevented from voting in the House and thus losing their voice while on leave (Bittner and Thomas 2020).

Achieving Political Parity—A Way Forward for Canada

While we have highlighted some pathbreaking women in this chapter, women who pushed boundaries, broke down barriers, and made important changes to Canadian politics and society, it is important to highlight the fact that women's representation is not an individual issue but a systemic one that requires institutional change to make progress. It is not up to individual women to improve their own chances of running, winning, and leading; they are not solely responsible for the creation or perpetuation of the many barriers that exist. What will lead to change in women's representation is institutional change, in particular institutional change initiated by parties and by governments.

First and foremost, parties have a big role to play. When parties take gender parity seriously, when they institute policies requiring affirmative action initiatives, we see change in the number of women candidates, in the number of racialized candidates, and in the representation of these groups in the House of Commons, the lower house of the Canadian Parliament. Research indicates that voters are not biased against women candidates and that when major parties nominate women in winnable ridings, voters will vote for them (Terry et al. 2019). Some may suggest that national quotas legislated by governments are key—indeed, there is plenty of research on quotas around the world that demonstrates they do work (e.g., Hughes et al. 2019). At the same time, efforts by parties can be made outside of national legislative action and can lead to major changes. The representation of women in the province of Quebec jumped to more than 40 percent in the provincial legislature after all the parties signed a parity pledge. We would also point to women's share of candidacies in the National Democratic Party, which is linked to their internal party policies on diversity. In the 2019 federal election, women made up 49 percent of National Democratic Party candidates, compared to 39 percent for Liberals and 32 percent for Conservatives.

Parties are powerful actors and can initiate major change in the Canadian political landscape. In addition to concerted recruitment efforts, parties can increase the supports they provide to nontraditional candidates and potential candidates from traditionally marginalized groups. Mentorship—and especially sponsorship—programs; campaign schools; dedicated funding support, including staffing, fundraising, and experienced volunteers; and paid campaign teams to assist women from diverse backgrounds to move from potentially interested, to nomination winner, to member of Parliament would bridge some of the systemic gaps that exist across demographic groups in social networks, access to funding, and relevant experience and skills.

Of course, legislation is the most immediately effective solution to many of society's problems. Research suggests that regulatory changes favoring family-friendly policies (e.g., maternity and paternity leaves, universal childcare, early childhood education) lead to greater labor force participation by women, and this leads to greater diversity in legislatures on a global scale (Thomas and Bittner 2017), including the presence of mothers in parliaments around the world. Government intervention, then, to provide supports to traditionally marginalized groups in society should further diversify legislatures and increase the representation not just of women writ large but of women from a diverse set of backgrounds, including Indigenous women, immigrant women, racialized women, women of different classes, and women with disabilities.

WOMEN IN U.S. POLITICS

American Women as Voters

In February 1921, less than a year after the ratification of the Nineteenth Amendment, representatives from over seventy women's organizations attended the unveiling of a sculpture in the U.S. Capitol Rotunda. Made of white marble, the Portrait Monument was gifted to Congress by the National Woman's Party and features detailed busts of three prominent suffragists—Lucretia Mott, Elizabeth Cady Stanton, and Susan B. Anthony—in front of a fourth uncarved pillar, which is believed to represent the unfinished work of the women's movement. An inscription on the statue proclaims, "Woman, first denied a soul, then called mindless, now arisen, declared herself an entity to be reckoned" (Boissoneault 2017). The very next day, Congress ordered the "blasphemous" inscription to be removed, and the monument was relocated to the Capitol Crypt beneath the floor of the Rotunda, where it would remain for the next seventy-six years. In 1997, with the passage of H.Con.Res.216, the Portrait Monument was moved back to its original location, prominently displayed in the Capitol Rotunda.

The story of the Portrait Monument's relocation, however, is not straightforward and reflects the complexities of women's struggle for representation in American politics. Women's groups pushing to relocate the statue to the Rotunda faced resistance from men—and some women—in Congress who did not want to use taxpayer money to fund the move. The National Congress of Black Women (NCBW) also stressed the historical inaccuracy of the monument and fought to replace it with one that would include Sojourner Truth, a Black abolitionist and women's rights activist and one of the most powerful voices of her generation (Painter 1996). In response to the NCBW, Representative Cynthia McKinney (D-GA), a member of the Congressional Black Caucus who had originally supported the relocation efforts, along with twenty-five cosponsors introduced a resolution to postpone moving the sculpture to the Rotunda. While ultimately unsuccessful in replacing Portrait Monument, the NCBW donated a bronze stand-alone bust of Sojourner Truth, which was approved by Congress, unveiled in 2009, and now sits in Emancipation Hall in the Capitol Visitor Center (Architect of the Capitol n.d.).

Like the politics surrounding the Portrait Monument, the suffrage movement was neither simple nor linear. By the time the Nineteenth Amendment was ratified in 1920, women in some states had already been legally voting for decades. Corrine McConnaughy's (2013) research on the woman suffrage movement underscores the significance of coalitional politics between enfranchised and disenfranchised groups in influencing political parties and state legislatures to support suffrage. Suffragists also faced many barriers, including opposition from an antisuffrage movement that was composed of men *and* women who were concerned about the moral degradation of traditional gender roles and the (white) family unit (Goodier 2013). Racial tensions—including the explicit racism of many suffragists—also created internal divisions within the movement and perpetuated the oppression of women of color (Free 2015).

The beginning of the woman suffrage movement in the United States is marked by the signing of the Declaration of Sentiments at the 1848 women's convention in Seneca Falls, New York. Among the many grievances listed in the document was a demand for the right to vote, although there was little activism on suffrage between the women's convention and the Civil War (Wolbrecht and Corder 2020). Following the Civil War and amid reforms that focused on Black citizenship and enfranchisement, women's rights activists—many of whom were active in the abolitionist movement—organized explicitly around women's suffrage (Wolbrecht and Corder 2020). Debates over the Fifteenth Amendment, which would give Black men the right to vote, divided the woman suffrage movement into those who supported the Fifteenth Amendment and those who would only support a suffrage amendment if it also included an end to sex discrimination.

The sacrifices of all suffragists in the United States should certainly be commemorated; members of the National Woman's Party were the first in American history to picket the White House, and women were jailed, beaten, and tortured for the right to vote. At the same time, the racist arguments made in support of the Nineteenth Amendment and the exclusion and segregation of Black women within the movement should also be interrogated; the work done by Black women, Indigenous women, Latinas, and Asian American women across the country to secure women's suffrage has often gone unacknowledged. Notably, even with the additions of the Fifteenth and Nineteenth Amendments, Indigenous women were denied U.S. citizenship until the passage of the Snyder Act in 1924. More generally, voting rights were—and continue to be—in a precarious position, as voter suppression efforts were not addressed until the passage of the 1965 Voting Rights Act, which has once again come under attack (see Hajnal, Lajevardi, and Nielson 2017).

One hundred years after the ratification of the Nineteenth Amendment, and during national uprisings for gender and racial justice, the United States must recognize its history of intersectional oppression and commit to structural solutions that address women's political underrepresentation (Collins 1990; Crenshaw 1989; Jordan-Zachery and Alexander-Floyd 2018). Indeed, the Portrait Monument's uncarved pillar situated behind three white suffragists, while symbolic of an unfinished fight for women's rights, is also emblematic of the erasure of the historic contributions and leadership of women of color in the suffrage movement and in formal electoral politics. Centering the experiences of marginalized women can paint a more accurate picture of the representation of women in national U.S. politics.

The voting behavior of women in the United States today highlights the importance of focusing not only on gender but also on the intersection of gender, race, education, religion, and so on (Gothreau 2021). Since the 1980s, women have registered and turned out to vote at higher rates than men. Gender gaps also exist in terms of vote choice, partisanship, and policy preferences, with women more often voting Democratic and taking more liberal positions on policy. But as Junn and Masuoka (2020) emphasize, the gender gap is also a race gap. While women, regardless of race, are more likely than their male counterparts to support the Democratic presidential candidate, a majority of white women have voted for the

Republican candidate since 2000. Complicating the gender gap in voting behavior is one way to better understand the distinct voting patterns *among* women—not just between men and women.

American Women as Members of the U.S. Congress

Figure 1.2 shows the percentage of women in the U.S. House of Representatives over time. Jeannette Rankin (R-MT), the first woman to serve in Congress, was elected in 1916, four years before women in the United States won the right to vote. It would be 48 years before the first woman of color, Patsy Mink (D-HI), and 102 years before the first Indigenous women, Debra Haaland (D-NM) and Sharice Davids (D-KS), would be elected to Congress (CAWP n.d.). These gaps highlight the fact that intersecting identities like race and ethnicity have always shaped women's access to political power in the United States. Nevertheless, women of color continue to make significant gains and bring important perspectives with them to elected office.

The 2018 midterm election resulted in the most diverse group of women in Congress. We saw the election of the first two Indigenous women, the first two Muslim women, and the youngest woman ever elected to Congress (CAWP n.d.). The 2020 election cycle was another record-breaking

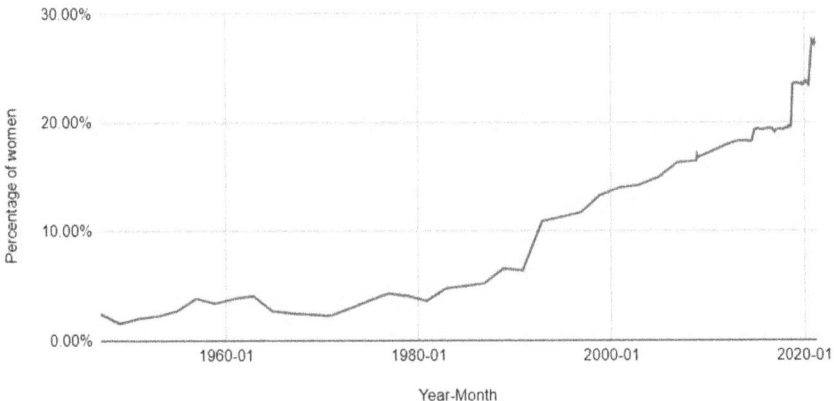

Figure 1.2 Percentage of Women in the United States House of Representatives (Inter-Parliamentary Union: Parline database on national parliaments, July 31, 2021).

Table 1.5   Women in the U.S. Congress

Chamber	Percentage of Women
House of Representatives	27.4
Senate	24
Total	**26.7**

Source: Center for American Women and Politics (2021c).

year for women (see table 1.5). Although the percentage of women of color is smaller than in the previous Congress, we continued to see notable firsts, including a record-breaking thirty-nine Republican women and the first Korean American women elected to Congress. Of the record 142 women currently serving in the 117th Congress, 49 (34.5 percent) are women of color (CAWP 2021d).

As more women are elected and gain seniority within their parties, they have also attained more powerful leadership positions within Congress. In 2007, Representative Nancy Pelosi (D-CA) became the first woman to be elected Speaker of the House, the highest-ranking woman in American political history; she served as Speaker from 2007 to 2011 and was elected again in 2019 and 2021 when Democrats gained control of the House.

American Women as Leaders

As of this writing, the United States has never had a woman president. Hillary Rodham Clinton made history in 2016 when she became the nation's first major-party presidential nominee. Falling short of winning the presidency, Clinton's race nevertheless brought women one step closer to cracking "the highest, hardest glass ceiling" (Clinton 2008). In the very next presidential election, six women—Representative Tulsi Gabbard (D-HI), Senator Kirsten Gillibrand (D-NY), Senator Kamala Harris (D-CA), Senator Amy Klobuchar (D-MN), Senator Elizabeth Warren (D-MA), and Marianne Williamson—ran for the Democratic nomination, marking the first time in U.S. history that more than two women had competed in the same major party's nomination process. While none of these women clinched the nomination, Kamala Harris, the daughter of Jamaican and Indian immigrants, was selected as Joe Biden's vice presidential running mate and was the nation's first woman of color on a major-party ticket. On January 21,

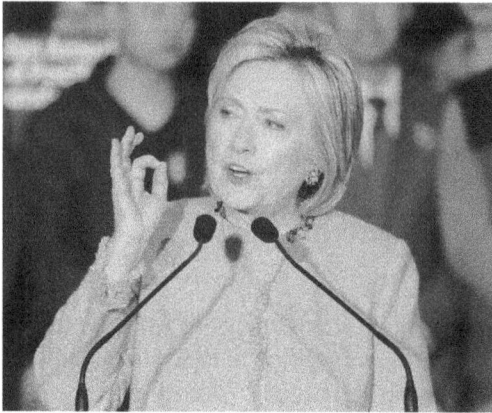

Hillary Clinton, the first woman presidential candidate in the United States. (Joe Sohm | Dreamstime.com)

2021, she was sworn in as the first woman of color, the first Black person, and the first South Asian person to hold the vice presidency of the United States.

Importantly, the women who made history in 2016 and 2020 walked on a path blazed by the women who had come before them. Decades before Hillary Clinton and Kamala Harris made their historic runs for the White House, Shirley Chisholm was the first woman to seek the Democratic nomination, running in 1972 under the slogan "Unbought and unbossed" (History, Art & Archives 2021). Geraldine Ferraro, who became Walter Mondale's running mate in 1984, was the United States' first major-party woman vice presidential candidate. On the other side of the aisle, Republican women have also made strides in presidential politics since 1964, when Margaret Chase Smith, a Republican senator from Maine, became the first woman in a major party to run for president. Sarah Palin, in 2008, made a historic run as the first woman vice presidential candidate on a Republican ticket, and Michele Bachmann and Carly Fiorina each sought the Republican presidential nomination in 2012 and 2016, respectively. Notably, there has yet to be a woman of color on any Republican presidential ticket—a general trend in Republican Party politics that is discussed further in this chapter.

Within the federal executive branch, a total of sixty-four women have held presidential cabinet or cabinet-level positions (CAWP 2021b). Of these sixty-four women, forty-one have been appointed by Democratic presidents and twenty-three by Republican presidents. Frances Perkins, the first woman to serve in a U.S. president's cabinet, was nominated by President Franklin Delano Roosevelt and served from 1933 to 1945. Under the Biden administration, a record eleven women have been nominated and confirmed to serve in such positions. Among these appointments is Secretary Debra Haaland, the first Indigenous woman to ever hold a

INDIGENOUS WOMEN AND U.S. POLITICS

Wearing a handmade ribbon skirt and traditional Laguna Pueblo moccasins at her swearing-in ceremony in March 2021, Secretary Debra Haaland became the first Indigenous cabinet secretary in U.S. history. Prior to her role at the Department of the Interior, she was one of the first two Indigenous women to serve in the U.S. Congress. Haaland's presence in U.S. government underscores the importance of political representation and the need to not only increase the *number* of women in elected office but also the *diversity* of women.

Haaland, who had previously represented New Mexico's First Congressional District, often notes that Indigenous Americans were denied the right to vote well into the twentieth century. Indeed, despite the passage of the Fifteenth and Nineteenth Amendments, it was not until 1962 that all Indigenous communities could vote—after New Mexico became the last state to enfranchise Indigenous voters.

In a Newsy interview, Haaland describes what it means to her to be one of the first Indigenous women elected to Congress: "Native Americans have gone through all of these eras of oppression and people making decisions for them, and so I have to work as hard as I can to make it better for people in the future" (Newsy 2020). While Haaland, like all members, worked on a wide range of issues, her unique perspective as an Indigenous woman helped her amplify the voices of communities that have long been overlooked. From increasing access to wireless services on tribal lands, to ensuring Indigenous communities received necessary funding during the COVID-19 pandemic, to inviting tribal leaders to committee hearings, Haaland's legislative work often focused on bettering the lives of Indigenous peoples.

cabinet position. A woman has not yet served as secretary of veteran affairs or secretary of defense.

Barriers to Political Parity in the United States

While women's presence in Congress has been on the rise, and while women of color are gaining prominence within the Democratic Party, there remain significant barriers on the road to political parity. In what follows, we discuss partisan discrepancies in women's representation and women's decisions to run for elected office. Understanding this landscape allows us to think more deeply and creatively about structural solutions to women's underrepresentation in the United States.

Significant Partisan Discrepancies

Reaching gender parity in American political institutions will require increasing women's representation in both the Democratic and Republican Parties. In recent years, Democratic women have come closer to parity within their party: in Congress, women are currently about 38 percent of the Democratic Caucus. Comparatively, only about 14 percent of all Republican members of Congress are women. Despite a record-breaking year for Republican women, the partisan gap in women's congressional representation persists. Why does this gap exist, and what can be done to close it?

One answer lies in the election of women of color. On the Democratic side, women of color are not only prominent leaders in the party; they have also been driving overall increases in women's representation (Carew 2016; Hardy-Fanta et al. 2006). Of the forty-nine women of color in Congress, forty-four (about 90 percent) are Democrats. Research has shown that the Republican Party's aversion to what it perceives to be **identity politics** and increasing use of racist rhetoric and policies make it challenging for women of color to navigate the tension between their partisan and social identities (Wineinger 2021). Simultaneously, Democratic women of color have in some ways been able to use their identities to their advantage, catering to the multiple social groups within their party's base (Bejarano 2013; Smooth 2006).

While all political candidates must learn to navigate gendered expectations on the campaign trail (Dittmar 2015b), Republican women face hurdles on the path to elected office that their Democratic women counterparts do not (Elder 2021). On average, women Republican congressional candidates raise less money than both Democratic women and Republican men. One reason for this discrepancy is that, unlike Democratic women, Republican women lack access to effective networks of women's **political action committees (PACs)**. While well-connected and well-funded PACs like EMILY's List exist to elect Democratic women, Republican women PACs such as the Susan B. Anthony List have comparatively limited funds and are less visible in the political arena (Och and Shames 2018). For example, according to the Center for Responsive Politics (opensecrets.org), EMILY's List raised $80.6 million and spent $79.6 million in the 2019–2020 cycles. The Susan B. Anthony List raised $1.6 million and spent $1.5 million. For Republican donors, who are often more concerned with ideological purity than with gender, candidate endorsements from women's organizations do not carry the same level of prestige that they do for Democratic donors

(Crowder-Meyer and Cooperman 2018). This uneven funding environment, among other factors, makes it challenging for Republican women to make it through their primary elections.

Another reason for Republican women's disproportionate underrepresentation in Congress is a partisan discrepancy in the gendered pipeline to office. Danielle M. Thomsen and Aaron S. King (2020) found that women, and to a greater extent Republican women, are underrepresented in three main potential candidate pools: lower-level officeholders, people named in the media as likely candidates, and lawyers who have made political contributions. Such underrepresentation in these potential candidate pools means that, to reach gender parity, Republican women must be much more likely to run for office than their male counterparts (Thomsen and King 2020). So, how do we elect more women? How do we increase women's representation at all levels of the pipeline? And how do we perhaps create a pipeline where women are already represented? Research on women's ambition for political office has grappled with these questions and provides suggestions for increasing and diversifying women's representation on both sides of the aisle.

"Ambition" for Elected Office

It is true that Republican women face unique hurdles to elected office, as previously noted, a common refrain among scholars and advocates is that "When women run, women win." That is, women candidates win elections at statistically similar rates as their male counterparts (Sanbonmatsu 2006). The bigger issue is that women are less likely than men to choose to run for office in the first place. Indeed, much of the literature on women's representation has focused on political ambition. Why is it that fewer women than men decide to run for office, and how can this issue be addressed in the United States?

Jennifer L. Lawless and Richard L. Fox (2005, 2010) have spearheaded research on women's political ambition and found that women in potential candidate pools are less likely than men to run for office. On some level, this gender gap in ambition can be attributed to gender role socialization. Indeed, young girls and boys are exposed to gendered notions of political leadership at a young age (Lay et al. 2019), and even as children, girls are less likely than boys to be interested in politics or a political career (Bos et al. 2020). As Lawless and Fox have noted, "The gender gap in political ambition results from longstanding patterns of traditional socialization that persist in U.S. culture" (2005, 6–7).

Cultural changes can certainly help to create an environment that is more hospitable to women in politics. Importantly, though, those changes need not (and perhaps should not) rely simply on encouraging women to conform to male standards of doing politics. Research on women who do run for office shows that women often make decisions about their political candidacies differently than men. For example, Susan J. Carroll and Kira Sanbonmatsu (2013) found that women take many paths to office, including from professions that are not traditionally considered part of the pipeline to elected office. Women also often make decisions that are relationally embedded, meaning they take into consideration how their decision to run will affect those around them (Carroll and Sanbonmatsu 2013). And compared to men, who tend to view politics as a career in and of itself, women tend to be motivated to run for office with specific policy interests or goals in mind (Thomas and Wineinger 2020).

All this is to say that if we are to increase women's political representation, we must consider the ways gender and race shape decisions to run for office and tailor our solutions accordingly. Women are already politically ambitious in that they care about and are active on issues that are important to them; convincing women to take the next step requires shifting the narrative around the costs, benefits, and nature of running for elected office (Shames 2017). For women to view elected office as worthwhile, it is important to send the message that the skills and qualifications women already possess are enough—and even valuable—in the political arena; that, even in a polarized era, women have made and continue to make policy differences while in office (Volden, Wiseman, and Wittmer 2013); and that barriers to office can be overcome (Dittmar 2015a). In the following section, we discuss how some of those barriers are already being addressed and what structural solutions should be implemented to make running for office a viable and appealing option for women.

Achieving Political Parity—A Way Forward for the United States

Increasing women's representation in the United States requires cultural changes as well as structural solutions that focus on recruiting women and decreasing the cost of running for office. Once again, it cannot simply be up to women to push for increased visibility and representation in politics. A commitment from men and women in both parties is important if we are to implement the institutional changes necessary to address women's political underrepresentation.

Women's organizations have been instrumental in training and funding women candidates, especially within the context of the United States, where parties have less power than in other countries. While many of the women who participate in campaign training programs have already expressed interest in running for office, research has shown that such programs can build women's campaign skills and increase access to important networks (Sanbonmatsu and Dittmar 2020). Once on the campaign trail, women's groups also support candidates monetarily and through endorsements, although this has been more significant for Democratic than Republican women (Crowder-Meyer and Cooperman 2018). Strengthening and promoting women's organizations on both sides of the aisle can help women candidates attain important resources and feel comfortable navigating the current political arena.

In the candidate-centered context of the United States, party organizations play a relatively limited role in elections, but that does not mean that they cannot play a larger role in actively recruiting and supporting women candidates. Including more women in party leadership positions (Crowder-Meyer 2013) and incentivizing male party leaders (Valdini 2019) to focus on women's representation can help women run for office and make it through their primaries. Traditionally, congressional party organizations like the Democratic Congressional Campaign Committee (DCCC) and the National Republican Congressional Committee (NRCC) do not endorse or support candidates in primary elections. As NRCC recruitment chair, Representative Elise Stefanik (R-NY) recruited one hundred women to run for office in 2018—but only one of them won. This experience motivated her to create Elevate PAC (E-PAC), a political action committee dedicated to supporting Republican women candidates in their primary elections. After initially denouncing her efforts to "play in primaries," party leaders are now supportive of Stefanik's initiative to address what she has called the "crisis" of Republican women's underrepresentation in Congress (Hagen 2019). Party organizations and party elites have a role to play in creating an environment that is hospitable to women candidates. Given the fact that Republican women's organizations struggle to obtain funding and visibility compared to their Democratic counterparts, the Republican Party has an especially critical role to play in recruiting and supporting women candidates.

Using legislation to address the specific needs of women and other marginalized candidates must also be a priority. Legislative efforts like Representative Katie Porter's (D-CA) Help America Run Act, which has passed the House and would allow campaign funds to be used to pay for childcare, elder care, and health insurance, can make it more feasible for a diverse array of candidates to run for office. The lack of access to childcare remains a significant cost for women candidates. Of the seventeen states that have allowed campaign money to be used for childcare, only six have codified that practice (CAWP 2021a).

Importantly, no single reform is the panacea to women's political underrepresentation in the United States. Women's diverse experiences, rooted in myriad intersecting identities, affect their decisions to run for office. Indeed, as Andrea Silva and Carrie Skulley (2019) have shown, factors that affect women's emergence as political candidates can vary based on racial identity. Thus, the implementation of a broad range of reforms—with particular attention to marginalized groups—can best help to increase women's overall representation.

CONCLUSION: INVESTING IN WOMEN AND CENTERING MARGINALIZED EXPERIENCES

Research has shown that the presence of diverse legislators leads to policy innovation and cross-party collaboration to introduce legislation that supports diverse groups in society (Holman and Mahoney 2018). Numerous studies from around the world have found that women's presence affects legislative outcomes and that women's presence and the presence of members of other traditionally marginalized groups helps to make institutional change in legislatures (Allen and Childs 2019; Bratton and Rouse 2011; Clark 2019; Dittmar, Sanbonmatsu, and Carroll 2018; Johnson and Josefsson 2016; O'Brien and Piscopo 2019). This means that institutional change designed to ensure greater diversity in the legislature is likely to lead to greater diversity in future legislative actions among representatives.

As we saw in the suffrage movements in Canada and the United States, feminist movements and women's interests may have significant overlap, but there are still groups of women and other marginalized groups who are overlooked or deliberately excluded. While **civil society** and social movements play an integral role in furthering equality and access to democracy, gradual improvement to women's representation in political leadership is not enough. In both countries, implementing systemic solutions centered on the experiences of marginalized women can more quickly lead us to gender parity and create institutions that better reflect the policy needs and desires of all.

REFERENCES

Allen, Peter, and Sarah Childs. 2019. "The Grit in the Oyster? Women's Parliamentary Organizations and the Substantive Representation of Women." *Political Studies* 67 (3): 618–638.

Archard, N. 2013. "Women's Participation as Leaders in Society: An Adolescent Girls' Perspective." *Journal of Youth Studies* 16 (6): 759–775.

Architect of the Capitol. n.d. "Sojourner Truth Bust." https://www.aoc.gov /explore-capitol-campus/art/sojourner-truth-bust

Bejarano, Christina E. 2013. *The Latina Advantage: Gender, Race, and Political Success.* Austin: University of Texas Press.

Bittner, Amanda and Melanee L. Thomas. 2020. "Making a Bad Thing Worse: Parenting MPs and the Pandemic." *Canadian Parliamentary Review* 43 (3): 14–19.

Boissoneault, Lorraine. 2017. "The Suffragist Statue Trapped in a Broom Closet for 75 Years." *Smithsonian Magazine*, May 12, 2017. https:// www.smithsonianmag.com/history/suffragist-statue-trapped-broom -closet-75-years-180963274/

Bos, Angela, Mirya Holman, Jill Greenlee, Zoe Oxley, and J. Celeste Lay. 2020. "100 Years of Suffrage and Girls Still Struggle to Find Their 'Fit' in Politics." *PS: Political Science & Politics* 53 (3): 474–478.

Bratton, Kathleen, and Stella M. Rouse. 2011. "Networks in the Legislative Arena: How Group Dynamics Affect Cosponsorship." *Legislative Studies Quarterly* 36 (3): 423–460.

Carew, Jessica D. 2016. "How Do You See Me? Stereotyping of Black Women and How It Affects Them in an Electoral Context." In *Distinct Identities: Minority Women in U.S. Politics*, edited by Nadia Brown and Sarah Allen Gershon, 95–115. New York: Routledge.

Carroll, Susan J., and Kira Sanbonmatsu. 2013. *More Women Can Run: Gender and Pathways to the State Legislatures.* New York: Oxford University Press.

Center for American Women and Politics (CAWP). n.d. "History of Women of Color in U.S. Politics." Rutgers University. https://cawp .rutgers.edu/history-women-color-us-politics

Center for American Women and Politics (CAWP). 2021a. "State Candidates and the Use of Campaign Funds for Childcare Expenses." Rutgers University, April 2021. https://cawp.rutgers.edu/use-cam paign-funds-childcare-expenses

Center for American Women and Politics (CAWP). 2021b. "Women Appointed to Presidential Cabinets." Rutgers University. https:// cawp.rutgers.edu/sites/default/files/resources/womenapptdtopres cabinets.pdf

Center for American Women and Politics (CAWP). 2021c. "Women in the U.S. Congress 2021." Rutgers University. https://cawp.rutgers.edu /women-us-congress-2021

Center for American Women and Politics (CAWP). 2021d. "Women of Color in Elective Office." Rutgers University. https://cawp.rutgers .edu/women-color-elective-office-2021

Clark, Christopher. 2019. *Gaining Voice: Causes and Consequences of Black Representation in the American States*. New York: Oxford University Press.

Clinton, Hillary Rodham. 2008. "Hillary Clinton Endorses Barack Obama." Transcript in *New York Times*, June 7, 2008. https://www .nytimes.com/2008/06/07/us/politics/07text-clinton.html

Collins, Patricia Hill. 1990. *Black Feminist Thought: Knowledge, Consciousness, and the Politics of Empowerment*. New York: Routledge.

Conn, Heather. 2019. *Canadian Encyclopedia*. English ed. Toronto: Historica Canada.

Crenshaw, Kimberle. 1989. "Demarginalizing the Intersection of Race and Sex: A Black Feminist Critique of Antidiscrimination Doctrine, Feminist Theory and Antiracist Politics." *University of Chicago Legal Forum* 1989 (1), article 8: 139–167.

Crowder-Meyer, Melody. 2013. "Gendered Recruitment without Trying: How Local Party Recruiters Affect Women's Representation." *Politics & Gender* 9 (4): 390–413.

Crowder-Meyer, Melody, and Rosalyn Cooperman. 2018. "Can't Buy Them Love: How Party Culture among Donors Contributes to the Party Gap in Women's Representation." *Journal of Politics* 80 (4): 1211–1224.

Department of Justice Canada. 2018. "Principles Respecting the Government of Canada's Relationship with Indigenous Peoples." https://www.justice.gc.ca/eng/csj-sjc/principles.pdf

Dittmar, Kelly. 2015a. "Encouragement Is Not Enough: Addressing Social and Structural Barriers to Female Recruitment." *Politics & Gender* 11 (4): 759–765.

Dittmar, Kelly. 2015b. *Navigating Gendered Terrain: Stereotypes and Strategy in Political Campaigns*. Philadelphia: Temple University Press.

Dittmar, Kelly, Kira Sanbonmatsu, and Susan J. Carroll. 2018. *A Seat at the Table: Congresswomen's Perspectives on Why Their Presence Matters*. New York: Oxford University Press.

Elder, Laurel. 2021. *The Partisan Gap: Why Democratic Women Get Elected but Republican Women Don't*. New York: NYU Press.

Free, Laura E. 2015. *Suffrage Reconstructed: Gender, Race, and Voting Rights in the Civil War Era*. Ithaca, NY: Cornell University Press.

Fulton, Sarah A. 2012. "Running Backwards and in High Heels: The Gendered Quality Gap and Incumbent Electoral Success." *Political Research Quarterly* 65 (2): 303–314.

Gidengil, Elisabeth, Joanna Everitt, and Susan Banducci. 2009. "Do Voters Stereotype Female Party Leaders? Evidence from Canada and New Zealand." In *Opening Doors Wider: Women's Political Engagement in Canada*, edited by Sylvia Bashevkin, 167–193. Toronto: UBC Press.

Goodier, Susan. 2013. *No Votes for Women: The New York State Anti-Suffrage Movement*. Chicago: University of Illinois Press.

Goodyear-Grant, Elizabeth. 2009. "Crafting a Public Image: Women MPs and the Dynamics of Media Coverage." In *Opening Doors Wider: Women's Political Engagement in Canada*, edited by Sylvia Bashevkin, 147–166. Toronto: UBC Press.

Gothreau, Claire. 2021. "Everything You Need to Know about the Gender Gap." Center for American Women and Politics, February 26, 2021. https://cawp.rutgers.edu/election-analysis/everything-you-need-know-about-gender-gap

Hagen, Lisa. 2019. "Elise Stefanik Seeks to Tackle GOP's Women 'Crisis' ahead of 2020." *The Hill*, January 21, 2019. https://thehill.com/homenews/campaign/426124-elise-stefanik-wants-to-tackle-gops-women-crisis-ahead-of-2020

Hajnal, Zoltan, Nazita Lajevardi, and Lindsay Nielson. 2017. "Voter Identification Laws and the Suppression of Minority Votes." *Journal of Politics* 79 (2): 363–379.

Hardy-Fanta, Carol, Pei-te Lien, Dianne M. Pinderhughes, and Christine M. Sierra. 2006. "Gender, Race, and Descriptive Representation in the United States: Findings from the Gender and Multicultural Leadership Project." *Journal of Women, Politics & Policy* 28 (3–4): 7–41.

History, Art & Archives, U.S. House of Representatives. 2021. "Shirley Chisholm Campaign Poster." August 9, 2021. https://history.house .gov/Collection/Listing/2005/2005-181-000/

Holman, Mirya R., and Anna M. Mahoney. 2018. "Stop, Collaborate, and Listen: Women's Collaboration in US State Legislatures." *Legislative Studies Quarterly* 43 (2): 179–206.

Hughes, Melanie M., Pamela Paxton, Amanda B. Clayton, and Pär Zetterberg. 2019. "Global Gender Quota Adoption, Implementation, and Reform." *Comparative Politics* 51 (2): 219–238.

Huncar, Andrea. 2016. "Maternity Leave for MLAs to Be Introduced by Alberta Government." *CBC News*, March 7, 2016. https://www .cbc.ca/news/canada/edmonton/maternity-leave-for-mlas-to-be -introduced-by-alberta-government-1.3479937

Ingram, Leigh-Anne. 2014. "Re-Imagining Roles: Using Collaborative and Creative Research Methodologies to Explore Girls' Perspectives on Gender, Citizenship and Schooling." *Educational Action Research* 22 (3): 306–324.

Johnson, Niki, and Cecilia Josefsson. 2016. "A New Way of Doing Politics? Cross-Party Women's Caucuses as Critical Actors in Uganda and Uruguay." *Parliamentary Affairs* 69 (4): 845–859.

Jordan-Zachery, Julia S., and Nikol G. Alexander-Floyd. 2018. *Black Women in Politics: Demanding Citizenship, Challenging Power, and Seeking Justice.* Albany: State University of New York Press.

Junn, Jane, and Natalie Masuoka. 2020. "The Gender Gap Is a Race Gap: Women Voters in US Presidential Elections." *Perspectives on Politics* 18 (4): 1135–1145.

Lawless, Jennifer L., and Richard L. Fox. 2005. *It Takes a Candidate: Why Women Don't Run for Office.* New York: Cambridge University Press.

Lawless, Jennifer L., and Richard L. Fox. 2010. *It Still Takes a Candidate: Why Women Don't Run for Office.* New York: Cambridge University Press.

Lay, J. Celeste, Mirya Holman, Angela Bos, Jill Greenlee, Zoe Oxley, and Allison Buffett. 2019. "TIME for Kids to Learn Gender Stereotypes: Analysis of Gender and Political Leadership in a Common Social Studies Resource for Children." *Politics & Gender* 17 (1): 1–22.

McConnaughy, Corrine M. 2013. *The Woman Suffrage Movement in America: A Reassessment.* New York: Cambridge University Press.

Moss, Erin, Henderikus Stam, and Diane Kattevilder. 2013. "From Suffrage to Sterilization: Eugenics and the Women's Movement in 20th Century Alberta." *Canadian Psychology Ottawa* 54 (2): 105–114.

Moyser, Melissa, and Amanda Burlock. 2018. "Time Use: Total Work Burden, Unpaid Work, and Leisure." Statistics Canada, Catalogue no. 89-503-X: 22.

Newsy. 2020. "The Capitol through Her Eyes." YouTube video, 6:39, July 20, 2020. https://www.youtube.com/watch?v=X7liVnJUB78

O'Brien, Diana, and Jennifer Piscopo. 2019. "The Impact of Women's Political Presence." In *Handbook of Women's Political Rights*, edited by Susan Franceschet, Mona Lena Krook, and Netina Tan, 53–72. New York: Palgrave Macmillan.

Och, Malliga, and Shauna Shames. 2018. *The Right Women: Republican Party Activists, Candidates, and Legislators.* Santa Barbara, CA: Praeger.

O'Neill, Brenda, and Elisabeth Gidengil. 2017. "Motherhood's Role in Shaping Political and Civic Participation." In *Mothers and Others: The Impacts of Family Life on Politics*, edited by Melanee Thomas and Amanda Bittner, 268–286. Toronto: UBC Press.

O'Neill, Brenda, Scott Pruysers, and David Stewart. 2021. "Glass Cliffs or Partisan Pressure? Examining Gender and Party Leader Tenures and Exits." *Political Studies* 69 (2): 257–277.

Painter, Nell Irvin. 1996. *Sojourner Truth: A Life, a Symbol.* New York: W. W. Norton & Company, Inc.

Sanbonmatsu, Kira. 2006. "Do Parties Know That 'Women Win'? Party Leader Beliefs about Women's Electoral Chances." *Politics & Gender* 2 (4): 431–450.

Sanbonmatsu, Kira, and Kelly Dittmar. 2020. "Are You Ready to Run®? Campaign Trainings and Women's Candidacies in New Jersey." In *Good Reasons to Run: Women and Political Candidacy*, edited by Shauna L. Shames, Rachel I. Bernhard, Mirya R. Holman, and Dawn Langan Teele, 193–202. Philadelphia: Temple University Press.

Sangster, Joan. 2018. *One Hundred Years of Struggle: The History of Women and the Vote in Canada*. Toronto: UBC Press.

Shames, Shauna. 2017. *Out of the Running: Why Millennials Reject Political Careers and Why It Matters*. New York: NYU Press.

Silva, Andrea, and Carrie Skulley. 2019. "Always Running: Candidate Emergence among Women of Color over Time." *Political Research Quarterly* 72 (2): 342–359.

Smooth, Wendy. 2006. "Intersectionality in Electoral Politics: A Mess Worth Making." *Politics & Gender* 2 (3): 400–414.

Terry, Jillian, Susan Piercey, Elizabeth Goodyear-Grant, and Amanda Bittner. 2019. "Opportunities for Growth in Women's Representation: The Direct Effects of Pro-Woman Attitudes." Paper presented at workshop on Party Organization and Gender organized by Bill Cross and Jeanette Ashe, Vancouver BC, June 3, 2019.

Thomas, Melanee, and Amanda Bittner, eds. 2017. *Mothers and Others: The Role of Parenthood in Politics*. Toronto: UBC Press.

Thomas, Melanee, and Marc André Bodet. 2013. "Sacrificial Lambs, Women Candidates, and District Competitiveness in Canada." *Electoral Studies* 32 (1): 153–166.

Thomas, Sue, and Catherine Wineinger. 2020. "Ambition for Office: Women and Policy Making." In *Good Reasons to Run: Women and Political Candidacy*, edited by Shauna L. Shames, Rachel I. Bernhard, Mirya R. Holman, and Dawn Langan Teele, 75–92. Philadelphia: Temple University Press.

Thomsen, Danielle M., and Aaron S. King. 2020. "Women's Representation and the Gendered Pipeline to Power." *American Political Science Review* 114 (4): 989–1000.

Tolley, Erin. 2015. *Framed: Media and the Coverage of Race in Canadian Politics*. Toronto: UBC Press.

Tolley, Erin. 2019. "Who You Know: Local Party Presidents and Minority Candidate Emergence." *Electoral Studies* 58: 70–79.

Trimble, Linda, Jane Arscott, and Manon Tremblay. 2013. *Stalled: The Representation of Women in Canadian Governments*. Toronto: UBC Press.

Trimble, Linda, and Manon Tremblay. 2005. "Representation of Canadian Women at the Cabinet Table." *Atlantis: Critical Studies in Gender, Culture & Social Justice* 30 (1): 31–45.

Valdini, Melody. 2019. *The Inclusion Calculation: Why Men Appropriate Women's Representation*. New York: Oxford University Press.

Volden, Craig, Alan E. Wiseman, and Dana E. Wittmer. 2013. "When Are Women More Effective Lawmakers Than Men?" *American Journal of Political Science* 57 (2): 326–341.

Wineinger, Catherine. 2021. "How Can a Black Woman Be a Republican? An Intersectional Analysis of Identity Claims in the 2014 Mia Love Campaign." *Politics, Groups, and Identities* 9 (3): 566–588.

Wolbrecht, Christina, and J. Kevin Corder. 2020. *A Century of Votes for Women: American Elections since Suffrage.* New York: Cambridge University Press.

TWO

Latin America and the Caribbean

Isabel Castillo and Krystoff Kissoon

This chapter analyzes women's political participation and representation in Latin America and the Caribbean regions. We must start by clarifying the boundaries, as there is no unique definition of which countries compose Latin America and which the Caribbean. There are generally two ways of understanding whether a country belongs in one or the other region: a geographical categorization and a cultural one. The geographical definition considers that countries in the mainland from Mexico to the Strait of Magellan in the south are Latin America, whereas the islands in the Caribbean Sea are the Caribbean region. The cultural definition is based on who the **colonizer** was—the Spanish, Portuguese, French, British, or Dutch empire. From the colonizers, countries inherited their language, religion, and institutions, so we often group them together. Latin American countries were former Spanish, Portuguese, and French colonies, and the Caribbean islands were former British colonies.

In this chapter, we will follow a mostly geographical definition, with some exceptions. Belize, in Central America, and Guyana and Surinam, in South America, will be considered Caribbean countries for their cultural traditions: the first two are former British colonies, whereas Surinam was a Dutch colony. Table 2.1 lists all the countries in each region.

Latin America has been a leader in terms of the representation of women in legislatures. A few years ago, it simultaneously had four women serving as presidents in their respective countries, including in the largest country in the region—Brazil. This notable achievement is largely related to the pioneer introduction of quotas and parity laws in the region. Progress, however, has been uneven. In some countries, women remain highly underrepresented in the legislature. Women of Indigenous origin and Afro-descendants face particular challenges to access power positions. And even in successful cases, such as Bolivia, the inclusion of women has not come without costs, which multiple episodes of violence against women politicians have made clear. Finally, in the executive arena, women presidents remain an exception.

While there have been significant advances in women's political representation in Latin America, progress in the Caribbean has moved at a slower pace. Nonetheless, women have been involved in politics across Caribbean states since **decolonization** and the passage of women's suffrage. Women have been engaged in social and political activism through

Table 2.1   Countries in the Latin American and Caribbean Regions

Latin America	Caribbean
Argentina (AR)	Antigua and Barbuda (AG)
Bolivia (BO)	Bahamas (BS)
Brazil (BR)	Barbados (BB)
Chile (CL)	Belize (BZ)
Colombia (CO)	Cuba (CU)
Costa Rica (CR)	Dominica (DM)
Ecuador (EC)	Dominican Republic (DO)
El Salvador (SV)	Grenada (GD)
Guatemala (GT)	Guyana (GY)
Honduras (HN)	Haiti (HT)
Mexico (MX)	Jamaica (JM)
Nicaragua (NI)	St. Kitts and Nevis (KN)
Panama (PA)	St. Lucia (LC)
Paraguay (PY)	St. Vincent and the Grenadines (VC)
Peru (PE)	Suriname (SR)
Uruguay (UY)	Trinidad and Tobago (TT)
Venezuela (VE)	

membership in women's groups and political parties and have contested and won seats in parliament across Caribbean states. Many Caribbean countries have also elected women heads of state and appointed women cabinet ministers. Notable progress in women's representation has been made in two Caribbean states, Haiti and Guyana, largely as a result of the adoption of quota systems. Despite these successes, women in the Caribbean overall continue to face barriers to achieving the highest levels of political participation, such as traditional gender stereotypes and patriarchal attitudes and the challenges of balancing domestic, professional, and political duties. However, as more women are attaining higher education and higher-income employment in the Caribbean, opportunities for increased women's participation in politics are on the rise.

WOMEN IN POLITICS IN LATIN AMERICA

Latin American Women as Voters

Women's suffrage in Latin America was achieved in two waves. A small group of countries—Ecuador, Brazil, and Uruguay—extended suffrage in the late 1920s and early 1930s, whereas the majority did so in the decade following the end of World War II. Table 2.2 clearly shows these two groups, considering the year women were legally able to vote in national elections. Overall, there was a thirty-two-year span between the first and last countries to enfranchise women.

In a few countries, women were first able to vote in local elections. For example, in Chile, women have been able to vote and run for office in municipal elections since 1934 but had to wait until 1949 to participate in national elections for the legislature and presidency. Similarly, in Bolivia, women had participated in local elections since 1945 but not until 1952 nationally. The logic behind these limited suffrage extensions was that local politics—for example, beautification of streets and parks, collecting garbage, and the like—was closer to traditional women's roles as homemakers and not where the big political issues were decided. As such, their participation was a smaller threat to traditional gender roles, where women were primarily in charge of domestic affairs and politics was the business of men.

The gradual expansion of suffrage was the dominant strategy more generally. The early republics tended to be, on paper, quite inclusive as suffrage restrictions—the most common being those based on income, sex,

Table 2.2   Date of Women's Suffrage

Country	Year
Ecuador	1929
Uruguay	1932
Brazil	1932
Cuba	1934
Dominican Rep.	1942
Guatemala	1945
Panama	1945
Venezuela	1946
Argentina	1947
Costa Rica	1949
Chile	1949
El Salvador	1950
Bolivia	1952
Mexico	1953
Colombia	1954
Peru	1955
Nicaragua	1955
Honduras	1955
Paraguay	1961

Source: Castillo (2019).

and education—were introduced throughout the nineteenth century. These restrictions were then slowly removed. Property and income restrictions and sometimes education requirements were removed first, reaching broad male suffrage. Then came women's suffrage, usually the single-largest expansion of the franchise, although Brazil, Chile, Ecuador, Guatemala, and Peru retained a literacy restriction. This literacy restriction mostly excluded Indigenous peoples and peasants, particularly women from those groups, as they had lower education rates.

Politicians tend to resist changing the rules of the game. Incorporating new voters always introduces a degree of electoral uncertainty, which is why this piecemeal or gradual strategy of suffrage expansion was so common. In some cases, however, **revolutionary governments** will implement bolder and broader changes all at once. For example, one of the first measures taken by the government after the 1952 Bolivian revolution was to immediately establish universal suffrage, removing the sex, income/occupation, and literacy restrictions. Through this measure, most women, Indigenous peoples, and peasants that had previously been excluded were incorporated into the electoral process.

That most Latin American countries did not enfranchise women until the 1940s and 1950s was not due to a lack of trying. The demand for women's suffrage started in the late nineteenth century in some countries and in the early twentieth century in others. There were multiple instances in which women's enfranchisement was debated by the legislature and ultimately dismissed. Two central reasons delayed women's inclusion. On the one hand, some political parties believed women would mostly support conservative parties. The reason behind this argument is that women at the time—and even today—tend to be more religious than men in terms of identifying with a particular religion as well as in terms of church attendance. As a Catholic region, parties believed this closeness between women and the Catholic Church would make them support conservative parties aligned with the church. As such, antireligious parties resisted giving women the vote. On the other hand, many politicians believed politics was an activity that should be reserved for men and that women's "natural" place was in the home. Moreover, some legislators argued that by participating in politics, women would abandon their children and family. These types of beliefs became less common with time, as women increasingly joined the workforce and took on new roles.

The Struggle for Suffrage in Latin America

Whereas in the early twentieth century it was mostly isolated voices—from both men and women—who asked for suffrage to be extended, by the 1940s, most countries saw a women's movement form. There are considerable differences in the region in the size and characteristics of these **first wave women's movements**. Argentina, Chile, Mexico, and Uruguay had some of the largest and strongest women's organizations that formed in the 1920s and 1930s. These movements generally had a broader set of demands; in addition to suffrage, they included equal civil rights, access and expansion of education, and protections for women workers and mothers. In other countries, such as Ecuador and Peru, similar women's organizations were very weak with limited membership.

Organizations were not the only ones pushing the debate on women's suffrage forward. In some cases, the desired reform was due to the role played by individual women. Matilde Hidalgo, from Ecuador, is an example. The first woman physician in her country, she registered to vote in 1924, arguing there were no legal impediments to do so, starting the path for some women to vote in that year's election and to be explicitly included in the constitution as citizens in 1929. A second interesting case is that of Berta Lutz, in Brazil, who was already a renowned figure when Getulio Vargas arrived in government through a **military coup** in 1930. Two years later, a new electoral code was being debated, but an initial draft included women's suffrage only for single women, widows, and married women with their husband's permission. In this scenario, women's organizations mounted a campaign to obtain suffrage in equal conditions as men. After Lutz and a few other women met directly with Vargas, they finally succeeded in their demand (Hahner 1990, 161–162).

A third example of one woman taking on a leading role was in the case of Eva "Evita" Duarte de Perón, in Argentina. Although Argentina had a strong and progressive feminist movement in the earlier part of the century, by the early 1940s, amid general political instability in the country, the movement had weakened. When **populist leader** Domingo Perón was elected to the presidency in 1946, his wife, Evita, led the campaign for women's suffrage, sidestepping the efforts of the traditional suffragist movement that was now opposed to Perón (Hammond 2011). Peronists finally succeeded in passing the suffrage law in 1947.

All these women as well as most of the members and leadership of women's organizations shared being from the middle and upper classes. The first generations of professionals, teachers, and women linked to male political elites formed the backbone of the movement. Working-class women were also starting to organize during the first part of the twentieth century, but their demands focused on working conditions and not suffrage. There were some exceptions to this general trend, with lower-class women joining the demand for equal political rights. For example, in Chile, the Movement for the Emancipation of Women, created in 1935, was a cross-class movement that incorporated women from the popular sectors in addition to professional women. Some individual feminists also stand out for not sharing the status and socioeconomic background of most feminists. Prudencia Ayala, from El Salvador, is one such figure. From

Indigenous and humble origins, she was a pioneer in the struggle for women's rights, mounting a (failed) presidential campaign in 1930, twenty years before women were able to vote.

Women's Political Engagement in Latin America

Before we review the current state of women's political participation and representation, it is important to note that women's suffrage was the beginning of a long road. Women incorporated into the electorate in a slow and gradual manner. Registration and turnout lagged men for decades, and very few women reached elected office, a trend that remained largely unchanged until the 1990s.

In addition to these trends, which are largely common to other regions in the world, Latin American women—and voters more generally—saw their political rights limited by frequent democratic interruptions. The second half of the twentieth century was filled with authoritarian regimes of different kinds, including military **dictatorships**, political dynasties, and **hegemonic** party systems. While some included noncompetitive elections, others suspended voting altogether. These regimes were not always problematic for women's rights. In fact, in thirteen out of the seventeen Latin American countries, suffrage was extended by nondemocratic regimes. But women often had to wait to exercise their voting rights, limiting the impact of their voice in the political process.

As women were incorporated into the electorate after men, there was a gender gap in turnout for decades. Currently, there are no big differences between men's and women's rates of electoral participation, even though there is some discussion about whether small gaps favor men (Carlin and Love 2015) or women (Carreras and Castañeda 2014), largely due to inconsistencies across survey data. In other forms of political participation, such as following and talking about politics, participating in political parties, political campaigns, and demonstrations or protests, there is greater consensus that women participate less than men (Espinal and Zhao 2015; Desposato and Norrander 2009). The reasons behind these differences include different patterns of **socialization** between men and women. One key factor seems to be access to employment, which provides women with economic independence, alters traditional gender roles, and provides exposure to new points of view, forms of communication, and sources of information. Since women participate at lower rates than men in the labor market, they have less access to these resources, and their overall level of political participation is lower.

Another key issue is whether men and women have different political preferences, that is, whether they tend to support different political parties. The literature refers to a traditional gender gap to point to the early decades of political participation, when women tended to favor parties more on the right relative to men. The modern gender gap reversed this trend and took place sometime around the 1980s in Europe and the United States. Do we see similar patterns in Latin America?

As with turnout, we do not have systematic data for the early phases of women's electoral participation, before the **third wave of democratization**. For recent decades, the traditional gender gap seems to persist, meaning that women tend to support more candidates to the right than men (Morgan 2015). The differences are small and only present in some years, but they seem to indicate that, compared to other regions, advancement toward gender equality has been slower. As before, the differences in voting preferences are related to women's autonomy, with women working outside the home voting more to the left and women conforming to traditional gender roles as homemakers preferring candidates on the right. Overall, we can conclude that in comparison to Europe and other advanced democracies, Latin America has not seen a clear change toward a modern gender gap. In turnout, the evidence is mixed, and there does not seem to be important differences between men's and women's participation rates overall. In other forms of participation as well as in terms of voting preferences, the traditional gender gap seems to have been reducing, but it still remains, indicating the persistence of traditional gender roles.

Latin American Women as Members of Parliament

The descriptive, or numerical, representation of women in legislatures in Latin America has generally improved in the last couple of decades, as seen in figure 2.1. Considering all countries, women now represent 33 percent of members of the lower or single chamber, up from 10 percent in 1997. In a little over twenty years, there has been a threefold increase. The figure also shows that the improvement in women's representation has been quite steady. If the trend continues, it might take another twenty years to achieve parity, although we can expect the curve to slow down as some countries achieve parity—not having more room to grow.

Looking beyond these general trends, table 2.3 shows there is great variation, with a range between 14.8 percent in Brazil and 51.7 percent in

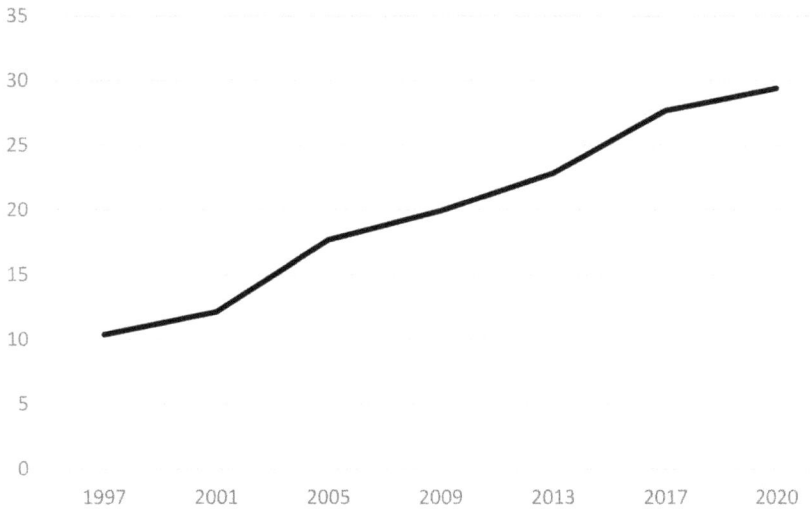

Figure 2.1 Evolution of Average Percentage of Women in the Legislature in Latin America, 1997–2020 (Inter-Parliamentary Union: Parline database on national parliaments, July 31, 2021).

Nicaragua—the country with the third-highest percentage of women in the legislature worldwide.

One important reason for the improvement of women's representation is the existence of legislative gender quotas, which are present in every Latin American country except Guatemala. Latin America was the pioneer region in the adoption of this type of electoral institution (see sidebar for the case of Argentina). Legislative quotas mandate a minimum percentage of women to be included as candidates that ranges from 20 percent to 50 percent in countries with parity laws. And although these laws have been generally effective, boosting the number of elected women in the twenty-first century, the results are not the same across countries.

The last column in table 2.3 indicates the difference between the percentage of women candidates and those that actually get elected. While some variation between the two numbers is to be expected, a larger difference indicates a less effective quota. For example, the laws of Honduras and Panama mandate that half the candidates must be women, but only 27.3 percent and 22.5 percent of their legislatures, respectively, are

Table 2.3   Women's Representation in Parliament and Legislative Quotas (as of 2022)

Country	Percentage of Women in Lower Chamber	Year Quota Adopted	Quota Size	Gap between Quota and Elected Women
Nicaragua	51.7	2012	50	−1.7
Mexico	50.0	1996	50	0
Costa Rica	47.4	1996	50	2.6
Bolivia	46.2	1997	50	3.8
Argentina	44.8	1991	30	−14.8
Peru	40.0	1997	30	−10
Ecuador	38.7	1998	50	11.3
Chile	35.5	2015	40	4.5
Colombia	28.9	1999	30	1.1
El Salvador	27.4	2013	30	3.3
Honduras	27.3	2000	50	22.7
Uruguay	25.3	2009	33	4.7
Panama	22.5	2007	50	28.5
Venezuela	22.2	1998	50	27.8
Guatemala	19.4	—	—	—
Paraguay	17.5	1996	20	2.5
Brazil	14.8	1997	30	15.2

Source: IPU (2022) and IDEA (2020).

actually composed of women. How successful this instrument is will depend on whether the law includes mechanisms for sanctioning parties that do not meet the quota, whether it mandates the order of the candidates or whether women must be placed in electable positions, as well as the electoral system more broadly. In this sense, there has been an important process of learning. The first laws adopted tended to be less effective, but successive reforms have often incorporated corrections and higher quota sizes.

ARGENTINA: PIONEER IN THE ADOPTION OF NATIONAL QUOTAS

In 1991, Argentina became the first country in the world to have a legislative quota law. This reform mandated that a minimum of 30 percent of candidates had to be women; otherwise, the party would not be allowed to compete. It also stated that women candidates should run in places with real chances of being elected. In the first election under the quota law in 1993, the percentage of women in the Chamber of Deputies rose from 5 percent to 14 percent. In 1995, under a strengthened quota law, women's seats rose to 27 percent, and a decade later, women's presence in parliament was at 36 percent. In the Senate, quotas started functioning in 2001 with similar results; in only two years, the Senate went from being 6 percent women to 36 percent.

The demands for a quota emerged with Argentina's transition to democracy in 1983. Women actively fought for democracy and massively joined political parties; by 1988, they represented 48 percent of party members nationwide. The new climate presented an opening for feminist movements to strengthen and question the roots of discrimination against women that highlighted the low representation of women in decision-making spaces (Lubertino 2003). Women in the Argentine Congress started to introduce bipartisan bills championing quotas and won bipartisan support as well as support from the president (Caminotti 2014). Once the quota became law, parties found ways to circumvent the quota. However, over time, quota loopholes were closed, and sanctions became more stringent. Gender quotas for legislative elections is now a consolidated feature of Argentine elections and has been internalized by political parties, who abide it without much trouble.

Spotlight on Women and Minorities in Latin America

The rest of this section will focus on two underrepresented groups that are particularly important in Latin America: Indigenous and Afro-descendant. Diversity is fundamental to have different voices and perspectives represented in decision-making spaces. The inclusion of more men and women from ethnic minorities and lower classes is still a pending task in many Latin American nations.

Who counts as Indigenous and Afro-descendant does not have a straightforward answer; currently, most countries ask whether citizens self-identify as Indigenous or Afro-descendant. Indigenous people constitute 62 percent of the population in Bolivia and 41 percent in Guatemala, the two countries with the largest Indigenous populations. On the other extreme are El Salvador and Brazil, with 0.2 percent and 0.5 percent, respectively (CEPAL 2014, 43). Afro-descendants range from 53.4 percent in Venezuela and 50.9 in Brazil to zero in Guatemala (Htun 2016, 26). There is, then, great variation in the racial and ethnic makeup of Latin American countries. In terms of the representation of Indigenous people, Bolivia had the highest number of Indigenous (40 percent) in its legislature in 2014. Guatemala had 13 percent, Peru had one Indigenous legislator, and Chile had none (Htun 2016, 35). Afro-descendants in Brazil were 20 percent of the legislature compared to over half the population (Htun 2016). In Ecuador, Afro-descendants were better represented with 6.6 percent of the legislature while being 7.2 percent of the national population. There is, then, a clear underrepresentation of both Afro-descendants and Indigenous peoples in Latin America that is more pronounced in countries with larger nonwhite populations. This reflects broader patterns of racism, where social, economic, and educational opportunities are not equally distributed.

The main exception is Bolivia. In 1995, the Indigenous in Bolivia constituted only 1 percent of elected members of Congress; after electing its first Indigenous president in 2005, Indigenous candidates were able to access elected offices in unprecedented numbers as part of the governing Movement Toward Socialism (MAS) party. Women also increased their access to the legislature after the 2009 constitution established parity in all government branches. At the intersection of both of these processes were Indigenous women, who reached 19 percent of seats in 2014 (Rousseau and Ewig 2017). Because numbers are so small in most countries, there are often no clear trends or significant differences between the representation of men and women from these minorities. For example, in 2013, Peru had three Afro-descendant legislators, and all three were women. In 2018, Chile elected two Indigenous to the lower chamber, both women. Countries with larger populations, such as Brazil with Afro-descendants or Bolivia with Indigenous, do show that women from these groups are less represented than men.

Unlike in the case of women with gender quotas, mechanisms to promote racial and ethnic inclusion are less common. In this case, the preferred mechanism has been reserved seats, where a number of seats are assigned to Indigenous peoples and are elected from a separate list. Bolivia, Ecuador, Mexico, Peru, and Venezuela have some form of mechanism to promote inclusion. Bolivia has seven lower house seats reserved for Indigenous peoples. Colombia has one in the Senate, and there is one for Indigenous and two for Black communities in the lower house. Venezuela has three reserved seats in the National Assembly. Peru has a quota mechanism specifically for the Amazonian region that states 15 percent of the party list must be composed of Indigenous candidates. In Mexico, there are twenty-eight special Indigenous districts where there is a high concentration of Indigenous peoples (Htun 2016, 15).

Latin American Women as Leaders

Latin American countries are all presidential systems, meaning that the legislature and the president are elected separately (as in the United States). The presidency is the most powerful and visible political office, which makes it particularly hard to reach for traditionally excluded groups, such as women. It is also a highly masculine office, with presidents traditionally seen as **patriarchs**, the nation's fathers (Reyes-Housholder and Thomas 2018). Because of this association between men and presidential power, women candidates are often criticized if perceived as too soft or maternal, which is equated with not presidential. At the same time, women are punished if they depart from traditional gender roles or are not seen as feminine, thus facing standards difficult to meet.

Compared to other regions, however, Latin America has made considerable progress by having seven women elected to the presidency since 1990. Table 2.4 lists all the women that have been elected president. Before 1990, no woman had been elected president, but in the last fifteen years, five countries have had women presidents, with three of them elected for a

Table 2.4   Women Presidents in Latin America, 1990–2022

Year	Country	President	Ideology
1990	Nicaragua	Violeta Chamorro	Center-right
1999	Panama	Mireya Moscoso	Right
2005/2013	Chile	Michelle Bachelet	Center-left
2007/2011	Argentina	Cristina Fernández de Kirchner	Center-left
2010	Costa Rica	Laura Chinchilla	Center-right
2010/2014	Brazil	Dilma Rousseff	Center-left
2021	Honduras	Xiomara Castro	Left

Source: Reyes-Housholder and Thomas (2018).

Michelle Bachelet, first woman president of Chile (2006–2010; 2014–2018). (Alexandre Paes Leme | Dreamstime.com)

second term. Four Central American and three South American countries have elected women to the executive, indicating that having women presidents is not exclusive of a particular subregion. The cases also indicate that there is no relationship between the president and her ideology, as the women presidents have been from the right, center-right, center-left and left.

Despite this progress, woman presidents remain an exception. Most countries in the region have yet to elect a woman, and no country has elected multiple women presidents. Between 2018 and 2021, no women presidents were in office (except for interim president Jeanine Añez in Bolivia); in late 2021, Xiomara Castro was elected to the presidency in Honduras. It thus remains to be seen whether the small wave of elected presidents in the past two decades was an exception or opened the door to women executives more broadly. Commonly, women are more likely to be included in lower-level offices—particularly as presidential running partners—to compensate for a lack of equality in executive leadership and to signal inclusion without fundamental change. In 2022, only six of fifteen countries have women as vice presidents (down from ten in 2020), including a woman of color in the case of Colombia, where Francia Márquez became the first Afro-descendant women to occupy that position in her country and the second in Latin America.[1] This growing incorporation of women as vice presidents increases the visibility of women in politics. Beyond that, it is unclear whether the vice presidency has any effect on women's participation in politics more broadly, for example, as a stepping stone for other elected offices.

---

[1] The other two countries, Chile and Mexico, do not have the institution of a vice presidency.

A final area or representation is the presidential cabinet. A cabinet is appointed to propose and implement the policies of the government. As highly visible offices, these can be important positions for careers in politics. In fact, of the recent women presidents, Bachelet, Chinchilla, and Rousseff were elected to the presidency after serving in their predecessors' cabinets. Women's presence in cabinets has seen an increase in the last few of decades. In 1990, only 7 percent of ministries were occupied by women. The number rose to 15 percent in the early 2000s and was 25 percent a decade later (Taylor-Robinson and Gleitz 2018). These numbers are similar to women in the legislature, indicating that as women enter one political arena, there seems to be greater awareness on the importance of including women in other arenas. Most women, however, are appointed in stereotypically feminine ministries, such as those related to social welfare issues (e.g., education, health, housing, women's issues), while they remain underrepresented in the traditionally masculine areas of security/interior and finance.

WOMEN IN POLITICS IN THE CARIBBEAN

Caribbean Women as Voters

The suffrage movement occurred in the Caribbean in the mid-eighteenth century, and women won the right to vote in Jamaica in 1919, Dominica and Trinidad and Tobago in 1925, and Guyana in 1928 (Shirley 2014, 19). The granting of suffrage rights in the Caribbean followed closely on the heels of the United Kingdom, which passed women's suffrage in 1918. The achievement of suffrage in the Caribbean was therefore linked to colonial ties between the United Kingdom and its former colonies. However, like suffrage laws in the United Kingdom, suffrage laws adopted by Caribbean states included discriminatory restrictions that excluded most women from accessing the vote. These restrictions included age, income, property tax, and literacy, which were imposed more severely on women than men (UN Women 2018, 11). This is hardly surprising given the historical process of slavery in the Caribbean, which disenfranchised most Black men and women as well as poor whites.

Faced with only **partial enfranchisement** because of these requirements, women activists in the Caribbean worked to level the playing field and enfranchise most women. For example, Janet Jagan, a women's rights activist in Guyana, cofounded the Women's Political and Economic Organization (WPEO), which led protests demanding universal suffrage and

Table 2.5   Date of Universal Adult Suffrage in the Caribbean

Country	Year
Antigua and Barbuda	1951
Bahamas	1962
Barbados	1950
Belize	1954
Dominica	1951
Grenada	1951
Guyana	1953
Haiti	1950
Jamaica	1944
St. Kitts and Nevis	1952
St. Lucia	1951
St. Vincent and the Grenadines	1951
Suriname	1948
Trinidad and Tobago	1946

Source: Buddan (2004).

brought awareness to other inequalities and issues women faced. Jagan successfully gained a seat in the general elections of 1953, the first election called under universal suffrage in Guyana. Similarly, in Barbados, the first general election after the introduction of adult suffrage in 1950 saw the election of the first woman to the **House of Assemblies**, Edna Ermyntrude Foster, known as Ermie Bourne. Universal adult suffrage was first passed in Jamaica and spread to the other Caribbean islands by 1962, spanning an eighteen-year period and constituting a **democratic revolution** (Buddan 2004, 135). The passage of adult suffrage in the Caribbean was a critical component of the legitimization of political parties, elections, constitutions, and political leadership (table 2.5).

The Struggle for Suffrage in the Caribbean

In the early twentieth century, women activists in the Caribbean did not limit their political participation to calls for full enfranchisement but engaged in many forms of activism for social and political change. For example, in Trinidad and Tobago, Audrey Jeffers became the first woman elected to the Port-of-Spain City Council in 1936. She founded the Coterie of Social Workers in 1921, which comprised only middle-class women and was concerned with educational opportunities for girls and the inclusion of middle-class women into salaried employment (Reddock 1994). In the long term, its goal was to improve the social, economic, and political status of Black middle-class women as well as men. Audrey Jeffers advocated for removing the legal barriers that excluded women from gaining access to the Legislative Council of Trinidad and Tobago and was successfully appointed in 1946 (Shirley 2014).

During the same period, in Jamaica, Mary Morris Knibb became the first woman to hold a political post when she won a seat in the 1939 local government elections. She was a social worker who was concerned with the plight of poor women and children, particularly the increasing number of illegitimate children and the extent to which their fathers neglected them. This led her to pursue a mass wedding initiative in which she marshaled over 150 weddings (Cooper 1995). The expectation was that marriage would improve the living conditions of women and children by providing them with family stability and access to legal redress. Morris Knibb gained favor among the population, and her election to local government in 1939 paved the way for many other women to run for seats in the 1944 general election (Shirley 2014). In 1944, Iris Collins of the Jamaica Labor Party became the first woman to win a seat in the House of Representatives, amassing 5,519 votes, whereas her closest contender, Allan George St. Claver Coombs, received a measly 1,683 votes.

Dominica also has a rich history in women's political activism. Phyllis Byam Shand Allfrey, born in Dominica in 1908, was a novelist and political activist who immigrated to the United States and England for several years until she returned to Dominica in 1954 (Paravisini-Gebert 1996). She was inspired by sociopolitical ideologies through her association with the Labor Party in England and became highly concerned for the working conditions of the poor, Black working class. Allfrey challenged the small, powerful elite who controlled the social, political, and economic systems and resources of Dominica and cofounded the Dominica Labor Party in 1955. However, because of her criticisms of the patriarchy and male hegemonic party politics, she was expelled from the Dominica Labor Party in 1962 in a coup. This led her to forge an alliance with another woman activist, Eugenia Charles, and to join the Dominica Freedom Party, where Allfrey won a seat in the 1970 general elections (Shirley 2014). As a result, an analysis of the lives and activism of Audrey Jeffers, Mary Morris Knibb, and Phyllis Byam Shand Allfrey reveal that while their middle-class backgrounds provided them with opportunities and access to political structures to change the status quo, they were challenging a sexist, patriarchal culture that often sought to exclude women from the highest levels of political leadership.

The period of the 1970s marked a significant transformation in the understanding of gender equality in the Caribbean. The unequal distribution of wealth, power, and resources coupled with the rise of Black identity and community power as a result of the Black Power movement produced a wave of radicalism in the region during this time. This radicalism was also driven by the rise of **second wave feminist** thought in the 1960s in the United States as well as global socialist ideologies, which transferred to the Caribbean (Shirley 2009). For example, various Caribbean countries introduced their own brand of socialism, such as **cooperative socialism** in Guyana and **democratic socialism** in Jamaica.

Women were drawn to the movements, especially in the case of the Black Power movement in Trinidad and Tobago, where they had even participated alongside men in violent encounters against the police (Pasley 2001). However, women were often marginalized within these hegemonic structures of Black patriarchy, and they often departed to form women's groups, where they had agency to advocate for issues that affected them as a constituency. Through leadership in these grassroots feminist groups, women activists did important work on the ground to improve women's access to the larger social, economic, and political structures. For example, women assembled to form the Housewives Association of Trinidad and Tobago (HATT) in 1972 and focused on issues such as consumerism, product standards, inflation, rape and violence against women, domestic workers rights, employer rights, nutrition, and other health-related issues (Shirley 2014). Leaders of HATT pursued advocacy and protest actions that challenged the state to turn its attention to women's issues and influenced a variety of legislative and policy changes concerning standards such as minimum wage. In addition, five members of HATT went on to contest the 1976 general elections, representing four different political parties as well as independent candidates. The legacy of HATT reveals that once a platform for women's advocacy is created, women are more likely to be included in the political structures of the state and represented in the democratic electoral process (Shirley 2014).

Similarly, in Jamaica, women led the reform movement during the 1970s. The ruling People's National Party, newly guided by a democratic socialist approach, supported the inclusion of women in the state's policy agenda. Women who were already within the structures of governance became inspired by democratic socialism and took a deeper interest in the plight of poor Jamaican women (Shirley 2014). For example, Mavis Gilmour and Lucille Mathurin Mair lobbied the prime minister to establish a governmental institution focused on transforming poor women's lives (Reddock 1998). As a result of this advocacy, the state implemented the Bureau of Women's Affairs, the first of its kind in the world, within the Office of the Prime Minister. The case of Jamaica reveals that despite a minority presence of women within established political structures, significant policy changes for women by women can be made (Reingold 2008).

In Guyana, during the period of the 1970s, women activists were less successful in gaining the autonomy to undertake feminist work outside of the established political structures. The political arms of the two oppositional women's political parties, the Women's Progressive Organization (WPO) and the Women's Revolutionary Socialist Movement (WRSM), were more committed to retaining their party's hegemonic control of the government rather than pursuing substantive feminist initiatives (Shirley 2014). In the late 1970s, an autonomous feminist group, WPA Women, emerged out of a larger political party and broke its ties to enable women to engage in feminist initiatives more freely. WPA Women successfully worked to transform the lives of poor women outside of established male hegemonic party structures, which often sought to co-opt feminism and marginalize the needs of women.

Caribbean Women as Members of Parliament

There is insufficient data on women's electoral participation compared to men in the Caribbean. However, there is sufficient data on other forms of women's political participation such as membership in parliament. Women in Caribbean states have made important contributions to the legislative agendas of their respective countries. Yet, the percentage of women members of parliament in the Caribbean significantly lags behind Latin America: 14.3 percent compared to 25.2 percent, respectively (Faieta, McDade, and Arias 2015, 8). The percentage of women's representation in

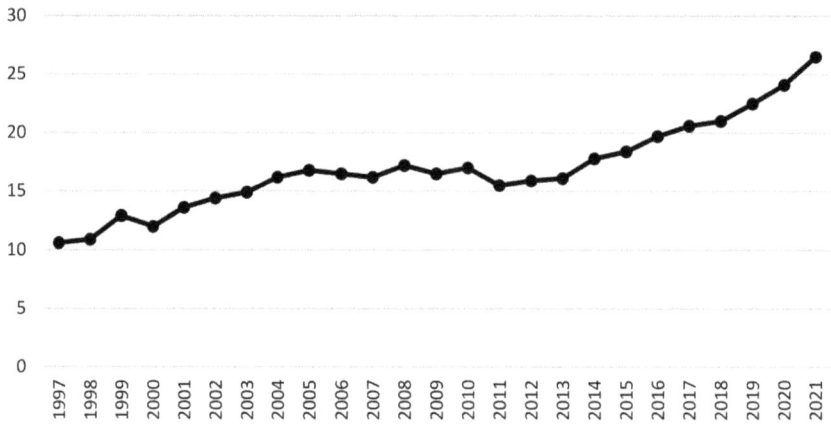

Figure 2.2 Average of Women in Parliament in Caribbean Region over Time (Inter-Parliamentary Union: Parline database on national parliaments, July 31, 2021).

Caribbean parliaments has remained virtually stagnant in the period 2000–2014: between 13.1 percent and 15.7 percent (Faieta, McDade, and Arias 2015, 25). Since 2012, representation has gradually improved, but it remains low compared to global and regional figures (Faieta, McDade, and Arias 2015, 25; figure 2.2).

In the Caribbean Community (CARICOM), only two countries have electoral gender quotas: Haiti and Guyana. The Republic of Haiti amended its constitution in 2012 to include a minimum quota of 30 percent for women at all levels, including public service (Article 17.1). It also requires that the structures and functions of all laws related to political parties must operate in accordance with the minimum 30 percent quota established in Article 17.1 (table 2.6).

The Cooperative Republic of Guyana has utilized a legislative candidate quota for over twenty years. The quota provision (Representation of the People Act, Section 11B) requires at least one-third (33 percent) of the candidates on a party's list be women for the constituencies in which that party is contesting. There is an additional requirement that at most 20 percent of the number of constituencies in which a party is contesting may contain no women. After the quota system was introduced in Guyana in 2000, the percentages of women parliamentarians steadily increased from

Table 2.6   Women in National Parliament in Caribbean Countries, 2021

Country	Percentage of Women in Lower House	Electoral Gender Quotas
Antigua and Barbuda (AG)	11.1	
Bahamas (BS)	12.8	
Barbados (BB)	20.0	
Belize (BZ)	12.5	
Cuba (CU)	53.4	
Dominica (DM)	34.4	
Dominican Republic (DO)	27.9	Yes
Grenada (GD)	46.7	
Guyana (GY)	35.7	Yes
Haiti (HT)	—	Yes
Jamaica (JM)	28.6	
St. Kitts and Nevis (KN)	25	
St. Lucia (LC)	16.7	
St. Vincent and the Grenadines (VC)	18.2	
Suriname (SR)	29.4	
Trinidad and Tobago (TT)	26.2	

Source: IPU (2021) and IDEA (2020).

20 percent in 2001 to 31.34 percent in 2011 (Faieta, McDade, and Arias 2015, 33–34).

Caribbean Women as Leaders

Women have held executive power in fourteen Caribbean states since 1980. Seven women have served as prime minister, and four women have served as president in the Caribbean (see table 2.7). Seven women have served or are currently serving as governors general, the chief

Table 2.7   Women Heads of State and Government of CARICOM Countries since 1980

Country	Function	Name	Period
Antigua and Barbuda	Governor general	Dame Louise Lake-Tack	2007–2014
Bahamas	Governor general	Dame Ivy Dumont	2001–2005
	Prime minister	Cynthia A. Pratt	05/4/2005–06/06/2005
Barbados	Governor general	Dame Nita Barrow	1990–1995
	Prime minister	Mia Mottley	2018–present
	President	Sandra Mason	2021-present
Belize	Governor general	Dame Elmira Minita Gordon	1981–1993
Dominica	Prime minister	Mary Eugenia Charles	1980–1995
Grenada	Governor general	Dame Cécile La Grenade	2013–present
Guyana	Prime minister	Janet Jagan	1997
	President	Janet Jagan	1997–1999
Haiti	Acting president	Ertha Pascal-Trouillot	1990–1991
	Prime minister	Michèle Pierre-Louis	2008–2009
Jamaica	Prime minister	Portia Simpson Miller	2006–2007 2011–2016
St. Lucia	Governor general	Dame Pearlette Louisy	1997–2017
St. Vincent and the Grenadines	Deputy governor general/Acting governor general	Monica Jessie Dacon	2001–2002
Trinidad and Tobago	Prime minister	Kamla Persad-Bissessar	2010–2015
	President	Paula-Mae Weekes	2018–present

Source: Faieta, McDade, and Arias (2015) updated by author in 2021 with data courtesy of Farida Jalalzai.

representative of the Crown in a Commonwealth country of which the British monarch is head of state. Among the CARICOM states, only St. Kitts and Nevis and Suriname have never had a woman head of state.

Women have also held executive power in the Caribbean by being appointed to cabinet ministerial positions. In 2014, 33 out of a total of 227 cabinet ministers in the CARICOM countries, or 14.5 percent, were women (Faieta, McDade, and Arias 2015, 37). Most countries have between 10 percent and 20 percent women ministers, which, given the small size of most cabinets, only translates to 1–4 women ministers in each cabinet. Haiti (35 percent), Grenada (30.8 percent), and Guyana (27.8 percent) have the highest percentage of women ministers, whereas Trinidad and Tobago (6.5 percent) and Suriname (5.6 percent) have the lowest percentage of women cabinet ministers (Faieta, McDade, and Arias 2015, 37).

Although women hold an average of 15 percent of ministerial portfolios in the Caribbean, they tend to be clustered in policy areas traditionally considered women's issues, such as social services, education, culture, youth, and gender affairs. They are rarely appointed to ministries such as commerce, industry, foreign affairs, development, or finance, which are dominated by men (Htun and Piscopo 2010). In Guyana, Carolyn Allison Rodrigues-Birkett served as minister of foreign affairs (2008–2015), and Karen Roslyn Vanessa Cummings most recently served in this position (2019–2020). In addition, Suriname had a woman minister of labor (2005–2010), a woman minister of foreign affairs twice (2000–2005 and 2005–2010), and its first woman minister of finance in 2010 (Faieta, McDade, and Arias 2015, 38).

BARRIERS TO POLITICAL PARITY IN LATIN AMERICA AND THE CARIBBEAN

Barriers to women's representation in Latin America include institutional, political, economic, and cultural factors. According to the historical sexual division of labor, politics is a male-dominated space, where for centuries women were largely excluded. And while this notion has partly changed in the last few decades, there is still a perception of women as newcomers who are entering a space where they do not belong. As such, women in politics often face resistance, both from colleagues and citizens at large. One manifestation of this resistance has been attempts to curve the implementation of gender quotas by forcing women to resign and male alternates taking their place or even having men pose as transgender women (Piscopo 2020).

Women politicians often face violence, whether physical, sexual, or psychological, that seeks to discourage them from participating in politics. In extreme cases, it can lead to the assassination of women politicians, as was the case of Rio de Janeiro's councilwoman Marielle Franco, a Black, feminist, and LGBT rights activist who was shot in her car in 2018. The phenomenon of violence against women in politics has only recently begun to be systematically analyzed by scholars, international and grassroots organizations, and lawmakers. One study conducted with women from legislatures across the world found that 81 percent have suffered psychological violence, including sexist remarks, death and rape threats, and harassment (IPU 2016). Another study conducted among political parties in Honduras found that women politicians acknowledged that violence was common (Torres García 2017).

In 2012, Bolivia became the first and only country in the world to specifically criminalize violence against women in politics (VAWIP). The concept of VAWIP highlights that the goal of the violence and harassment suffered by women in politics is for them to leave politics by forcing women to step down as candidates or resign political office. Behind these acts of violence and discrimination is the notion that politics is a space for men only. Although women politicians face violence and harassment around the world, its inclusion in domestic legal frameworks is rare. Why did Bolivia pass this law? Why have six other Latin American countries discussed similar proposals?

Local activists were key to making the phenomenon visible. It was mostly politicians serving as mayors and in local councils, the ones that were subject to VAWIP. In the early 2000s, activists made clear that existing legislation on violence against women could not be used for VAWIP, as regular laws focus on domestic or intimate partner violence. In the case of VAWIP, perpetrators can be fellow politicians (from the same or opposing parties), civil servants, or private citizens. To fill this gap, the first VAWIP bill was drafted in 2004.

The bill was pushed by feminist and Indigenous activists and politicians, with renewed impetus once Evo Morales, the first Indigenous president, was elected in 2005, initiating a process of broad social and political change. But it was only after the murder of councilwoman Juana Quispe that the bill received attention in the legislature, finally becoming law in 2012. This law defines harassment and violence against women in politics and lists seventeen acts of harassment and violence, such as pressuring women to step down, withholding female politicians' salaries, and even restricting women's speech in workplace commissions, committees, and the like. The law considers both administrative sanctions, when public employees are the harassers, and criminal charges, including possible prison sentences.

A key to the success of the bill was feminist activists calling attention to the issue by presenting violence against women in politics not as a women's rights issue but a problem that violates democratic principles (Restrepo Sanín 2020). In particular, VAWIP is understood as limiting women's political rights and their representation in the political sphere, key elements in a democracy. This framework was successful in Bolivia and has diffused to other countries in the region. Ecuador, Peru, Mexico, Costa Rica, Honduras, and Colombia have discussed similar legislation, and the phenomenon has gained increased attention in the last decade.

In Bolivia, up to 2019, not a single case had a criminal sentence, despite dozens of complaints. Challenges persist for more effective implementation. The law, however, has been successful in making violence against women in politics visible, generating better information and awareness of some of the challenges faced by women in politics.

Women candidates and politicians in Caribbean countries tend to be disadvantaged by established practices of recruitment by political parties and internal party selection for political offices (UN Women 2018, 14). In terms of campaign funding, women do not typically have access to social networks from which to derive donations, and when they run for elections, they must do so on their own dime. Rural women and women whose occupations are in lower-income sectors do not enjoy the same job flexibility and access to political networks as women and men living in urban areas and in higher-income sectors necessary to pursue political office while maintaining their income. Women in the Caribbean also continue to bear the brunt of domestic duties, such as household management and child-rearing, and in addition to the struggles of balancing these unpaid duties with their professional lives, they must balance both their domestic and work responsibilities with political campaigning to run for office (UN Women 2018, 15).

Caribbean women who have successfully entered the political sphere have largely been from the middle and upper classes, allowing them to participate in politics from home and providing them with exposure and access to political networks and resources through marriage and family ties. For example, the current prime minister of Barbados, Mia Mottley, has a long family history in politics. Her grandfather, Earnest Mottley, was the first mayor of Bridgetown and a parish-level politician for many years. Mottley's father was also a member of the Barbados House of Assembly (UN Women 2018, 15). Successful women politicians in the Caribbean have also gained access to political networks through involvement in civic groups, labor unions, and women's organizations. For example, Janet Jagan, the former president of Guyana (1997–1999), was a member of the British Guianese Labor Union, helped found the Women's Political and Economic Organization (WPEO) and the Political Affairs Committee (PAC), and even cofounded the People's Progressive Party together with her husband (UN Women 2018, 15).

In general, the patriarchal culture of most Caribbean states discourages women from seeking political office, and they are often discouraged by their own families as well as the political parties (UN Women 2018, 12). A significant barrier that women face is the perception that they are unsuitable for leadership positions that require tough decision-making. Women are also held to traditional gender roles associated with their biological sex that dictate what kind of behavior is socially acceptable for men and women. As a result of these societal gender biases, women who seek political office find their personal lives more strictly scrutinized by the public and media than their male counterparts.

For example, in Trinidad and Tobago, opposition senator Khadijah Ameen experienced criticism from her political opponents based on her status as a divorced mother (UN Women 2018, 12). Societal perceptions around her status as a woman also limited her opportunities for political campaigning, such as when she decided not to campaign in bars because they are seen as predominantly masculine spaces. If she were to be seen publicly drinking a beer, it would be perceived more negatively than if a male politician were to be seen campaigning in this way. Sabrina Mowlah-Baksh, the former deputy mayor of San Fernando in Trinidad and Tobago, experienced the same form of discrimination during her first local campaign for being present in bars (UN Women 2018, 12). Women also face more scrutiny than men for the way they dress, constituting a form of political harassment that discourages highly suitable and qualified women candidates for office from running.

While women in the Caribbean also generally face the barrier of societal expectations of their role in the home, they do not experience these challenges in the same way. For example, East Indian women in the Caribbean often experience expectations beyond the immediate family and are straddled with additional responsibilities to their extended families, exacerbating this barrier for them. Kamla Persad-Bissessar, the former prime minister of Trinidad and Tobago (2010–2015), has described the challenges she faces not only as a woman but as a woman of East Indian descent (UN Women 2018, 14). She was the leader of the United National Congress (UNC), a majority male East Indian party, and thus the forms of campaigning and political leadership she pursued had to take place within the context of entrenched East Indian and particularly Hindu religious and cultural ideals. In this way, the race, ethnicity, and religion of women in the Caribbean often intersect with their gender to shape their political opportunities and experiences.

ACHIEVING POLITICAL PARITY—A WAY FORWARD FOR LATIN AMERICA AND THE CARIBBEAN

The barriers to women's equal representation respond to deeply entrenched notions of appropriate gender roles and behaviors. Whether consciously or inadvertently, men in power positions tend to support and promote the careers of other men, whom they deem more fitting, putting up obstacles for women's access to elected office. Changing these beliefs usually takes time, which is why the number of women in the legislature and executive powers has taken decades to improve and is still far from parity.

The experience of Latin American countries shows that despite existing disadvantages, strong feminist mobilization can push for the introduction of mechanisms that lead to greater representation, such as gender quotas. Then, after some change has been achieved, it is possible to push for further reform, whether it is improving existing quota laws or through new institutions. For example, Chile finally adopted a quota in 2015, after many years of debates. But once this initial step was achieved and more women entered Congress, an active feminist movement was able to push for further mechanisms to increase representation when the opportunity presented itself. As a result, Chile had the first constitutional proposal drafted by a convention composed of an equal number of men and women (see sidebar).

The experience of Caribbean countries reveals a similar pattern of strong feminist mobilization overcoming institutional barriers such as political party recruitment practices and sociocultural barriers such as gender biases. Women, particularly from the upper and middle classes,

PARITY IN CHILE'S CONSTITUTIONAL CONVENTION

After an unprecedented process of protests and social mobilization demanding deep changes to curve the country's multiple forms of inequality, political parties in Chile agreed to carry out a process to draft a new constitution. The campaign for a parity convention in charge of drafting the new constitution was led by a feminist coalition of civil society organizations, professional societies, and a group of congresswomen from both government and opposition parties. The debate focused on the electoral rules to be used and how women would ultimately be represented, leading to demands for a parity convention where women and men were equally represented.

The Women Political Scientists' Network suggested an electoral formula requiring candidate lists to be equally composed of men and women and seats to be assigned so that an equal number (or a difference of one in districts with an odd number of representatives) of men and women are elected within each district. For example, if a district elects three representatives and all three are women, the elected candidate with the least votes must be replaced by the man with the most votes on that same list. This system secured that no gender would have more than 55 percent of representatives or less than 45 percent. After months of intense debate, everyone agreed on an electoral formula that would guarantee a parity convention.

Arguments regarding the need to achieve equal representation of women as a requirement for a true democracy became commonplace, reflecting important cultural changes. On October 25, 2020, a broad majority of citizens approved initiating the process to draft a new constitution and chose the fully elected convention. As a result, although it ended up being rejected in a plebiscite, Chile had the first constitutional proposal written by a constitutional body composed of an equal number of men and women.

have entered the highest levels of executive and legislative office and further organized within these institutions through strategies such as forming women's factions of the political parties. Gender quotas have also proven highly effective in increasing women's representation in parliament, such as Guyana's candidate quota system that was adopted in 2001 and led to a significant increase in women parliamentarians by 2011.

Although the greater representation of women can lead to a backlash, it generally has an important positive effect in normalizing the access of women to power positions. Women's presence in office has a symbolic effect by setting an example for others, which is particularly relevant for younger women and girls, who can grow up having role models. In conclusion, the main path to achieve parity is building on previous successes, having strong civil society organizations that can promote and propose changes when there are windows of opportunity, and being vigilant on the correct implementation of existing mechanisms to promote inclusion.

REFERENCES

Buddan, Robert. 2004. "Universal Adult Suffrage in Jamaica and the Caribbean since 1944." *Social and Economic Studies* 53 (4): 135–162.

Caminotti, Mariana. 2014. "Ideas, legados y estrategias políticas en la reforma de las reglas de selección de candidatos: la ley de cuotas pionera de Argentina." [Ideas, Legacies and Political Strategies in Candidate Selection Rules Reform: The Pioneering Quota Law in Argentina]. *Revista Uruguaya de Ciencia Política* 23 (spe): 65–85.

Carlin, Ryan E., and Gregory J. Love. 2015. "Who Is the Latin American Voter?" In *The Latin American Voter: Pursuing Representation and Accountability and Challenging Contexts*, edited by Ryan E. Carlin, Matthew M. Singer, and Elizabeth J. Zechmeister, 31–59. Ann Arbor: University of Michigan Press.

Carreras, Miguel, and Néstor Castañeda. 2014. "Article Who Votes in Latin America? A Test of Three Theoretical Perspectives." *Comparative Political Studies* 47 (8): 1079–1104.

Castillo, Isabel. 2019. "Explaining Female Suffrage Reform in Latin America: Motivation Alignment, Cleavages, and Timing of Reform." PhD diss., Northwestern University, Evanston, IL.

CEPAL. 2014. *Los pueblos indígenas en América Latina: Avances en el último decenio y retos pendientes para la garantía de sus derechos.* [Indigenous Peoples in Latin America: Advances in the Last Decade and Pending Challenges for the Guarantee of Their Rights]. Santiago: UN-CEPAL.

Cooper, Carolyn. 1995. *Noises in the Blood: Orality, Gender and the "Vulgar" Body of Jamaican Popular Culture.* Durham, NC: Duke University Press.

Desposato, Scott, and Barbara Norrander. 2009. "The Gender Gap in Latin America: Contextual and Individual Influences on Gender and Political Participation." *British Journal of Political Science* 39 (1): 141–162. https://doi.org/10.1017/S0007123408000458

Espinal, Rosario, and Shanyang Zhao. 2015. "Gender Gaps in Civic and Political Participation in Latin America." *Latin American Politics and Society* 57 (1): 123–138. https://doi.org/10.1111/j.1548-2456 .2015.00262.x

Faieta, Jessica, Susane McDade, and Rebeca Arias. 2015. *Where Are the Women? A Study of Women, Politics, Parliaments and Equality in the CARICOM Countries.* Panama: United Nations Development Programme.

Hahner, June Edith. 1990. *Emancipating the Female Sex: The Struggle for Women's Rights in Brazil, 1850–1940.* Durham, NC: Duke University Press.

Hammond, Gregory. 2011. *The Women's Suffrage Movement and Feminism in Argentina from Roca to Perón.* Albuquerque: University of New Mexico Press.

Htun, Mala. 2016. *Inclusion without Representation in Latin America: Gender Quotas and Ethnic Reservations.* Cambridge and New York: Cambridge University Press.

Htun, Mala, and Jennifer Piscopo. 2010. "Presence Without Empowerment? Women in Politics in Latin America and the Caribbean." *Global Institute for Gender Research.* http://webarchive.ssrc.org /pdfs/Mala_Htun_and_Jennifer_M._Piscopo-Presence_without _Empowerment_CPPF_Briefing_Paper_Dec_2010_f.pdf

IDEA (International Institute for Democracy and Electoral Assistance). 2020. "Gender Quotas around the World." https://www.idea.int /data-tools/data/gender-quotas

IPU (Inter-Parliamentary Union). 2016. "Sexism, Harassment and Violence against Women Parliamentarians." *Issues Brief* (October). https:// www.ipu.org/resources/publications/issue-briefs/2016-10/sexism -harassment-and-violence-against-women-parliamentarians

IPU. 2021. "Historical Data on Women in National Parliaments." https:// data.ipu.org/historical-women

IPU. 2022. "Monthly Ranking of Women in National Parliaments." https:// data.ipu.org/women-ranking?month=9&year=2022

Lubertino, María José. 2003. "Pioneering Quotas: The Argentina Experience and Beyond." In *The Implementation of Quotas: Latin American Experiences. Workshop Report*, 32–40. Stockholm: IDEA.

Morgan, Jana. 2015. "Gender and the Latin American Voter." In *The Latin American Voter: Pursuing Representation and Accountability and Challenging Contexts*, edited by Ryan E. Carlin, Matthew M. Singer, and Elizabeth J. Zechmeister, 143–168. Ann Arbor: University of Michigan Press.

Paravisini-Gebert, Lizabeth. 1996. *Phyllis Shand Allfrey: A Caribbean Life*. New Brunswick, NJ: Rutgers University Press.

Pasley, Victoria. 2001. "The Black Power Movement in Trinidad: An Exploration of Gender and Cultural Changes and the Development of a Feminist Consciousness." *Journal of International Women Studies* 3 (2): 24–40.

Piscopo, Jennifer M. 2020. "When Do Quotas in Politics Work? Latin America Offers Lessons." *Americas Quarterly* (October).

Reddock, Rhoda E. 1994. *Women Labour and Politics in Trinidad and Tobago*. Kingston: Ian Randle Publishers.

Reddock, Rhoda E. 1998. "Women's Organizations and Movements in the Commonwealth Caribbean." *Feminist Review* 59 (Summer): 57–73.

Reingold, Beth. 2008. *Legislative Women: Getting Elected, Getting Ahead*. Boulder, CO: Lynne Rienner Publishers.

Restrepo Sanín, Juliana. 2020. "Criminalizing Violence against Women in Politics: Innovation, Diffusion, and Transformation." *Politics & Gender* 18 (1): 1–32.

Reyes-Housholder, Catherine, and Gwynn Thomas. 2018. "Latin America's Presidentas: Overcoming Challenges, Forging New Pathways." In *Gender and Representation in Latin America*, edited by Leslie A. Schwindt-Bayer, 19–38. Oxford and New York: Oxford University Press.

Rousseau, Stéphanie, and Christina Ewig. 2017. "Latin America's Left-Turn and the Political Empowerment of Indigenous Women." *Social Politics: International Studies in Gender, State & Society* 24 (4): 425–451.

Shirley, Beverly. 2009. "An Examination of the Transformative Potential of Caribbean Feminisms in Trinidad, Barbados, Guyana and Jamaica in the 1970s." PhD diss., University of the West Indies, Mona.

Shirley, Beverly. 2014. "Crossing over the Barriers: A Historical Journey of Women's Political Leadership in the Anglophone Caribbean." In *Politics, Power and Gender Justice in the Anglophone Caribbean: Women's Understandings of Politics, Experiences of Political Contestation and the Possibilities for Gender Transformation*. IDRC Research Report 106430-001, by principal investigator Gabrielle Jamela Hosein and lead researcher Jane Parpart. Ottawa: International Development Research Centre.

Taylor-Robinson, Michelle M., and Meredith Gleitz. 2018. "Women in Presidential Cabinets: Getting into the Elite Club?" In *Gender and*

Representation in Latin America, edited by Leslie A. Schwindt-Bayer, 39–55. Oxford and New York: Oxford University Press.

Torres García, Isabel. 2017. *Violencia contra las mujeres en la política. Investigación en partidos políticos de Honduras.* [Violence against Women in Politics: Research in Political Parties in Honduras]. USAID, PADF, and NDI. https://oig.cepal.org/sites/default/files/investigacion_violencia_politica.pdf

UN Women. 2018. *Women in Political Leadership in the Caribbean.* https://parlamericas.org/uploads/documents/WomensPolitical LeadershipUNWomen.pdf

THREE

Europe

Michela Cella and Elena Manzoni

Europe is the western peninsula of the Eurasian continent bordered by the Atlantic Ocean in the west; the Mediterranean, Caspian, and Black Seas in the south; the Arctic Ocean in the north; and the Ural Mountains in the east, although the eastern demarcation is contested. In this chapter, the following countries are considered part of Europe: all twenty-seven members of the **European Union (EU)**, the Balkan region (Albania, Bosnia and Herzegovina, Kosovo, Macedonia, Montenegro, and Serbia), Andorra, Belarus, Greenland (formally belonging to Denmark), Iceland, Liechtenstein, Moldova, Monaco, Norway, San Marino, Switzerland, Turkey, Ukraine, and the United Kingdom.[1]

European culture and institutions may appear homogeneous to an outside viewer, and certainly they are to some extent. Yet, European countries differ in terms of political systems, socioeconomic conditions, and cultural traditions, which all impact the extent to which women are represented in politics. Europe is therefore particularly interesting, as it offers the possibility to compare countries, most of which are quite similar in terms of economic indicators but differ, in some cases substantively, in terms of cultural and historical background, gender attitudes and roles, and institutional makeup. Understanding the causes of these differences

---

[1] The European Union member states are Austria, Belgium, Bulgaria, Croatia, Cyprus, Czech Republic, Denmark, Estonia, Finland, France, Germany, Greece, Hungary, Ireland, Italy, Latvia, Lithuania, Luxembourg, Malta, Netherlands, Poland, Portugal, Romania, Slovakia, Slovenia, Spain, and Sweden.

and how they are reflected in different levels of participation of women in politics are important in understanding how to improve the political environment, particularly in those countries that seem to have fallen behind. This chapter guides the reader through the history and the contemporaneity of the condition of women in politics in Europe, offering an interpretation as to what are the most relevant barriers to gender equality in politics and suggesting possible solutions.

WOMEN AS VOTERS

The notion of citizenship as a status conferring certain rights and duties took root in Europe after the French Revolution, with the growing role of the **bourgeoisie** in the public sphere and the growth of the **nation-state**. But the idea of citizenship was a gendered concept because women were completely left out from this process of nation-state building and democratization. Some lonely voices immediately advocated for equal rights for women, but it took over a century for these voices to become loud and numerous enough to make women's participation in public life a matter of political debate. One of the first notable exceptions is Marquis de Condorcet, who in 1790 published his appeal for women's political rights based on their equality with men. Only a year later, Olympe de Gouges, in her Declaration of the Rights of the Woman and the Female Citizen, argued for equal rights, especially political rights. But they were both clearly ahead of their times (Blom 2012).

Women were viewed as carriers of traditional values, and political actors presumed that giving women the right to vote would have boosted the support of more conservative parties. For this reason, women's enfranchisement did not receive the immediate support of progressive parties. For many **socialist** parties, workers' rights and class struggle took precedence over women's enfranchisement. Socialist parties also did not want to cooperate with many women's associations, as they were connected to the educated classes. In addition, women's associations, which began their activity in Europe around the mid-1850s, often gave priority to other issues, such as education, employment, and professional development, while proletarian (working-class) women fought harder for equal pay, the extension of protection of maternity rights, and employment protection. The women's right to vote was not a priority for many political and social actors. Nevertheless, the struggle for women's suffrage provided the first occasion for an international mobilization for women's rights. This form of suffragism was born in England, but it spread across the globe and obtained the result of the International Woman Suffrage Association being established between 1899 and 1902 that soon recruited women of all social classes.

Most European countries chose to enfranchise women in a piecemeal fashion by granting limited form of political participation to groups of women. In some countries (including the United Kingdom in 1894, Sweden in 1862, and Denmark in 1908) women were granted the vote in local elections while being still excluded from the national elections. Countries with greater equality between men and women were the first to grant political rights to women at the beginning of the twentieth century. Scandinavian countries (Finland in 1906, Denmark in 1908, and Norway in 1913) granted enfranchisement of women (even if partial) early because the clear-cut separation between home (the private sphere) and labor (the public sphere) in agrarian societies was missing, as both women and men performed paid labor on the farm. Thus, it was easier to recognize women as being part of the public sphere (Rubio-Marín 2014).

The private sphere is the area of the home and family where women perform unpaid care work in support of their husbands' outside employment. Traditionally, women's role as wives and mothers meant women's main responsibility was to care for the children and elderly while also performing all household chores. In contrast, the public sphere is the domain of politics and business dominated by men who are active members of the paid workforce. The public/private dichotomy associates different gender norms for men and women: caring for women and work and leadership for men. These gender norms translate into gendered expectations on what it means to be a man or a woman. For example, women are traditionally supposed to be caring, emotional, weak, compassionate, and gentle individuals, whereas men are associated with traits such as powerful, strong, decisive, aggressive, and rational. Based on these social norms, society developed gender role expectations about the appropriate roles men and women can perform in society. It is no coincidence that professions such as education or health care are dominated by women, while leadership positions in politics and business are dominated by men.

A second set of countries granted partial or universal women's suffrage in the period between the two World Wars. The first country to do so was the United Kingdom. The question of women's suffrage had already been widely debated before the war, but it was opposed by the Liberal prime minister, Lord Asquith, on the grounds that women's enfranchisement would have favored the Conservatives (Hills 1981). The war interrupted the activities of the suffragist movement, but the shortage of workers during and immediately following World War I created a demand for women workers and allowed women to enter the workforce. Women's increased labor force participation together with the change in the political leadership translated into a partial women's enfranchisement in 1918. Women heads of household (aged thirty or above) and women married to heads of household (aged thirty-five or above) were granted the right to vote, which was expanded to universal suffrage in 1928.

Germany and Spain also granted suffrage to women in the period between the two World Wars. In Germany, suffrage came with the **Weimar Republic**, where universal suffrage for both sexes (above age twenty) was granted in 1918, when it was included in the Constitution of the Weimar Republic. Spain granted universal suffrage in 1931. In both countries, women's suffrage was short lived with the establishment of the Franco regime in Spain and the **Third Reich** under Hitler in Germany. While Franco completely removed women's right to vote granted in 1931, German women could still vote but not stand as candidates. Nevertheless, the Nazi Party actively sought the support of women voters in the 1932 elections through the prominent use of women speakers during the election campaign (Durham 1998). All **fascist** movements in Europe ended up being anti-feminists, stressing the role of women as mothers and women's importance in securing the future of the nation by bearing as many children as possible. Thus, as before, women's place continued to be in the home, not the public sphere of politics or business.

The remaining European countries granted women suffrage after World War II, when women's enfranchisement became an important element of modern democracy, beginning with France in 1944. In other words, women received the right to vote when states either became independent (Malta in 1947 and Cyprus in 1960) or when countries established modern democracies through the rewriting of their constitution. The delay in granting women the right to vote was due to either lack of political support or the weakness of the women's movement.

A whole different process unfolded in the **Soviet Union** and its republics (Armenia, Azerbaijan, Belarus, Georgia, Kazakhstan, Kyrgyzstan, Moldova, Russia, Tajikistan, Turkmenistan, Ukraine, and Uzbekistan) and in the Baltic states (Latvia, Lithuania, and Estonia) and the **communist** countries that joined the Warsaw Pact (Albania, Bulgaria, Czechoslovakia, East Germany, Hungary, Poland, and Romania), which was a mutual defense organization to counter the threat posed by the North Atlantic Treaty Organization (NATO). Despite being **authoritarian** regimes, communist ideology stressed equal rights between men and women and thus preserved universal suffrage during the Cold War period. In some communist states, like Bulgaria (1947), Romania (1946), and the former Yugoslavia (1945), women were granted the right to vote for the first time under communist regimes (table 3.1).

The European continent is also home to two of the most surprising latecomers in granting political rights to women: Switzerland and Liechtenstein. The first Swiss association in support of women's suffrage was founded in 1909. For decades, it tried to modify, through popular petitions or in court, laws that excluded women from the right to vote. In 1958, well into the last wave of enfranchisement, a referendum to enfranchise women was held and decided on by an all-male populace. Unsurprisingly, the referendum was defeated 66.9 percent to 33 percent. A decade later, Switzerland wanted to sign the European Convention of Human Rights without recognizing gender equality, which triggered another wave of protests that culminated in a second referendum in 1971 that passed by 65.7 percent to 34 percent. Although the referendum granted women the right to vote on the federal level, local elections rules were left to the **cantons** to decide. In 1990, Appenzell Inner Rhodes was the last canton to allow women to vote after the Swiss Supreme Court ruled that the canton was violating the Swiss constitution. In Liechtenstein, it took women four referenda to obtain the right to vote. The first three referenda (in 1968, 1971, and 1973) were defeated, while the 1984 referendum was won by a narrow margin of 51.3 percent to 48.7 percent. Finally, nearly eighty years after women's enfranchisement was introduced in Finland in 1906, all European women could vote.

Women's Political Engagement

More than a century has passed since the enfranchisement of Finnish women. Women's turnout remained low in the first few elections after women's enfranchisement in all European countries. On average, it took four to five electoral cycles to close the turnout gap between men and women (Aidt and Dallal 2008). Somewhat counterintuitively, countries that introduced women's enfranchisement later closed the turnout gap between men and women faster than countries that granted enfranchisement earlier. In some countries today, such as Germany, Finland, Spain, Slovenia, Sweden, and Poland, women vote in higher percentages than

Table 3.1   Three Waves of Suffrage in Europe

Before WWI	Between WWI and WWII	After WWII
Denmark (1915)	Albania (1920)	Andorra (1973)
Finland (1906)	Austria (1918)	Belgium (1921)
Iceland (1915)	Belarus (1919)	Bosnia and Herzegovina (1949)*
Norway (1913)	Czech Republic (1920)**	Bulgaria (1944)
	Estonia (1918)	Croatia (1945)
	Germany (1918)	Cyprus (1960)
	Hungary (1918)	France (1944)
	Ireland (1928)	Greece (1952)
	Latvia (1918)	Italy (1945)
	Lithuania (1918)	Kosovo (1946)*
	Luxembourg (1919)	Liechtenstein (1984)
	Moldova (1978)	Macedonia (1946)*
	Netherlands (1919)	Malta (1947)
	Poland (1918)	Monaco (1962)
	Russia (1918)	Montenegro (1946)*
	Slovakia (1920)**	Portugal (1976)
	Spain (1931)	Romania (1946)
	Sweden (1921)	San Marino (1973)
	Turkey (1934)	Serbia (1946)*
	Ukraine (1919)	Slovenia (1945)
	United Kingdom (1928)	Switzerland (1971)

* As part of former Yugoslavia.
** As part of former Czechoslovakia.

Source: Data from IPU database with the exception of Moldova, for which we report the first introduction of women's suffrage in 1940, when Moldova was annexed to the Soviet Union. http://archive.ipu.org/wmn-e/suffrage.htm

men. Overall, turnout is heterogeneous across countries, ranging from the 80 percent of Sweden, Denmark, and the Netherlands to the 50 percent in Croatia, Slovenia, Portugal, and Greece.

Women have been making full use of their vote, but how have they been voting? From the time of their enfranchisement until the 1970s and 1980s, women had been leaning to the right and voting for conservative parties more than men did. This traditional gender gap has steadily been decreasing, and starting in the 1980s, women and men have roughly voted for right and left parties at the same rate. Yet, for the past thirty or forty years, we have been witnessing the emergence of the modern gender gap, where women are more likely than men to vote for leftist parties. The reasons are many. Leftist parties are more concerned with women having an active role in society and the labor market. Women seem to have a higher risk aversion and therefore may ask for more social and economic protection from the state. And religious and traditional values have steadily declined in importance. This phenomenon is present in most European countries, albeit with varying intensity. For example, a 2008 study found a modern gender gap in all countries in Europe except for Hungary, Slovenia, Poland, Ireland, the Czech Republic, and Slovakia (Abendschön and Steinmetz 2014). The greatest modern gender gaps were found in Norway and Switzerland, while Portugal and France had the smallest modern gender gaps. Most interestingly, the gender gap seems to vary by age cohort (Shorrocks 2018). Among older women, we still find a traditional gender gap; older women are more likely to vote for conservative parties, while younger generations exhibit signs for a modern gender gap, with young women voting for leftist parties in greater numbers than young men.

WOMEN AS MEMBERS OF PARLIAMENT

Most European countries have yet to achieve gender-balanced parliaments, where women make up at least 40 percent of members of parliament. Large differences remain even within each country when we consider different institutional levels. Women's presence in parliament increases when we move from local parliaments to national parliaments to the European Parliament. The average percentage of women across national parliaments in Europe has increased in the past years (see figure 3.1) to 30.5 percent (January 2021).

Table 3.2 shows the statistics for each European country in a ten-year span (from 2011 to 2021).

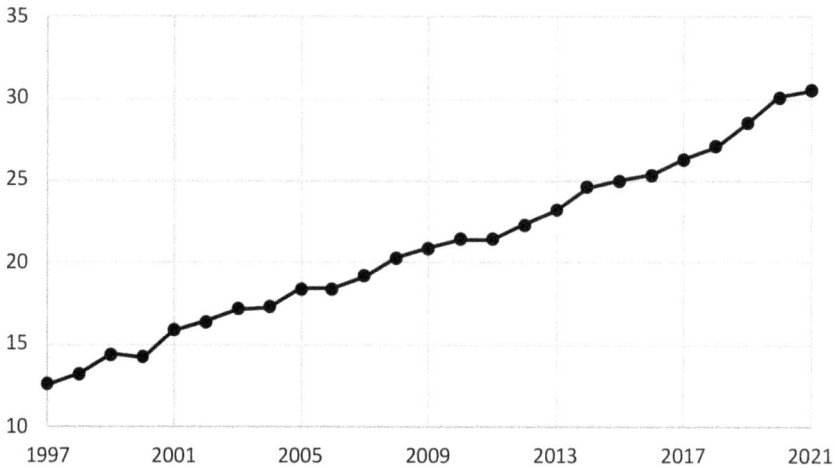

Figure 3.1 Average Percentage of Women in Parliaments (Inter-Parliamentary Union: Parline database on national parliaments, July 31, 2021).

When compared to a decade earlier, the data for national parliaments show a leap forward in several countries in southern and eastern Europe and in the Balkans; for example, France, Serbia, Italy, and Albania experienced increases of 20.6, 17.6, 14.4, and 13.1 percent, respectively. It is interesting to notice that while the Balkan countries do not have the highest share, they are the group of countries that has shown the strongest gain, and now they are ahead of most of the southern European and former communist countries. One reason for this increase is that most of these countries have introduced electoral gender quotas that have led to a greater share of women in parliament. For example, Albania introduced legislative electoral gender quotas in 2008 when only 7 percent of the members of parliaments were women. The law states that, "for each electoral zone, at least 30 percent of the multi-member list and/or one of the first three names on the multi-member list must be from each gender." Albania is the perfect example because of advantageous institutional elements: a proportional electoral system with multimember districts in addition to an effective legal quota that includes a ranking requirement for women and men (see the introduction for a more detailed explanation of institutional structures and quotas). In addition, Article 175, Electoral Code 2015, imposes not only financial sanctions but also a remedy for quota noncompliance:

Table 3.2 Percentage of Women in National Parliament on January 2011 Compared to January 2022

Country	2011 (%)	2021 (%)	Country	2011 (%)	2021 (%)	Country	2011 (%)	2021 (%)
Albania	16.4	29.5	Greece	17.3	21.7	North Macedonia	32.5	39.2
Andorra	35.7	46.4	Hungary	9.1	12.6	Norway	39.6	44.4
Austria	27.9	39.9	Iceland	42.9	39.7	Poland	20	28.3
Belarus	31.8	40	Ireland	13.9	22.5	Portugal	27.4	40
Belgium	39.3	42	Italy	21.3	35.7	Romania	11.4	18.5
Bosnia and Herzegovina	16.7	26.2	Kosovo	NA	32.5*	Russia	14	15.8
Bulgaria	20.8	27.1	Latvia	20	29	San Marino	16.7	33.3
Croatia	23.5	31.1	Liechtenstein	24	12	Serbia	21.6	39.2
Cyprus	12.5	21.4	Lithuania	19.1	27.7	Slovakia	15.3	22.7
Czech Republic	22	23	Luxembourg	20	31.7	Slovenia	14.4	26.7
Denmark	38	39.7	Malta	8.7	13.4	Spain	36.6	44
Estonia	22.8	27.7	Moldova	18.8	24.8	Sweden	45	47
Finland	40	46	Monaco	26.1	33.3	Turkey	9.1	17.3
France	18.9	39.5	Montenegro	11.1	24.7	Ukraine	8	20.8
Germany	32.8	31.5	Netherlands	40.7	33.3	United Kingdom	22	33.9

* The data for Kosovo come from EIGE (n.d.) and refers to 2020-Q4.

Source: Data from Inter-Parliamentary Union database (January 2011 and January 2021).

POLITICAL EQUALITY IN THE EUROPEAN PARLIAMENT

The European Parliament, the parliament of the European Union, is directly elected every five years. The percentage of women increased from 15.2 percent in 1979, the first time the European Parliament election took place, to 40.4 percent in the latest election in 2019 (European Parliament 2019).

Each EU member state has a fixed number of representatives based on the country's population size, ranging from six representatives for the smallest state to ninety-six representatives for the largest member state, Germany. The percentage of women elected to the European Parliament varies widely by EU member state. As of 2021, Finland (57.1 percent) and Spain (52.4 percent) elected more women to the European Parliament than men, while Cyprus (no women), Romania (18.2 percent), and Greece (23.8 percent) elected the lowest percentage of women (European Parliamentary Research Service 2021). Luxembourg, Latvia, Malta, Slovenia, and Denmark all elected equal numbers of men and women to the European Parliament.

Interestingly, countries often elect more women to the European Parliament than their national parliaments. In 2019, this still holds true for all but four EU member states (Belgium, Cyprus, Lithuania, and Slovakia). The greatest discrepancy is Malta, with 36.6 percent more women in the European Parliament than in national parliament, followed by Hungary (+25.4 percent), Slovenia (+23.3 percent), Ireland (+22.5 percent), and Latvia (+21 percent). On average, twenty-three of the twenty-seven EU member states elected 11 percent more women to the European Parliament than their national parliaments. This difference is largely due to how voters perceive the importance of the parliament: voters are more likely to vote for women, and parties are more likely to nominate more women candidates for parliaments that voters and parties perceive as being less powerful and important (Xydias 2016).

Malliga Och

"In case of non-compliance with the gender quota provisions, the Central Election Commission (CEC) shall impose a fine of ALL 1,000,000 (approximately €7120). In addition, the CEC shall replace each candidate with the next candidate in the list belonging to the least represented gender, until the gender quota is reached." As a result, the share of women members of parliament has quickly and continuously increased: 18 percent of women were elected in 2013 and 28 percent in 2017.

In Europe, quotas are widespread; approximately 72 percent of countries have adopted them in one way or another (IDEA n.d.). The most common type of quotas in Europe are legislated candidate quotas. Table 3.3 summarizes the quotas in place in European countries.

Table 3.3   Electoral Gender Quotas in Europe

Country	Quotas at the National Level
Albania	Legislated quotas for the single/lower house
Austria	No
Belgium	Legislated quotas for the single/lower house
	Legislated quotas for the upper house
Bosnia and Herzegovina	Legislated quotas for the single/lower house
Croatia	Legislated quotas for the single/lower house
Cyprus	No
Czech Republic	Legislated quotas for the upper house
France	Legislated quotas for the single/lower house
	Legislated quotas for the upper house
Germany	No
Greece	Legislated quotas for the single/lower house
Hungary	No
Iceland	No
Ireland	Legislated quotas for the single/lower house
Italy	Legislated quotas for the single/lower house
	Legislated quotas for the upper house
Kosovo	Legislated quotas for the single/lower house
Lithuania	No
Luxembourg	No
Malta	No
Moldova, Republic of	Legislated quotas for the single/lower house
Montenegro	Legislated quotas for the single/lower house
Netherlands	No
North Macedonia, Republic of	Legislated quotas for the single/lower house
Norway	No
Poland	Legislated quotas for the single/lower house
Portugal	Legislated quotas for the single/lower house
Romania	No

(Continued)

Table 3.3   (*Continued*)

Country	Quotas at the National Level
San Marino	Legislated quotas for the single/lower house
Serbia	Legislated quotas for the single/lower house
Slovakia	No
Slovenia	Legislated quotas for the single/lower house
Spain	Legislated quotas for the single/lower house
	Legislated quotas for the upper house
Sweden	No
Switzerland	No
Ukraine	No
United Kingdom	No

Source: Data from IDEA (n.d.).

In late 2022, the number of women in parliament has risen even further. Twelve countries now have a share of women above 40 percent: Iceland (47.6 percent), Sweden (46.1 percent), Andorra (46.4 percent), Finland (45.5 percent), Spain (43 percent), Belgium (42.7 percent), Switzerland (42.5 percent), North Macedonia (41.7 percent), Austria (41 percent), Netherlands (40.7 percent), the Republic of Moldova (40.6 percent), Slovenia (40 percent), and Norway (45 percent) (IPU 2022). It is worth noting that in late 2022 only three countries are left with fewer than 20 percent of women in parliament: Romania (19.1), Cyprus (14.3 percent), and Hungary (14.1 percent).

WOMEN AS LEADERS

The first women prime ministers in Europe were the United Kingdom's Margaret Thatcher (elected May 1979) and Portugal's Maria de Lourdes Pintasilgo (elected August 1979). The tenure of Maria de Lourdes Pintasilgo was rather short, as it lasted only until January 1980, and no woman has become prime minister of Portugal since her tenure. Margaret Thatcher, on the contrary, was the longest-serving prime minister of the twentieth century in Great Britain. In 2013, Theresa May became the second woman prime minister of Great Britain (2013–2016), and Liz Truss

MARGARET THATCHER

Margaret Thatcher, First Women Prime Minister of the United Kingdom (1979–1990). (David Fowler | Dreamstime.com)

Margaret Thatcher was a British politician who became the leader of the Conservative Party (1975–1990) and the first woman prime minister (1979–1990). She was the longest-serving prime minister and has been influencing worldwide politics ever since.

Thatcher's nickname, the "Iron Lady," was first used by a Russian newspaper, and she immediately embraced it. True to her nickname, she declared war on Argentina following its invasion of the Falkland Islands, a British colony 300 miles off the Argentinean coast. The war's success and an improving economy were prominent reasons for her second electoral victory in 1983.

Thatcher was probably the first woman who really did shatter the glass ceiling, and she undeniably challenged gender stereotypes by proving that a woman could become the leader of one of the most powerful countries in the world. Undoubtedly, though, she did it in a very individualistic way and never saw herself as a part of larger movement that supported the advancement of women in politics or in society generally. She strongly opposed any affirmative action, claiming that a woman should rise through merit alone, and she refused to approve government-funded childcare that would have helped working mothers.

If Thatcher ever appealed to women as a group, she did so by claiming to be a housewife, and her political language was focused on women as a part of a household: for example, owning your own home, setting the household budget, and choosing the best school for your children. Thus, despite having risen above traditional gender roles, she reinforced them with her politics.

ANGELA MERKEL

Angela Merkel was the German chancellor, equivalent to a prime minister, from 2005 to 2021. Born in Hamburg (West Germany), she was raised in communist East Germany. Like Margaret Thatcher, she has a scientific background: Merkel has a PhD in quantum chemistry and worked as a scientist until 1989, when the Berlin Wall fell. She then entered the world of politics, first in East Germany, as the deputy spokesperson of the government, and then in unified Germany, as the minister for women.

Angela Merkel, first woman Chancellor of Germany (2005–2021). (Markwaters | Dreamstime.com)

Merkel is at ease with male-dominated environments, yet she was aware of the effects of male dominance in politics: "I find the tendency that certain male politicians have constantly to assert themselves rather unpleasant. . . . When that happens, I feel almost physically oppressed and would prefer not to be there" (Kornelius 2013). Early in her political career, she had difficulty with the gendered nature of the job. In an official trip to Moscow in 1990, journalists wrote about her new coat and shoes instead of focusing on the political details of the trip. Today, she is known for her unique dress style, a soberly cut pantsuit in many different colors, that is (mostly) not commented on. She has also succeeded in shielding her private life from the scrutiny of the media so that her being twice married and childless has not been a topic of discussion.

In her speech for the one hundredth anniversary celebration of women's suffrage in Germany, Merkel acknowledges her positive effect as a role model (to the point that Mattel produced a Barbie with her look), but she is also aware that this is not enough. Germany has a long way before reaching gender equality, and her presence should not be an excuse to slow down the process.

URUSLA VON DER LEYEN

The European Commission represents the executive branch of the European Union. In 2019, Ursula von der Leyen became the first woman elected to the presidency of the European Commission. Throughout her career, von der Leyen was an outspoken advocate for women's equality in Germany in her previous positions as the minister for families, women, seniors, and youth matters; as the minister of labor and social affairs; and as the first woman minister of defense. She has been one of the main forces in introducing gender-equitable parental leave and quotas for women on corporate boards in German law as well as in creating a more women-friendly German military.

As the European Commission president, von der Leyen nominated the most gender-balanced commission in the European Union's history, with twelve out of twenty-seven commissioners—the equivalents of cabinet ministers—being women. Notably, many of the women commissioners have been assigned to policy portfolios that are not traditionally feminine, such as competition, energy, transport, and financial stability. Women are also three of the seven vice presidents.

Finally, von der Leyen has set out a very ambitious Gender Equality Strategy for the 2020–2025 period that prioritizes four goals: political parity, equal pay, equal participation and opportunities in the labor market, and gender-based violence and stereotypes. In addition, the strategy calls for greater gender mainstreaming in the policy-making process. This means that the European Commission will systematically include a gendered perspective in all stages of the policy process and actively consider the impact of each policy decision on overall gender equality in the European Union.

became the third prime minister of Great Britain in September 2022. Her premiership, however, was short-lived, Truss only governed for 44 days.

As of late 2022, nine countries had a woman prime minister (Estonia, Finland, France, Georgia, Iceland, Lithuania, Moldova, Serbia, and the United Kingdom) and seven countries had a woman president (Estonia, Georgia, Greece, Hungary, Kosovo, Moldova, and Slovakia). Estonia and Moldova are the only two countries that has both a woman prime minister and a woman president. This is the highest number ever achieved in Europe. Since Thatcher's rise to power, Europe has seen a total of fifty-eight tenures of either women prime ministers or presidents (see table 3.4).

The level of women's presence in executive positions is much lower than in legislative bodies. The share of women cabinet members has reached 30.6 percent in 2020 in Europe (see table 3.5). European countries once again show a widespread heterogeneity. In 2020, the largest share of

Table 3.4 List of Women Executive Leaders in Europe (Excluding Interim Leaders)

Country	Office	Name	Estonia
Belgium	Prime minister	Sophie Wilmès	2019–2020
Croatia	Prime minister	Jadranka Kosor	2009–2011
	President	Kolinda Grabar-Kitarovic	2015–2020
Denmark	Prime minister	Helle Thorning-Schmidt	2011–2015
Estonia	Prime minister	Mette Frederiksen	2019–2021
	President	Kersti Kaljulaid	2016–present
	Prime minister	Kaja Kallas	2021–present
Finland	President	Tarja Halonen	2000–2012
	Prime minister	Anneli Tuulikki Jaatteenmaki	April 2003–June 2003
	Prime minister	Mari Kiviniemi	2010–2011
	Prime minister	Sanna Marin	2019–present
France	Prime minister	Edith Cresson	1991–1992
	Prime minister	Elizabeth Borne	2022–present
Georgia	President	Salome Zurabishvili	2018–present
Germany (East)	President	Sabine Bergmann-Pohl	May 1990–October 1990
Germany (Unified)	Chancellor	Angela Merkel	2005–2021
Greece	President	Katerina Sakellaropoulou	2020–present
Hungary	President	Katalin Novák	2022–present
Iceland	President	Vigdis Finnbogadottir	1980–1996
	Prime minister	Jóhanna Sigurðardóttir	2009–2013
	Prime minister	Katrín Jakobsdóttir	2017–present

Ireland	President	Mary McAleese	1997–2011
	President	Mary Robinson	1990–1997
Kosovo	President	Atifete Jahjaga	2011–2016
	President	Vjosa Osmani	2021–present
Latvia	President	Vaira Vike-Freiberga	1999–2007
	Prime minister	Laimdota Straujuma	2014–2016
Lithuania	Prime minister	Kazimiera Danuta Prunskiene	1990–1991
	President	Dalia Grybauskaitė	2009–2019
	Prime minister	Ingrida Šimonytė	2020–present
Malta	President	Agatha Barbara	1982–1987
	President	Marie-Louise Coleiro Preca	2014–2019
Moldova	Prime minister	Zinaida Greceanîi	2008–2009
	Prime minister	Maia Sandu	June 2019–November 2019
	President	Maia Sandu	2020–present
	Prime minister	Natalia Gavriliţa	2021–present
Norway	Prime minister	Gro Harlem Brundtland	February 1981–October 1981
			1986–1989
			1990–/1996
Poland	Prime minister	Erna Solberg	2013–2021
	Prime minister	Hanna Suchocka	1992–1993
	Prime minister	Ewa Kopacz	2014–2015
	Prime minister	Beata Szydło	2015–2017

(Continued)

Table 3.4 *(Continued)*

Country	Office	Name	Estonia
Romania	Prime minister	Viorica Dăncilă	2018–2019
Serbia	Prime minister	Ana Brnabić	2017–present
Slovakia	Prime minister	Iveta Radičová	2010–2012
	President	Zuzana Čaputová	2019–present
Slovenia	Prime minister	Alenka Bratušek	2013–2014
Sweden	Prime minister	Magdalena Andersson	2021–2022
Switzerland	President	Ruth Dreifuss	1999–1999
	President	Micheline Calmy Rey	January 2007–December 2007
	President	Doris Leuthard	2010–2011
	President	Eveline Widmer-Schlumpf	January 2012–December 2012
	President	Simonetta Sommaruga	January 2015–December 2015
			January 2020–December 2020
Turkey	Prime minister	Tansu Çiller	1993–1996
Ukraine	Prime minister	Yuliya Tymoshenko	January 2005–September 2005
			2007–2010
United Kingdom	Prime minister	Margaret Thatcher	1979–1990
	Prime minister	Theresa May	2016–2019
	Prime minister	Liz Truss	2022–present
Yugoslavia	Prime minister	Milka Planinc	1982–1986

Source: Data courtesy of Farida Jalalzai (excludes interim or appointed leaders).

women members of government was recorded in Sweden (49.6 percent), followed by Finland (46 percent), Spain (44 percent), Belgium (42 percent), and France (41 percent). At the bottom of the list, women accounted for less than 20 percent of the members in Turkey (17.3 percent), Malta (13.4 percent), Hungary (12.6 percent), and Lichtenstein (12 percent). In late 2022, there were nine parity cabinets in the European Union: Belgium, Spain, France, the Netherlands, Portugal, Finland, Sweden, Liechtenstein, and Albania; six of the cabinets were majority women cabinets with Spain (60.9 percent) and Albania (70.6 percent) having the largest share of women in cabinet (EIGE 2022).

Although women's presence in cabinets has increased, there is continued evidence suggesting some gender segregation in the allocation of portfolios at the cabinet level. Women continue to more often hold stereotypical feminine portfolios that deal with issues such as education, health care, and childcare than masculine portfolios that focus on issues such as crime, immigration, the economy, and national security. However, over the last decade, the problem of "pink ghettos," where women are confined to feminine portfolios, has steadily narrowed. Most noticeable, women have been appointed to the defense ministry with increased frequency. In 2014, a photo of the Swedish, German, Dutch, and Norwegian defense ministers captioned "True power girls" went viral (Taylor 2014). In the photo, you see Ursula von der Leyen (first woman defense minister of Germany; now the first woman president of the European Commission), Jeanine Hennis-Plasschaert (first Dutch woman defense minister), Karin Enström (third Swedish woman defense minister), and Ine Eriksen Søreide (fifth Norwegian woman minister of defense) sitting next to each other at the Munich Security Conference. The first woman defense minister of Spain also made headlines when she inspected the troops while seven months pregnant. Why do we see women taking over one of the most masculine portfolios? New research shows that countries are most likely to appoint women defense ministers when they have a higher number of women in parliament or have elected women chief executives and when the countries are less engaged in fatal disputes, spend less on the military, or do not have a military dictatorship (Barnes and O'Brien 2018).

In December 2019, the seventy-sixth government of Finland was elected, and its characteristics are unprecedented even for a country like Finland, where gender equality is far more advanced than in other European regions. The government was formed by a five-party coalition, the Social Democratic Party, the Centre Party, the Green League, the Left Alliance,

Table 3.5   Women in Cabinet Positions in Q4 2010 and Q4 2020

Country	2010 (%)	2020 (%)
Albania	NA	29.8
Austria	27.9	39.3
Belgium	40	42
Bosnia and Herzegovina	NA	26.2
Bulgaria	22.1	27.1
Croatia	24.8	31.1
Cyprus	12.5	22.2
Czech Republic	22	22.5
Denmark	37.6	39.7
Estonia	22.8	29.7
Finland	39.5	46
France	19.2	41
Germany	32.6	31.2
Greece	17	21.7
Hungary	8.8	12.6
Iceland	41.3	39.7
Ireland	13.9	22.5
Italy	21.1	35.9
Kosovo		32.5
Latvia	19	29
Liechtenstein	24	12
Lithuania	19.1	26.2
Luxembourg	20	31.7
North Macedonia	34.2	35.8
Malta	8.7	13.4
Montenegro		25.6
Netherlands	41.3	32
Norway	39.1	40.8
Poland	19.8	28.5

Table 3.5 *(Continued)*

Country	2010 (%)	2020 (%)
Portugal	30.4	39.5
Romania	11.4	22.2
Serbia	22.4	39.4
Slovakia	16	22.7
Slovenia	15.9	26.7
Spain	36.9	44
Sweden	45.6	49.6
Turkey	8.9	17.3
United Kingdom	22	33.8
Average	**24.6**	**30.6**

Source: Data from EIGE (2022). Data for Andorra, Belarus, Monaco, Moldova, Russia, San Marino, and Ukraine are missing.

and the Swedish People's Party. All five parties are led by women (Senna Marin, Katri Kulmuni, Maria Ohisalo, Li Andersson, and Anna-Maja Henriksson, respectively), and all but one of them are under thirty-five years of age. In addition, twelve out of nineteen ministers were women. This raised gender balance issues, as this government composition violated the Finnish convention that each gender must be represented by at least 40 percent of cabinet members and men accounted for only 37 percent of ministers. For the first time, gender imbalance went in an unexpected direction, suggesting that parity is a reality in Finland.

BARRIERS TO POLITICAL PARITY

European politics is shaped and governed by political parties, much more so than in the United States, where independent candidates can breakthrough in primaries without an explicit party endorsement (Piscopo 2019). Consequently, the role of women in the political arena is very much correlated with women's participation in parties' activity and organization. Women have been active in European political parties since the very beginning, but for many years, they were involved as support staff to the old boys' club, where important decisions were made. Many women formed women groups within political parties to voice their concerns and demands. Still present today, internal women's groups play an important part in representing women's issues within parties. Although in the public debate some view these organizations as a form of segregation, others consider them a networking opportunity for women party members (Childs and Kittilson 2016). Still, political parties remain a men's playground, with roughly two-thirds of party members being men (OCSE 2014). In 2020, men constitute 100 percent of major-party leaders in more than a third of European countries. Moreover, there is no country where is a larger share of women leading political parties than men, and only Finland reaches an equal share between men and women leaders and deputy party leaders.

Parties play a very important role when filling the candidate list in proportional electoral systems, deciding who gets on the ballot and in which position. Although proportional representation is generally considered more favorable to women and other minorities, and being a candidate is the necessary first step, the probability of success also depends on the details of the rule and the ballot. For example, the abovementioned position on the ballot is a key component to electoral success, as candidates at the top of the list have a strong advantage, even in those systems where voters can influence the rank order of the party list (so-called open list PR systems).

Some countries, like those of northern Europe, have an egalitarian culture, while others are characterized by a male-dominated political culture in which it is still unusual to observe women with political power. It is worth noting that at least in terms of expressed opinions ("Special Eurobarometer 465" n.d.), most European citizens think that gender equality is important to ensure a fair and democratic society. In this 2017 survey, 44 percent of men and 62 percent of women declared that their own country would benefit from more women in decision-making positions, and 70 percent of citizens were in favor (strongly or somewhat) of legal measures to ensure parity between men and women in politics.

Despite so many voters being strongly in favor of a more balanced representation, the gender political power index varies across European countries. The index measures gender equality in decision-making positions through the representation of women in national parliaments, government, and regional/local assemblies. In 2020, countries' index scores varied from 94.9 (out of 100, which denotes full gender equality) for Sweden to 17.8 for Hungary, with an average of 56.9 for EU countries. This variance in gender equality may be partially explained with the presence of an unconscious bias in the electorate. Voters are not openly sexist but still unconsciously associate gender traits and stereotypes to the likelihood of being a successful politician. For example, 69 percent of respondents believe that women are more likely than men to make decisions based on their emotions, a characteristic that is typically not desired in political representatives. Likewise, 35 percent of citizens think that women are less ambitious than men and are less interested in positions of political responsibility. These beliefs may lead voters to accept the status quo without much need for questioning and intervention in favor of increasing women's presence in politics. Finally, in many European countries, particularly in eastern Europe, a political career is still not an easy and socially accepted choice. For example, 44 percent of European citizens still think that the most important role for a woman is to take care of her home and family. The agreement is particularly high in former communist countries, where over 70 percent of respondents in Bulgaria, Hungary, Poland, the Czech Republic, Latvia, Lithuania, Slovakia, and Estonia agree with the statement.

It is worth noting that the gap in political careers cannot be explained with the supply argument according to which women typically do not possess the professional characteristics that are deemed essential for a politician. If we look at education, for example, women have overtaken men in most countries in getting a college degree. In 2017, the percentage of women aged twenty-nine to thirty-four having obtained a tertiary education qualification in the European Union was 44.7 percent, while the one for men stood at 34.8 percent. Unfortunately, countries do not necessarily tap into the full potential available to them. In the European Union, only 68.2 percent of women were employed in 2019 compared to 79.6 percent of men. Further, 45 percent of those women were employed in knowledge-intensive occupations, which require advanced degrees, while men were employed at a rate of only 29.4 percent. In addition, while boardrooms remain a predominantly male environment, the share of women who are presidents, members, and employee representatives of boards in the largest listed companies in the European Union increased from 8.5 percent in 2003 to 30 percent in 2020. However, many women are appointed to board positions that have little supervisory or decision-making powers.

One of the problems is that political activism, at least at the very beginning, is extremely resource consuming both in terms of time and financial resources, and women are often lacking both. On average, the gender pay gap is 16 percent across Europe. Further, women are more frequently found in low-paying jobs and part-time employment, which means that they have lower individual resources to devote to launching a political campaign. Time is another binding constraint for women in Europe; despite a reasonably ubiquitous and developed **welfare state**, women are still the main providers of child and elderly care as well as responsible for most household chores. European women spend twenty-two hours per week on average on care and household work compared to nine hours spent by men. Thus, women already carry a double burden of paid employment and unpaid care work. A political career represents a triple burden for which most women simply have no time unless they have a supportive spouse that can alleviate the care burden at home.

For women who successfully enter the political arena, life does not become easier. Parliaments are still male dominated, and despite official statements supporting equality of access and opportunity, old norms are difficult to modify. Women representatives find it difficult to make their voices heard or to break into the unofficial networks where political agendas are set and decisions are truly made (Criado Perez 2019). To combat these barriers, the European Union has provided assessment tools and guidelines to move national parliaments toward gender-sensitive parliaments. For example, some parliaments have established gender equity bodies whose aim is to ensure equal opportunities to influence the legislative process. The Swedish parliament was the first parliament to set up a Speaker's Gender Equality group in 1995. The group's objective is to facilitate women's ability to fulfill their duties as members of parliament in a masculinized environment with entrenched power structures (Freidenvall and Erikson 2020). Groups like the one in Sweden provide a series of recommendations and guidelines to make parliaments more inclusive and women friendly. For example, some organizations suggested that children should be allowed in the voting chambers so that parents can fully participate in parliamentary debate and proceedings. Another recommendation included that parliaments should offer long-term childcare, including short-term provisions for emergencies and school holidays. In addition, recommendations included that parliaments should set clear working schedules in advance in addition to limiting meeting times to school hours and school holidays to enable parents to plan ahead and consequently improve the work-life balance of representatives. Finally, one recommendation stated that parties should develop a list of skills necessary to be successful in politics to demystify politics and encourage more women to step forward as candidates.

ACHIEVING POLITICAL PARITY—A WAY FORWARD FOR EUROPE

So far, we have discussed how obstacles to gender equality in Europe can be categorized as coming from political parties, from traditional cultures, and from a lack of work-life balance. How can these barriers be removed or at least weakened? Countries in Europe have different views on the type of policies necessary to increase the participation of women in politics. The incremental track model, for example, the one adopted by Nordic countries, focuses intervention on capacity-building activities aimed at either improving women's political skills or easing their struggle to combine political activities and personal life (Freidenvall, Johansson, and Dahlerup 2013). These interventions include political candidate schools for women and mentoring projects, which were introduced following the European Union's efforts for gender equality in a variety of areas of public life.

For example, several women's associations gathered under the umbrella of the European Women's Lobby, which lobbies in for gender-balanced policies and funding in the EU. Among the programs promoted by the European Women's Lobby and its members is a program to train and support women candidates in Ireland and a think tank on gender parity in the Czech Republic. Other policies aim to make politics more women friendly by providing free childcare and modifying meeting hours to ease the work-life balance problem. The road to parity is therefore slow and made of small increments, which will in turn lead to parity over time, slowly erasing current gender prejudices against women in and systemic barriers to politics.

In contrast, the fast-track model proposes affirmative action policies as the main way to achieve gender balance via electoral gender quotas. Quotas are the natural intervention to address the lack of women candidates when it is caused by a hostile party environment, as they change the incentives of parties when choosing whom to nominate. Quotas may also be effective in reducing voters' gender stereotypes, as being exposed to women politicians may decrease prejudices that will persist even when quotas are removed (Cella and Manzoni 2022; De Paola, Scoppa, and Lombardo 2010). The Spanish case illuminates the benefits of the fast-track model. Spain is a relatively young democracy, with the first democratic elections being held in 1977 following the death of General Francisco Franco in 1975. Because Spain was a very traditional society, gender issues and women's political representation were not high on the agenda; the first four elections resulted in parliaments with fewer than 10 percent of members being women. Things began to change when the leftist parties, mainly the Spanish Socialist Party (PSOE), adopted a voluntary party quota of 25 percent in 1988, which was raised to 40 percent in 1997. The steady increase in the number of women elected finally resulted in the reform of the General Election Act in 2007 that introduced a legislative gender quota of 40 percent.

Under the new quota law, not more than 60 percent of candidates are allowed to be of the same gender (which in turn means no less than 40 percent of the other one). This quota requirement is applied to every five positions on the party list. By introducing a ranking requirement, parties could no longer place women at the bottom of the list, where they had little chance of being elected, while still formally adhering to quota requirements. The sanctions for nonadherence to the quota requirements are also very explicit: party lists that do not satisfy the requirements cannot participate in the election. The new quota law applies to all elections, from local to general elections, except for the state senate and municipal elections for cities with fewer than 3,000 people.

Quotas have had a visible effect. The Spanish lower house has seen a portion of women legislators of around 40 percent for nearly a decade and at present stands at 43 percent. A more equal Spanish parliament has spilled over to greater gender-balanced cabinets. For example, on the June 5, 2018, the ministers of the Spanish Socialist Party's new government were sworn in at the Zarzuela Palace. The cabinet had the highest number of women ministers in any government in Europe, with eleven out of seventeen ministries being led by women, amounting to 61 percent of the cabinet. Notably, women were given very important ministries, such as finance, justice, industry, and work, going well beyond the usual set of equality, education, welfare, and health. In the second Sanchez government, which began its work in January 2020, women ministers make up 48 percent of the cabinet. While not a parity cabinet, it signifies important and continued progress toward the equal representation of women. Most importantly, the trends toward more balanced cabinets have been maintained under conservative governments.

To summarize, despite a relative homogeneity in GDP and the peculiar geographical proximity, the level of success of European women in participating and influencing political life is quite heterogeneous. We go from near parity in the Scandinavian countries to greater women's underrepresentation in Mediterranean countries, with the recent exception of Spain.

On top of that, there are the countries of the former Eastern bloc, where the advent of capitalism in the last thirty years has fostered a revival of traditional roles that were, at least formally, absent from communist regimes. In those countries, women's presence in parliament fell from near parity to below 10 percent. However, we can witness a lot of progress across Europe for women as voters, members of parliament, and executive leaders. Yet, a lot remains to be done. While Europe has seen some remarkable examples of women leadership in politics, such as British prime minister Margaret Thatcher and German chancellor Angela Merkel, over a century after the first European women were granted the right to vote, women remain a minority in the elected legislatures of most European countries.

REFERENCES

Abendschön, S., and S. Steinmetz. 2014. "The Gender Gap in Voting Revisited: Women's Party Preferences in a European Context." *Social Politics* 21 (2): 315–344.

Aidt, T. S., and B. Dallal. 2008. "Female Voting Power: The Contribution of Women's Suffrage to the Growth of Social Spending in Western Europe (1869–1960)." *Public Choice* 134: 391–417.

Barnes, Tiffany D., and Diana Z. O'Brien. 2018. "Defending the Realm: The Appointment of Female Defense Ministers Worldwide." *American Journal of Political Science* 62 (2): 355–368. https://doi.org/10.1111/ajps.12337

Blom, I. 2012. "A Transnational Comparison of the Struggles for Women's Suffrage in the Nordic Countries during the Long 19th Century." *Scandinavian Journal of History* 37 (5): 600–620.

Cella, M., and E. Manzoni. 2022. "Gender Bias and Women's Political Performance." *European Journal of Political Economy*. https://doi.org/10.1016/j.ejpoleco.2022.102314

Childs, S., and M. C. Kittilson. 2016. "Feminizing Political Parties: Women's Party Member Organizations within European Parliamentary Parties." *Party Politics* 22 (5): 598–608.

Criado Perez, C. 2019. *Invisible Women: Exposing Data Bias in a World Designed for Men*. London: Vintage.

De Paola, M., V. Scoppa, and R. Lombardo. 2010. "Can Gender Quotas Break Down Negative Stereotypes? Evidence from Changes in Electoral Rules." *Journal of Public Economics* 94: 344–353.

Durham, M. 1998. *Women and Fascisms*. London: Routledge.

EIGE. 2022. Gender Statistics Database. National governments: ministers by seniority and function of government. https://eige.europa.eu/gen der-statistics/dgs/indicator/wmidm_pol_gov__wmid_natgov_minis

EIGE. n.d. "Gender Statistics Database." https://eige.europa.eu/gender-sta tistics/dgs/browse/wmidm

European Parliament. 2019. "Women in the European Parliament." September 12, 2019. https://www.europarl.europa.eu/news/en/headlines /society/20190226STO28804/women-in-the-european-parliament -infographics

European Parliamentary Research Service. 2021. "Share of Women in the European Parliament." March 1, 2021. https://epthinktank.eu/2021 /03/01/women-in-politics-in-the-eu-state-of-play/share-of-women -in-the-european-parliament/

Freidenvall, L., E. Johansson, and D. Dahlerup. 2013. "Electoral Gender Quota Systems and Their Implementation in Europe: Update 2013." Publications Office, European Parliament, Directorate-General for Internal Policies of the Union.

Hills, J. 1981. "Britain." In *The Politics of the Second Electorate: Women and Public Participation: Britain, USA, Canada, Australia, France, Spain, West Germany, Italy, Sweden, Finland, Eastern Europe, USSR, Japan*, edited by J. Lovenduski and J. Hills, 8–32. Abingdon, UK: Routledge.

IDEA. n.d. "Gender Quotas Database." https://www.idea.int/data-tools /data/gender-quotas

IPU (Inter-Parliamentary Union). 2022. "Monthly Ranking of Women in National Parliaments." https://data.ipu.org/women-ranking?month =9&year=2022

Kornelius, S. 2013. *Angela Merkel: The Chancellor and Her World*. London: Alma Books.

OCSE. 2014. *Handbook on Promoting Women's Participation in Political Parties*. Warsaw, Poland: OSCE Office for Democratic Institutions and Human Rights.

Piscopo, J. M. 2019. "The Limits of Leaning In: Ambition, Recruitment, and Candidate Training in Comparative Perspective." *Politics, Groups and Identities* 7 (4): 817–828.

Rubio-Marín, R. 2014. "The Achievement of Female Suffrage in Europe: On Women's Citizenship." *International Journal of Constitutional Law* 12: 4–34.

Shorrocks, Rosalind. 2018. "Cohort Change in Political Gender Gaps in Europe and Canada: The Role of Modernization." *Politics & Society* 46 (2): 135–175.

"Special Eurobarometer 465." n.d. https://data.europa.eu/data/datasets /s2154_87_4_465_eng?locale=en

Taylor, Adam. 2014. "Why a Picture of Four Female European Politicians Went Viral This Weekend." *Business Insider*, February 3, 2014. https://www.businessinsider.com/picture-of-female-european-politi cians-went-viral-2014-2

Xydias, Christina. 2016. "Discrepancies in Women's Presence between European National Legislatures and the European Parliament: A Contextual Explanation." *Political Research Quarterly* 69 (4): 800–812.

FOUR

Middle East and North Africa

Michaela Grančayová

This chapter addresses women's political representation and participation in the Middle East and North Africa (MENA). It discusses the history and notable cases of women's political engagement in the region as well as women's current political situation. More specifically, the chapter discusses the levels of women's representation in the region's national legislatures and executive branches and provides several examples of MENA's successful women politicians. The chapter also analyzes the barriers that prevent women in the region from entering the political realm and offers several solutions that might possibly boost women's political participation and representation.

Because MENA is a diverse region with no universal definition, it is necessary to specify how the term is used throughout the chapter. According to the most common definition, MENA is the geographical area that comprises all Arab states (Algeria, Bahrain, Egypt, Iraq, Palestine, Jordan, Kuwait, Lebanon, Libya, Morocco, Oman, Qatar, Saudi Arabia, Syria, Tunisia, United Arab Emirates, and Yemen) and two or three non-Arab states (Israel, Iran, and from time to time also Turkey). Sometimes, other countries with similar customs and traditions or linguistic features are included as well (e.g., Afghanistan, Pakistan). However, for the purpose of this chapter, I will stick to the former definition (all Arab states and three non-Arab countries). Additionally, this area consists of five subregions (see table 4.1) that represent various ethnic groups (e.g., Arabs,

Table 4.1   MENA Subregions

Arabian Peninsula	Fertile Crescent	Maghreb	Nile Valley	Northern Tier
Bahrain, Kuwait, Oman, Qatar, Saudi Arabia, United Arab Emirates, Yemen	Iraq, Israel, Jordan, Lebanon, Palestine, Syria	Algeria, Libya, Morocco, Tunisia	Egypt	Iran, Turkey

Kurds, Persians, Turks) and types of government (e.g., republics such as Egypt, monarchies like Saudi Arabia, and theocratic (religious) republics like Iran).[1]

WOMEN AS VOTERS

Even though all the MENA countries now grant women suffrage and support their political participation, the achievement of women's suffrage varied greatly across the region. In 1934, Turkey became the first MENA country that allowed women to vote and stand as candidates in elections. Several other countries soon followed Turkey in granting women suffrage: Israel in 1948, Lebanon in 1952, and Egypt in 1956. In contrast, women in Saudi Arabia were allowed to vote for the first time in 2015—the last country in the region to adopt universal suffrage (table 4.2).

Even though suffrage came relative late for many women in the region, MENA women were always highly visible and politically active citizens. This was mainly true regarding their participation in protests and demonstrations. For example, women played a significant role during the 1979 Islamic Revolution in Iran. In addition to demonstrations, they also participated in armed battles, fighting side by side with men. Even **Ayatollah Ruhollah Khomeini**, Iran's supreme religious leader (1979–1989), praised the country's women for their active participation in the uprising (Shojaei, Samsu, and Asayeseh 2010, 261). Moreover, some acts of the Iranian constitution that was drafted after the revolution recognized the importance of protecting "women's social and political rights" (Shojaei and Samsu and Asayeseh 2010, 262). Yet, women remain marginalized and cannot enjoy

---

[1] Many of these countries are "republics" only on paper (formally). In practice, they are often secular dictatorships.

Table 4.2   Enfranchisement for Women in the Middle East and North Africa

Country	Year of Suffrage
Turkey	1930, right to vote; 1934, full suffrage
Israel	1948
Syria	1949, right to vote; 1953, full suffrage
Lebanon	1952
Egypt	1956
Tunisia	1959
Algeria	1962
Iran	1963
Morocco	1963
Libya	1964
Yemen	1967, the People's Democratic Republic of Yemen; 1970, Yemen Arab Republic (in 1990, the People's Democratic Republic of Yemen and the Yemen Arab Republic were merged into the Republic of Yemen)
Jordan	1974
Iraq	1980
State of Palestine	1994
Qatar	1999
Bahrain	2001
Oman	2003, universal suffrage; 1994, voting rights for a number of women chosen by Sultan Qabus
Kuwait	2005
United Arab Emirates	2006
Saudi Arabia	2011, exercised for the first time in 2015

Sources: Infoplease (2017); IPU (n.d.); *Gulf News* (2015).

Tunisian woman voting in the polling station in Tunisia elections October 23, 2011. (Smandy I Dreamstime.com)

some of the political rights that their male counterparts have, most importantly having a major say in significant political decisions. In September 2022, the death of Mahsa Amin, a young Kurdish woman who died after her arrest by the morality police for wearing her headscarf incorrectly, sparked large scale protests in the country. Iranian women took to the streets decrying the Iranian theocratic regime, calling for an end to the country's religious rule, and protesting the regime's brutality against women. They showed their anger and solidarity with Mahsa Amin by burning their headscarves and cutting their hair.

In a similar fashion, Egyptian women played an important role during the country's major historical events. For instance, they were the leaders of the 1919 revolution against the British occupation (Allam 2017). Several Egyptian women were also highly active in political journalism. One of the most prominent figures was Fatma al-Youssef, a former Lebanese actress who established the political magazine and later a newspaper called *Rose al-Youssef*. Both media outlets made important contributions to the literary and cultural movement of the country by providing writers and poets with a platform to advance their political ideas (Osman 2013). Women were also among the leaders of the 2011 Arab Spring protests and their aftermath. The Arab Spring was a series of revolutionary uprisings against authoritarian regimes in the region that led to the ousting of prominent Arab leaders, such as Egyptian president Hosni Mubarak (1981–2011) and his Tunisian counterpart Zine el-Abidine Ben Ali (1987–2011).

Even though women had played a prominent role in the 1919 protests against the British, they were often denied the right to vote and had to wait until 1956 for enfranchisement. Once eligible to vote and to stand as candidates in elections, Rawya Ateya became the first Egyptian woman to be elected to the country's parliament and the first woman parliamentarian in the Arab world in 1957. Kuwaiti women were also politically active. Women played a prominent role during the 1990 Iraqi occupation of Kuwait (Tetreault 2001). Despite their active role in the resistance movement against the Iraqis, Kuwaiti women had to wait until 2005 to gain suffrage and thus were among the last women to become enfranchised.

Turkish women also have a long history of political participation. Mustafa Kemal Ataturk (1923–1938), the father of modern Turkey and the country's first president, supported women's civil and political participation and granted equal citizenship to men and women early in the history of the country (Kasapoglu and Ozerkmen 2011, 98). In 1923, Nezihe Muhiddin, a Turkish women's rights activist, founded both the country's first political and its first women party , Kadinlar Halk Firkasi (Women's People Party). Although the party was almost immediately banned, its establishment nevertheless marks an important milestone for MENA women. After the party was banned, Muhittin founded the Turkish Women's Union (Turk Kadinlar Birligi, TKB), which gave an important impetus to the first wave of feminism in Turkey (Leake 2012).

When it comes to voting, women generally turnout at lower levels than men in MENA countries. For example, in the 2009 municipal elections in Morocco, women's turnout was only 45 percent. In contrast, 57 percent of the country's men voters cast their ballot in the same elections (Abdul-Latif and Serpe 2010, 18). In Libya, the gender gap is stark: 59 percent of women compared to 84 percent of men took part in the 2012 General National Congress elections.

In several countries, the Arab Spring did not considerably move the needle when it comes to women's voter turnout. According to the 2015 research conducted by the Transitional Governance Project (as cited in Benstead and Lust 2015), women's participation in the first transnational elections in Egypt, Libya, and Tunisia was lower than men's participation. For instance, in the 2011–2012 transnational parliamentary elections in Egypt, only 58 percent of women cast a ballot in comparison to 77 percent of men. Before the Arab Spring, 47 percent of men and 24 percent of women turned out in elections (Transitional Governance Project 2015, as cited in Benstead and Lust 2015).

In contrast, in the Tunisian 2011 Constituent Assembly elections, women's turnout was 65 percent, whereas men's turnout was 75 percent (Transitional Governance Project 2015, as cited in Benstead and Lust 2015). According to the 2015 Transitional Governance project (as cited in Benstead and Lust 2015), Tunisia had already tried to close the gender gap in voting pre–Arab Spring efforts: 34 percent of both men and women stated that they had voted prior to the 2010–2011 revolution in the country. In Lebanon, women's turnout in the country's 2009 and 2018 parliamentary elections were slightly higher than men's turnout. In the 2009 elections, 80 percent of women turned out compared to 78 percent of men (Abdul-Latif and Serpe 2010, 18). In the country's 2018 elections, the situation was similar; 50.8 percent of women voted in comparison to 49.2 percent of men (UNDP Lebanese Elections Assistance Project 2018, 5).

In conclusion, even though MENA women have frequently played significant roles in their countries' political destinies, they have often faced considerable marginalization. In some cases (especially in the Gulf countries), they had to wait for suffrage until the twenty-first century. Overall, the situation has been gradually improving, and in the recent past, women have moved slightly closer to achieving political parity with men. The following section will discuss MENA women's political presence today.

WOMEN AS MEMBERS OF PARLIAMENT

Women's political representation in the MENA countries' legislatures is among the lowest in the world, and the data on the current political representation of women in the MENA region provide a mixed picture. Women constitute 16.8 percent of all members of parliaments in the MENA region (IPU 2022a; figure 4.1).

Among the countries with the highest number of women in national parliaments are the United Arab Emirates (50 percent), Israel (30 percent), Iraq (28.9 percent), Egypt (27. 7 percent), Tunisia (26.3 percent), Morocco (24.1 percent) and Saudi Arabia (19.9 percent). The region's countries with the lowest number of women in parliament are Yemen (no women), Kuwait (1.6 percent), Oman (2.3 percent), Qatar (4.4 percent), and Iran (5.6 percent) (IPU 2022b; table 4.3).

The percentage of women members of parliaments in MENA countries is often influenced by the type of electoral system that the countries adhere to. According to Adams (2018), countries that use proportional representation electoral systems usually have more women members of parliament

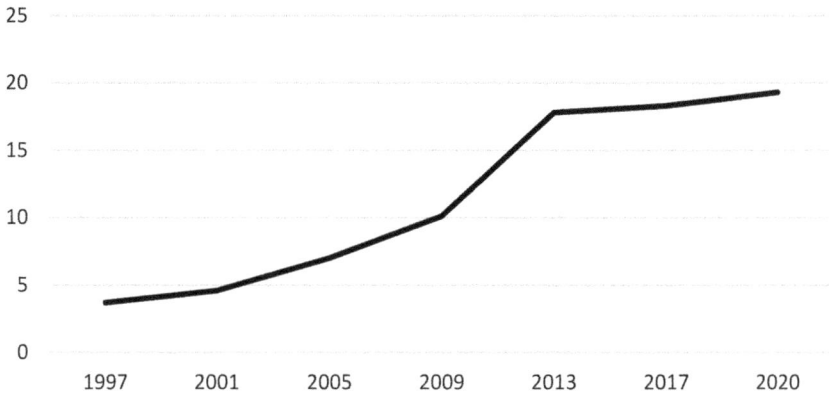

Figure 4.1 The Percentage of Women Members of Parliaments in the MENA Region, 1997–2020 (Inter-Parliamentary Union: Parline database on national parliaments, July 31, 2021).

than those that follow a different type of system (e.g., majoritarian or mixed-member systems). Israel, Tunisia, and Morocco all use proportional representation electoral systems and on average have more women members of parliament than MENA countries with different electoral systems. The same can be said about Iraq that until very recently (2021) also followed the system of proportional representation. However, there are some exceptions to the rule. For example, Egypt uses a majoritarian electoral system but has more women members of parliament than Lebanon, which follows a proportional representation electoral system (27.7 percent compared to 6.3 percent, respectively). This difference is most likely because Egypt has an electoral gender quota while Lebanon does not. Still, in general, regarding the number of women members of parliament, MENA countries with proportional representation electoral systems tend to do better than those that use a different system.

During the Arab Spring (2010–2011), women were among the main initiators of protests, actively participated in demonstrations, and encouraged other women to join them. Their participation did not come without risk because women were subjected to sexual harassment. In Egypt, women were even subject to forced virginity tests, which is an examination of female genitalia that aims to determine whether a woman is a virgin. In the renewed wave of protest in the 2011 post–Arab Spring Egypt, this

Table 4.3   The Percentage of Women Representatives in the National Parliaments of the MENA Region

Country	Percentage of Women Representatives	Electoral Gender Quota	Details on the Quota
United Arab Emirates	50	Reserved seats	50% of seats reserved for women
Israel	30		
Iraq	28.9	Reserved Seats	Not less than 25% of seats reserved for women
Egypt	27.7	Reserved Seats	At least 25% of seats reserved for women
Tunisia	26.3	Legislated candidate quota	"Candidates shall file their candidacy applications on the basis of parity between men and women" (Article 16 of Decree 35 as cited in IDEA)
Morocco	24.1	Reserved Seats	60 reserved seats for women and 30 reserved seats for both men and women under 40
Saudi Arabia	19.9	Reserved seats	20% of seats reserved for women
Turkey	17.4		
Libya	16.5	Legislated Candidate Quota	"Candidates shall be arranged on the basis of the alternation among male and female candidates vertically and horizontally" (Article 15 of the 2012 Law on the Election of the National General Congress as cited in IDEA)

Country	%	Quota Type	Details
Bahrain	15.0		
Palestine	13.0	Legislated Candidate Quota	Among candidates must be about 20% of women
Jordan	12.3	Reserved Seats	15 reserved seats for women
Syria	11.2		
Algeria	8.1	Legislated Candidate Quota	20%–50% of candidates have to be women "depending on the number of seats in each electoral district" (Article 2 of the 2012 Law for the Representation of Women as cited in IDEA)
Lebanon	6.3		
Iran	5.6		
Qatar	4.4		
Oman	2.3		
Kuwait	1.6		
Yemen	0.0		

Sources: International Institute for Democracy and Electoral Assistance (2021); IPU (2022b).

practice was used against women protestors to dissuade them from taking part in the demonstrations. Despite these challenges, MENA women courageously bore all the mistreatments and significantly contributed to the fall of the **autocratic regimes**. More importantly, they proved the skeptics who claimed that women could not be politically active citizens and that they should tend to their household and family duties wrong. By taking part in popular protests, MENA women proved that (1) women are equally interested in politics and in their countries' destiny as men are and that (2) women are important political actors keen on transforming their polities.

After the Arab Spring, women in many MENA countries started to more actively participate in the countries' political life, promoting women's rights and running for political office. Women also partook in the constitution drafting process, most notably in Tunisia and Egypt. In Egypt, five out of fifty members of the committee responsible for writing the new constitution were women (ESCWA 2017, 11). Similarly, women made up 24 percent of the Tunisian Constituent Assembly (ESCWA 2017, 11). Even though these numbers may seem relatively small, for many MENA women, this was a major success. For the first time, they were able to enter a space that traditionally was exclusively "reserved for men" (ESCWA 2017, 11).

Women's political representation increased in the Arab countries of the region, especially after the Arab Spring (see table 4.4). When comparing the percentages from 2009, 2016, and 2022, the number of women representatives has increased in almost every country in the MENA region. The highest increase occurred in those countries that went through the Arab Spring protests (e.g., Egypt, Tunisia), those that granted women the right to vote and stand as candidates in elections (e.g., Saudi Arabia), and those that adopted gender quotas.

In Egypt, women's political representation increased from 1.8 percent in 2009 to 14.9 percent in 2016 and 27.7 percent in 2022. In the 2009 Tunisian election, women won 27.6 percent of parliamentary seats. This percentage rose to 31.3 percent in 2016 and 35.9 percent in 2018. In Bahrain, the number of women representatives jumped from 2.5 percent in 2010 to 7.5 percent in 2016 to 15 percent in 2022. In Saudi Arabia, the percentage of women members of parliament increased from no women members in 2009 to 19.9 percent in both 2016 and 2022, after Saudi Arabia granted women the right to vote—the last country in the world. In Morocco, women constituted 10.5 percent of all the members of the parliament in 2009. Women's presence in parliament increased to 20.5 percent in 2016 and to 24.1 percent in 2022. The increase of women in parliament largely

Table 4.4   The Percentage of Women in the MENA Parliaments in 2009 and 2016

Country	2009 (%)	2016 (%)
Algeria	7.7	31.6
Bahrain	2.5	7.5
Egypt	1.8	14.9
Iran	2.8	5.9
Iraq	25.5	26.5
Israel	18.3	26.7
Jordan	6.4	15.4
Kuwait	7.7	2.0
Lebanon	3.1	3.1
Libya	7.7	16.0
Morocco	10.5	20.5
Oman	0.0	1.2
Qatar	0.0	0.0
Saudi Arabia	0.0	19.9
Syria	12.4	13.2
Tunisia	27.6	31.3
Turkey	9.1	14.9
United Arab Emirates	22.5	22.5
Yemen	0.3	0.0

Source: IPU national averages as December 31, 2009, and December 1, 2016.

occurred due to the 2012 change in the country's electoral gender quotas by the Moroccan king Mohammed VI, who increased the number of reserved seats from thirty to sixty seats (ESCWA 2017, 41–42). In the United Arab Emirates, the percentage of women representatives jumped from 22.5 percent in 2009 and 2016 to 50 percent in 2021, when the country established a reserved seat quota of 50 percent.

After the initial euphoria of the Arab Spring and the subsequent increase of the number of women members of parliament in MENA countries, some countries have been experiencing the opposite trend in recent years. In Algeria, the percentage of women representatives increased from 7.7 percent in 2009 to 31.6 percent in 2016. However, the percentage dropped to 8.1 percent in 2022. Likewise, Tunisia had 35.9 percent women in parliament in 2018, and it dropped to 26.3 percent in 2022. On the surface, Tunisia seems to promote gender equality, but women still face a political space that is patriarchal and misogynistic (Gouvy 2021). Women endure hate speech and verbal abuse or the outright reluctance of male politicians to nominate women candidates (Gouvy 2021). Even when nominated, women's presence is often instrumentalist to present the political party as progressive (Gouvy 2021). Nevertheless, when it comes to women's political rights, Tunisia still remains one of the region's top performers. This can be attributed to the fact that Tunisia was trying to lower the gender gap and achieve women's political parity even prior to the Arab Spring. For instance, the country's 1956 Personal Status Code granted women equality and gave them equal marriage and divorce rights (Benstead and Lust 2015). More generally, in 2010 and 2011, local women may have still truly believed in the revolution and its achievements. By 2021, after many unfulfilled revolutionary promises (Gouvy 2021), women may have felt disillusioned and not wanted to stand as candidates in elections, adding to a decrease in the number of women in parliament.

Among the region's worst performers when it comes to political parity are Yemen and Kuwait. In both countries, the percentage of women representatives continues to decrease. In Yemen, the Arab Spring events plunged the country into a civil war that brought a general marginalization of women's rights. In Kuwait, in the 2020 parliamentary elections, people did not prioritize women's candidates because traditional gender attitudes and beliefs still dominate Kuwaiti society (Holleis 2020). Neither Yemen nor Kuwait implemented any type of gender quotas that would help to boost women's political representation.

In contrast, ten countries in the region have implemented some type of electoral gender quotas to boost women's political representation, most commonly legislative candidate quotas and reserved seats. Among the countries that use legislative candidate quotas are Algeria, Libya, Tunisia, and Palestine (see table 4.3). The system of reserved seats is used by Egypt, Morocco, Iraq, Jordan, Saudi Arabia, and the United Arab Emirates. Most electoral gender quotas have been adopted in Arab countries and have contributed to an increase in women representatives from 10 percent to 18 percent in the period from 2012 to 2017 in these countries (Masad 2020).

Consistent with other regions, countries that have adopted either legislative candidate quotas or reserved seats have more women in parliaments that those that do not have any electoral gender quotas in place (see table 4.3). Thus, the United Arab Emirates, Egypt, Iraq, Tunisia, Algeria, Morocco, Saudi Arabia, Libya, and Jordan all have more women in parliament than Arab countries without electoral gender quotas.

Morocco is one example of the positive impact of electoral gender quotas. Morocco has been using reserved seats since 2002. Initially, the quota reserved 35 seats out of 325 seats for women. Following the Arab Spring protests, King Mohammed VI of Morocco increased this number to 60 out of 395 seats (ESCWA 2017, 40, 41). The quota changes boosted women's political representation from 10.5 percent in 2009 to 24.1 percent in 2022. Nevertheless, the quota design still has its flaws. According to a 2010 study conducted by the International Foundation for Electoral Systems (IFES), 96 percent of Moroccan women and 85 percent of Moroccan men do not know about the quota (IFES 2010, 20). Awareness of the quota changes with education levels: 12 percent of Moroccan women with a secondary or higher education say they have "a fair amount of knowledge" on the subject, 10 percent state they are slightly aware of the topic, and 78 percent of women claim they do not know anything about it (IFES 2010, 20). Moreover, the general support for the electoral gender quotas is higher among women than men. In Morocco, 71 percent of women "somewhat support" the gender quotas in comparison to 60 percent of men (IFES 2010, 21). Thus, as the Moroccan case demonstrates, even though the system of gender quotas in the region has helped boost women's political representation, more could be done to raise public awareness.

WOMEN AS LEADERS

When it comes to women in the executive, the overall picture is once again mixed. Even though several women have served as their countries' leaders (see table 4.5), they remain the exception and not the rule. Tansu Ciller was the first and only woman prime minister of Turkey. Golda Meier was the first and only woman prime minister of Israel (1969–1974) as well as the minister of internal affairs (1970), the minister of foreign affairs (1956–1966), and the minister of labor (1949–1956). In October 2021, Najla Bouden Romdhane became the first woman prime minister of Tunisia as well as the first woman prime minister in the Arab world. Not a single woman in the region has served as president, although several

Table 4.5   Women Executive Leaders in MENA

Country	Office	Name	Tenure
Tunisia	Prime minister	Najla Bouden	2021–present
Turkey	Prime minister	Tansu Ciller	1993–1996
Israel	Prime minister	Golda Meir	1969–1974

Source: Data courtesy of Farida Jalalzai (excludes interim or appointed leaders).

women ran as candidates in presidential elections. For example, in 2011, Bothaina Kamel became the first woman to run for the presidential office in Egypt. In 2018, Sarwa Abdul Wahid was the first woman in Iraq to run for presidential office.

While women have been noticeably absent from premiership and the presidency, some women have served as vice prime ministers. Zeina Akar Adra served as the deputy prime minister of Lebanon from January 2020 until September 2021. During the presidency of Mohammad Khatami (1997–2005), Masoumeh Ebtekar served as the vice president of Iran.

The number of women ministers in the region has slightly increased in the recent years. Considering that most women in MENA, particularly in the Gulf region, were not allowed to vote or stand for election until recently, their presence in cabinets is a breakthrough for women's rights in the region. As of now, every MENA country (with the exception of Yemen) has at least one woman minister in its cabinet. The countries with the highest number of women ministers include Lebanon (31.6 percent), the United Arab Emirates (27.3 percent), Israel (25 percent), Egypt (24.2 percent), and Algeria (14.7 percent) (IPU 2021). Among these countries, Lebanon has the highest share of women ministers (31.6 percent), whereas the United Arab Emirates has the highest number (9) of them. Women in the United Arab Emirates' cabinet oversee portfolios such as the Ministry of Culture and Youth (Noura Al Kaabi, 2020–present), Community Development (Najla bint Mohammad al-Awar, 2016–present), Public Education Affairs (Jameela Salem Al Muhairi, 2016–present), and the Ministry for Youth Affairs (Shamma Al Mazrui, 2016–present). Having women in charge of strategically important cabinets, the United Arab Emirates serves as a role model for other countries in the region in terms of boosting women's political participation and representation.

More recently, Egypt has been trying to increase the percentage of women in cabinets. Today, the country has the highest number of women ministers since 1962 (Bar'el 2018), with eight out of thirty-four ministers being women. Women oversee the Ministry of Healthcare (Hala Zayed, 2018–present), the Ministry of Planning, and Economic Development (Hala Hilmi al-Saeed, 2018–present), and the Ministry of Culture (Ines Abdel-Dayem, 2018–present). One possible reason for the presence of several women in cabinet is the efforts by President Abdel Fattah el-Sisi (2014–present) to present Egypt as a country that has political opportunities for all, women included. Women remain the exception in the cabinets of Kuwait (6.7 percent), Iran (6.7 percent), Qatar (7.1 percent), and Iraq (9.1 percent) (IPU 2021). The MENA countries with the lowest number of women ministers include Kuwait Qatar and Saudi Arabia.

As is common across the world, most women ministers in the MENA region oversee cabinet portfolios that are typically associated with women's issues, such as education, culture, women, and/or family affairs. Appointing women to traditional feminine cabinet positions reinforces the stereotypical image of women as being best suited for areas that are associated with their traditional roles as mothers, wives, and household providers. However, some women have been appointed to ministries that are traditionally masculine domains. In 2019, Raya al-Hassan (Lebanon) became the first woman minister of interior in the Arab world. Before holding this position, al-Hassan was appointed (as the first Lebanese woman) the minister of finance (2009–2011). In 2020, Zeina Akar Adra

SHAMMA AL MAZRUI—UNITED ARAB EMIRATES

Shamma Al Mazrui is the current minister of state for youth in the United Arab Emirates (UAE) and a former research analyst at the UAE embassy in Washington, DC. In the past, she also served as a public policy analyst at the UAE Mission to the United Nations. At the time of her appointment to her first ministerial position in 2016, as the Emirati minister of state for youth affairs, Al Mazrui was only twenty-two years old. This made her the youngest government minister in the world.

Being both very young and a woman, Al Mazrui serves as a role model for those Emirati women who have political aspirations but previously might have felt discouraged to run in elections. She is a good example of a MENA woman who has achieved an important political position and can in turn influence state affairs in her country.

Source: United Arab Emirates: The Cabinet (2021).

FARROKHROO PARSA—IRAN

Farrokhroo Parsa constitutes a very interesting case of an Iranian woman politician. Born into the family of the editor of the woman's magazine *Jahán e-Zanan* ("Women's World"), Parsa soon became both politically and publicly active. Among her various activities, she became involved in the education of female prisoners and the campaign for women's suffrage. In 1963, Parsa was elected to Iranian parliament, where she actively fought for women's rights. For instance, she dedicated her time to amending Iranian laws that concerned women and family. In 1968, she was appointed the Iranian minister of education and thus became the first woman in Iran to hold a cabinet position.

Even though Parsa was a strong advocate for women's rights and gender equality and had held important positions in the country's legislature and executive, fate was very cruel to her. After the 1979 Islamic Revolution and the implementation of several laws that curtailed women's rights, she felt disillusioned and frequently participated in protests opposing the country's transformation into an Islamic republic. As a result, she was arrested, charged with several "crimes," and was executed by firing squad in 1980.

Sources: Bahrami (2005); Jecks (2009).

(Lebanon) was appointed as the first Arab woman minister of defense. Lamia Zribi (2016–2017) served as the minister of finance in Tunisia, Sahar Nasr (2015–2019) led the Ministry of International Cooperation in Egypt, and Nihal Ali al-Awlaqi (2016–2020) oversaw the Ministry of Legal Affairs in Yemen. Appointing women to more powerful cabinet positions allows them to demonstrate their competence and qualifications to make decisions that are at the core of governance and, hopefully, weakens stereotypes that politics are a man's job.

BARRIERS TO POLITICAL PARITY

Considering that historically women in the MENA region were publicly and politically active, it is surprising that when it comes to political parity, women are still underrepresented. The popular explanation that MENA women are not interested in politics or that they are too shy to take part in politics will simply not suffice. Despite the governments' efforts and the implementation of gender quotas in several countries, barriers and obstacles still exist for those women who want to pursue a career in politics. In the MENA region, these barriers can be divided into two main categories: sociocultural and institutional barriers (ESCWA 2017, 19). Readers should keep in mind that the region is not homogeneous, and, consequently, not all the barriers can be universally applied to all the countries in the MENA region. Still, what follows is a summary of the most common barriers that are usually mentioned when discussing the low percentage of the MENA women in the region's legislatures and executives.

Sociocultural Barriers to Women's Political Parity in the MENA

One of the greatest hurdles for women in politics is the traditional culture dominant across the MENA region that is characterized by conservative gender attitudes. As the majority of the MENA countries are predominantly Muslim, Islam plays a significant role in people's lives. The discrimination of MENA women often stems from a particular interpretation of the Quran and other religious texts that the governments and religious authorities then "appropriate … to justify discrimination against women" (Kharroub 2015). Thus, in Muslim societies, women are often treated as "second-class citizens" (Abbott and Teti 2017) whose main role is to complement their husbands as obedient wives and bearers of children, not as independent political leaders or policy makers. This means that many countries in the region support the division of labor and gender-related roles based on the person's biological sex. Thus, women in the region are generally expected to concern themselves with the realm of the household (i.e., cooking, raising up children, shopping) and not with the public or political spheres, which are perceived as male domains. This traditional view of womanhood is reinforced in the countries' civil and **sharia** (Islamic) laws.

Sharia influences all spheres of public as well as private life. It regulates marriage and divorce norms as well as inheritance and custody (Lomazzi 2020). Thus, for instance, in Qatar (which combines civil law with sharia), unmarried women under the age of twenty-five are not allowed to travel abroad without the permission of their male guardian (e.g., husband, father, brother, uncle). Moreover, women also need their guardian's consent if they wish to marry or obtain a government scholarship. Even some reproductive health care is unavailable to women without obtaining the permission of their husbands (Human Rights Watch 2021a). In countries that follow a more conservative interpretation of Islam (especially the Gulf States), politics are a male-only affair. If women decide to break with

religion and cultural traditions, their political participation is often inter-
preted as an inappropriate demonstration of feminism, which is seen as a
Western product imposed by international (Western) powers that must be
rejected (ESCWA 2017, 23). Consequently, women running for office are
often greeted with doubt, mocking, and even discrimination.

In addition, Muslim families tend to have closer and more intimate family ties than their Western counterparts. Families are led by a patriarch who
traditionally controls all family activities. Research conducted by Michael
Robbins and Kathrin Thomas (2018, 14) found that 85 percent of men and
69 percent of women in Algeria, 75 percent of men and 69 percent of
women in Egypt, 66 percent of men and 59 percent of women in Tunisia,
and 65 percent of men and 50 percent of women in Morocco believe that
the "husband should have the final say in family decisions." Furthermore,
women in Egypt, Morocco, Lebanon, and Palestine claim that men frequently see it as their right to control their wives' personal freedoms, such
as the clothes the wife chooses to wear or the time when the couple has
sexual intercourse (El Feki, Heilman, and Barker 2017, 10). This means that
men and other older male family members control and impose their will on
women and younger members of the household. Typically, the patriarchs
perceive women as ineffective and inefficient leaders and consider politics
to be an inappropriate and unsafe activity for women (ESCWA 2017, 22).

Traditional gender attitudes are commonly prevalent in the rural parts
of the MENA region. However, traditional attitudes are not limited to the
region's rural and thus poorer areas. It is also present in rich petrostates
such as Saudi Arabia, Kuwait, and Qatar. For instance, as previously mentioned, unmarried Qatari women under the age of twenty-five cannot travel
abroad without the permission of their male guardian (Human Rights
Watch 2021a). Similarly, women in Saudi Arabia who are younger than
twenty-one cannot travel abroad without the approval of their male guardian (Human Rights Watch 2019). Moreover, women in the United Arab
Emirates are not eligible to receive financial support from their husband if
they are not willing to have sex with him "without 'a lawful excuse', [or if
the woman – emphasis the author] abandons the marital home or prevents
her husband from entering the marital home" (Decree on Federal Law No.
5 of 2020 art. 2 as cited in Human Rights Watch 2021b).

These attitudes toward women and their role in the society often further
translate into the perception of politics as an unsatisfactory and even dangerous place for women. Consequently, women politicians sometimes face
several stereotypes that try to diminish their presence in politics. For

example, a recent study conducted in Qatar showed that both men and women in the country believe that "males make better political leaders than women do" (Al-Tamimi 2016). This prevalent belief is also confirmed by 2018 research on the rights and roles of women in the MENA region (Robbins and Thomas 2018, 9–13). According to its findings, 81 percent of Algerians, 79 percent of Egyptians, 74 percent of Jordanians, and 71 percent of Palestinians believe that men are better politicians than women. In contrast, in Morocco, Tunisia, and Lebanon, agreement with this statement is a little bit lower: 56 percent of Moroccans, 55 percent of Tunisians, and 52 percent of Lebanese think that men make better politicians than their female counterparts. Unsurprisingly, this belief is mainly held by men. On average, men are 73 percent more likely to agree with this statement than women (Robbins and Thomas 2018, 13). Less educated people are also more likely to agree that men are better politicians than women than people with secondary or higher education.

The prevalent belief that men are better political leaders than women has changed somewhat in recent years. In 2006, 67 percent (72 percent of men and 63 percent of women) held this notion. In 2011, 70 percent (78 percent of men and 62 percent of women) did. In 2013, the opinion was held by 60 percent (68 percent of men and 52 percent of women). In 2016, 67 percent (73 percent of men and 61 percent of women) believed that men are better leaders than women. Greater trust in women's political ability, especially in 2013, can be linked to the initial euphoria and the effects of the Arab Spring and the reforms in Jordan and Morocco (Robbins and Thomas 2018, 13). In contrast, after 2016, the renewed prioritization of male political abilities over those of women might relate to rising insecurity in the region, with civil wars in Yemen and Syria as well as terrorist attacks throughout the region, and a commonly held belief that during insecure times men can manage better than women (Young 2003).

Despite prevalent views that men make better politicians than women, it seems that people would not have a problem with a woman serving as head of state or head of government. In 2016, this attitude was supported by 55 percent of men and 69 percent of women through research conducted in Morocco, Jordan, Palestine, Tunisia, Egypt, and Algeria (Robbins and Thomas 2018, 10). In general, women across the region tend to support the idea of a woman leader more than men (Robbins and Thomas 2018, 9). Again, people with secondary or higher education (with the exceptions of Jordan and Palestine) are more likely to support women serving as executive leaders (Robbins and Thomas 2018, 10). Over time, we can observe

VIOLENCE AGAINST TUNISIAN WOMEN POLITICIANS

Even when women politicians succeed in entering the political realm, they often endure various forms of violence to marginalize their role in politics. In Tunisia, a 2015 survey found that 53.5 percent of women said they have been the target of violence in the public space; 78 percent reported psychological violence; 41.2 percent faced physical violence; and 75.4 percent experienced sexual violence (Chouakri 2019, 17). Another study of forty-five party members (both men and women) from nine Tunisian political parties revealed that many of the country's women politicians have experienced some type of violence that stemmed from their political activity (Chouakri 2019). Violence against women politicians is multifaceted and includes, but is not limited to, threats against women representatives occurring within their own family structure that prevents women from being political active, personal attacks and harassment on social media, or purposeful exclusion of women from party decision-making structures (Chouakri 2019, 20).

A vivid example of the violence that women in politics endure happened in Tunisia on June 30, 2021. Independent male politician Sahbi Smara repeatedly hit Amir Moussi in the face, a woman member of the Tunisian parliament and the president of Al-Dustur al-Hurr (The Free Constitutional Party) party, during a parliamentary debate (Middle East Monitor 2021). Moussi was later verbally insulted by Seif El-Din Makhlouf, another Tunisian male politician (Raghd 2021). There was no apparent reason for the attack (Middle East Monitor 2021) and the incident caught the attention of both Tunisian and foreign media. Because of the violence endured by Moussi, the Tunisian parliament banned both Smara and Makhlouf "from taking the floor for three consecutive sittings" (The New Arab 2021). Thus, as also this incident demonstrates, a lot must be done to create an enabling environment, where women politicians would feel safe to work on their agendas and contribute to the political life of their country.

changes in attitudes. In 2006, 60 percent of people in these countries (51 percent of men and 70 percent of women) supported the idea of a woman president or prime minister. In 2011, this idea was supported by 57 percent of people (48 percent of men and 66 percent of women) and by 62 percent of people in 2016 (55 percent of men and 69 percent of women).

Institutional Barriers to Women's Political Parity in the MENA Region

Across the MENA region, politics remains largely a male-dominated space where men hold key positions in the executive and the legislature as well as in party machineries. Thus, women face an uphill battle if they want to break into the male-dominated spaces; in some circumstances, this might discourage women to run in the first place.

For one, women struggle to raise the necessary funds to mount a political campaign (Ohman 2016), as the region is marked by low women's labor force participation (around 27 percent in 2015 compared to 77 percent for men) and high unemployment rates for women. There are several factors that contribute to women's unemployment (ILO 2017, 2). First, women with higher education have lower chances to find employment. While women with university degrees in the Gulf States can find a job more easily (ILO 2016), "on average the unemployment rate of women with finalized tertiary education in the region is still over 50 percent after one year of job search" (Gatti et al. 2013, as cited in ILO 2017, 3). Second, MENA women are discouraged from working outside the house once they are married and face discriminatory labor laws and practices that limit selections of jobs that are available and deemed as suitable for women (Mcloughlin 2013). Third, businesswomen tend to have a hard time accessing financial resources, as banks and other financial institutions are more distrustful of businesswomen than of businessmen (Mcloughlin 2013). Taken together, all these challenges create almost insurmountable barriers for women to generate enough income to mount a political campaign.

In addition to financial barriers, women often lack access to professions that have traditionally been paths into political careers, such as law, academia, and business. According to the International Labor Organization (ILO), when compared to the rest of the world, the MENA region has the lowest number of women working in managerial positions (ILO 2016). In Tunisia and Palestine, countries with the highest percentage of women in managerial positions in the region, women still only make up 15 percent of managers and supervisors.

While several MENA countries have gender quotas in place (see table 4.3), quotas are often ignored to the detriment of women's political participation. For instance, political parties often place women candidates on less electable positions on their party lists. In 2006, a 15 percent quota for women was approved by the then president of Yemen Ali Abdullah Saleh. Despite the quota, only two, rather than forty-five, women were elected to parliament (Nasser 2019). At this moment in time, Yemen no longer has an electoral gender quota. Even when women enter parliament with the help of gender quotas, parliamentary rules can be weaponized against women. For example, in the Libyan parliament, meetings were scheduled for late at night, when it was not socially acceptable for women to be outside the home (United Nations Development Programme Libya 2015, as cited in Congressional Research Service 2020).

Outside parliament, women are faced with media that either completely ignores them or only marginally covers them. Thus, women struggle to campaign and gain the trust and, ultimately, the vote from citizens. Even when the media is reporting on women politicians, media reports frequently comment on the women politicians' looks, hairstyles, or makeup preferences but seldom on their political agenda. For instance, in 2018, Egyptian newspaper *Al-Masry-Al-Youm* (Egyptian Today) published an in-depth article on the country's new women ministers. However, instead of being interested in their portfolios, the newspaper gave space to fashion experts and psychologists who commented on the ministers' appearance, style of clothing, and the quality of their skin (Bar'el 2018). Thus, the minister of healthcare, Hala Zayed, was praised for her blue dress, and the minister of investments and international cooperation, Sahar Nasr, was congratulated on her choice of makeup. While media reports did briefly discuss ministers' educational background, reports did not pay much attention to the work they do (Bar'el 2018). Likewise, women ministers in Egypt constantly deal with local media that are more interested in their style of clothing or "tone of speech" (Bar'el 2018) than their political work. Of course, this problem is not limited solely to women politicians; inappropriate portrayals of women in the media are an issue in the whole of the MENA region. This stems from the general tendency of the regional media to portray women as predominantly gentle, docile, and weak creatures who do not participate much in public life (Allam 2008).

ACHIEVING POLITICAL PARITY—A WAY FORWARD FOR THE MENA REGION

The previous pages offered a mixed picture on the status of women in politics across the MENA region. Even though MENA women have become more interested in politics and many states have been trying to enhance women's political participation and representation, women still encounter many barriers and obstacles that prevent them from taking a more active role in politics. To overcome these barriers, MENA countries could implement several measures that would boost the number of women politicians. In what follows, this section offers several possible solutions that could enhance political parity, such as promoting and financing feminist and **nongovernmental organizations** (NGOs), educating the public on women's rights, providing gender equity training to local media, and reforming electoral gender quotas.

MENA countries should promote and finance the activities of feminist groups, NGOs, and women's rights groups, whose work is crucial to promoting women's presence in politics (ESCWA 2017, 26, 65). Among the region's most visible and prominent organizations are Nazra for Feminist Studies and the Voice of Libyan Women. Nazra for Feminist Studies is an independent Egyptian feminist group that promotes the voice and rights of women in the MENA region. It organizes various exhibitions, lectures, and speeches that empower women and emphasize the connections between the feminist movement and social and political mobilization (Nazra for Feminist Studies n.d.). The organization also strongly supports women's political engagement and educates the public on the effect of discrimination against women in the home that hinders their participation in the public sphere (Nazra for Feminist Studies n.d.). Moreover, as one of the most notable feminist and human rights organizations in the country, Nazra played a prominent role in the documentation of abuses that many Egyptians suffered during the Arab Spring and in its aftermath. Nazra also joined the coalition of women's groups that advocated for the inclusion of women's rights in the new constitution. During the 2011 parliamentary elections, Nazra also "supported 16 women candidates from underprivileged parts of Egypt and empowered them to run for election" (Right Livelihood 2016). In 2014, Nazra (together with other groups) successfully lobbied for the expansion of the definition of sexual crimes in the country's Penal Code, which made sexual harassment a crime in Egypt for the first time (Right Livelihood 2016). Despite its achievements, Nazra and its leader, Mozn Hassan since 2016, have been persecuted by the Egyptian regime as part of President Abdel Fattah el-Sisi's crackdown on free speech and human rights and the organizations and individuals that promote it.

Another example is the Voice of Libyan Women, an NGO that tries to foster respect for women and their political rights. The organization aims to increase women's political participation and to economically empower women (Voice of Libyan Women n.d.). It has published several documents on economic empowerment of women and their role in resolving conflicts and promoting peace. Women's organizations across the region are instrumental in promoting women's political empowerment, and larger financial support could be tremendously beneficial in pushing women's advancement in politics and the public sphere more generally.

Public education campaigns centered on women's political rights is another approach that could foster greater political participation among women (ESCWA 2017, 63). Because most MENA countries are strong patriarchal societies, it is necessary to educate both men and women on the benefits of women's political empowerment (ESCWA 2017, 63). At the same time, women must be equally informed about the political rights available to them. Any education about women's rights and the importance of women's political engagement must start early, ideally during primary and secondary schooling. Schools themselves should (with the help of national organizations responsible for the advancement of women's rights) educate children and their parents on women's rights. Likewise, any public awareness campaigns should target mothers because mothers are responsible for the upbringing of their children. Over time, early childhood education on women's political rights could advance women's social and political rights and promote their political participation and parity in the MENA region in the long run.

Local media could also help advance women's political rights in the region (ESCWA 2017, 63). As mentioned earlier, media operating in MENA countries present a significant barrier to women's political parity: media outlets offer limited airtime for women candidates or completely ignore them. If they do report on women candidates, they focus on their appearance rather than their political agenda. Thus, media outlets should be encouraged to (1) cover women candidates as much as men candidates and (2) focus their reporting on substantial political issues rather than a candidate's appearance or fashion. By promoting women's agendas and their political activities, the media could inspire more women to stand as candidates in elections. In Algeria, the National Democratic Institute (NDI) supports a local women journalists' organization called Femmes en Communication (Women in Communication) in order "to enhance information integrity around the global COVID-19 pandemic, including through the provision of credible information about the pandemic's effects on women" (NDI 2021). Moreover, Femmes en Communication tries to depict women in a more positive way and overcome negative stereotypes. Additionally, it spotlights women from varied professions and background who could serve as role models for the country's inhabitants (NDI 2021).

While the number of women members of parliaments in several countries has slightly increased due to the introduction of electoral gender quotas, many male politicians still view electoral gender quotas as a rule that they must contend with rather than support. One solution to this problem of male resistance is reforming electoral gender quotas and including effective sanctions for noncompliance. These sanctions should include monetary fines for political parties that do not comply with electoral gender quotas. In addition to adopting sanctions for noncompliance, quota targets should be increased. Moreover, the quota system should "reach the Beijing baseline (30 percent) and normalize the presence of women in all structures of decision making, including the legislative, judiciary and executive branches as well as local governance" (ESCWA 2017 64). Where quotas do not exist yet, electoral gender quotas should be incorporated into the constitution. Any quota reform also needs to include a rank-order rule that prevents parties from putting women in unelectable positions. Once quotas are in place, MENA governments should raise public awareness about quotas to encourage more women to run.

To conclude, MENA women were always politically active citizens. They took part in demonstrations and popular uprisings, such as the 1979 Islamic Revolution in Iran, the resistance against the 1990 Iraqi occupation of Kuwait, and most recently the Arab Spring. Today, MENA women are allowed to vote and to stand as candidates in elections. Women's political participation in countries such as the United Arab Emirates, Egypt, and Morocco has improved thanks to the Arab Spring and the introduction of electoral gender quotas. Women in these countries now hold several ministerial positions, and the percentage of women in national parliaments has increased as well. However, even when women enter politics, they still encounter many barriers and obstacles. In some countries such as Kuwait and Oman, political parity remains a distant dream. All in all, despite women's efforts and contributions to the political life of their countries, much needs to be done before MENA women can reach political parity.

REFERENCES

Abbott, Pamela, and Andrea Teti. 2017. "Against the Tide: Why Women's Equality Remains a Distant Dream in Arab Countries." The Conversation. April, 20, 2017. https://theconversation.com/against-the -tide-why-womens-equality-remains-a-distant-dream-in-arab -countries-74410

Abdul-Latif, Rola, and Lauren Serpe. 2010. "The Status of Women in the Middle East and North Africa: A Grassroots Research and Advocacy Approach: Preliminary Findings from Surveys in Lebanon and Morocco." International Foundation for Electoral Systems (IFES),

WAPOR Conference 2010. https://www.ifes.org/sites/default/files/a
_grassroots_research_and_advocacy_approach_0.pdf

Adams, Kimberly. 2018. "The Significant Influence of Proportional Representation and Democratization on the Share of Female Parliamentarians in Middle Eastern and North African (MENA) Countries." *International Journal of Arts and Sciences* 11 (1): 237–252.

Allam, Nermin. 2017. *Women and the Egyptian Revolution: Engagement and Activism during the 2011 Arab Uprisings.* Cambridge: Cambridge University Press.

Allam, Rasha. 2008. "Countering the Negative Image of Arab Women in the Arab Media: Toward a 'Pan-Arab Eye' Media Watch Project." Middle East Institute, June 2, 2008. https://www.mei.edu/publica tions/countering-negative-image-arab-women-arab-media-toward -pan-arab-eye-media-watch

Al-Tamimi, Noor Khalifa. 2016. "Qatari Women's Engagement in Politics." *QSCIENCE*, March 2016. https://www.qscience.com/content /papers/10.5339/qfarc.2016.SSHASP2414

Bahrami, Ardavan. 2005. "A Woman for All Seasons: In Memory of Farrokhrou Parsa." Iranian.com, May 9, 2005. https://www.iranian.com /ArdavanBahrami/2005/May/Parsa/index.html

Bar'el, Zvi. 2018. "Egypt Has a Record Number of Female Ministers. But Outside the Parliament, It's a Man's World." *Haaretz*, June 19, 2018. https://www.haaretz.com/middle-east-news/egypt/2018-06-19 /ty-article/.premium/the-deceptiveness-of-egypts-appointment-of -female-ministers/0000017f-e74d-df2c-a1ff-ff5d0c2d0000

Benstead, Lindsay J., and Ellen Lust. 2015. "The Gender Gap in Political Participation in North Africa." Middle East Institute, September 24, 2015. https://www.mei.edu/publications/gender-gap-political -participation-north-africa

Chouakri, Yasmina. 2019. "Violence against Women in Political Parties: Analysis of the Situation in Tunisia." National Democratic Institute, February 2019. https://www.ndi.org/sites/default/files/02-12-2019 _Tunisia%20%281%29.pdf

Congressional Research Service. 2020. "Women in the Middle East and North Africa: Issues for Congress." November 27, 2020. https://fas .org/sgp/crs/mideast/R46423.pdf

El Feki, S., B. Heilman, and G. Barker, eds. 2017. *Understanding Masculinities: Results from the International Men and Gender Equality*

Survey (IMAGES)—Middle East and North Africa: Executive Summary. Cairo and Washington, DC: UN Women and Promundo-US. https://imagesmena.org/wp-content/uploads/2017/05/IMAGES-MENA-Executive-Summary-EN-16May2017-web.pdf

ESCWA (Economic and Social Commission for Western Asia). 2017. *Women's Political Representation in the Arab Region.* Beirut: United Nations. https://archive.unescwa.org/sites/www.unescwa.org/files/publications/files/women-political-representation-arab-region-english.pdf

Gatti, Roberta, Matteo Morgandi, Rebekka Grun, Stefanie Brodmann, Diego Angel-Urdinola, Juan Manuel Moreno, Daniela Marotta, Marc Schiffbauer, and Elizabeth Mata Lorenzo. 2013. "Jobs for Shared Prosperity: Time for Action in the Middle East and North Africa." Washington, DC: World Bank. ttps://openknowledge.worldbank.org/handle/10986/13284

Gouvy, Constantin. 2021. "Decade after Revolution, Tunisia's Women Face Uphill Battle." Al Jazeera, January 17, 2021. https://www.aljazeera.com/news/2021/1/17/a-decade-after-revolution-tunisias-women-face-an-uphill-battle

Gulf News. 2015. "Timeline of Women's Right to Vote around the World." December 12, 2015. https://gulfnews.com/world/gulf/saudi/timeline-of-womens-right-to-vote-around-the-world-1.1635917

Holleis, Jennifer. 2020. "Kuwait's New All-Male Parliament Is a Blow for Women's Rights." Deutsche Welle, December 10, 2020. https://www.dw.com/en/kuwaits-new-all-male-parliament-is-a-blow-for-womens-rights/a-55897172

Human Rights Watch. 2019. "Saudi Arabia: Travel Restrictions on Saudi Women Lifted." August 22, 2019. https://www.hrw.org/news/2019/08/22/saudi-arabia-travel-restrictions-saudi-women-lifted

Human Rights Watch. 2021a. "Qatar: Male Guardianship Severely Curtails Women's Rights." March 29, 2021. https://www.hrw.org/news/2021/03/29/qatar-male-guardianship-severely-curtails-womens-rights

Human Rights Watch. 2021b. "UAE: Greater Progress Needed on Women's Rights." March 4, 2021. https://www.hrw.org/news/2021/03/04/uae-greater-progress-needed-womens-rights

IFES (International Foundation for Electoral Systems). 2010. "The Status of Women in the Middle East and North Africa: A Grassroots Research and Advocacy Approach: Preliminary Finding from

Surveys in Lebanon and Morocco." https://www.ifes.org/sites
/default/files/a_grassroots_research_and_advocacy_approach_0
.pdf

ILO (International Labour Organization). 2016. "Women in Business and
Management: Gaining Momentum in the Middle East and North
Africa: Regional Report." https://www.ilo.org/beirut/publications
/WCMS_446101/lang--en/index.htm

ILO. 2017. "Promoting Women's Empowerment in the Middle East and
North Africa: A Rapid Evidence Assessment of Labour Market
Interventions." https://www.ilo.org/wcmsp5/groups/public/---ed_emp
/documents/publication/wcms_563865.pdf

Infoplease. 2017. "Women's Suffrage: When and Where Did the Women
Earn the Right to Vote?" February 11, 2017. https://www.infoplease
.com/history/womens-history/womens-suffrage

International Institute for Democracy and Electoral Assistance. 2021.
"Gender Quotas Database." August 2021. https://www.idea.int/data
-tools/data/gender-quotas

IPU (Inter-Parliamentary Union). 2009. "Women in National Parliaments:
Situation as of 1 December 2009." August 2021. http://archive.ipu
.org/wmn-e/arc/classif311209.htm

IPU. 2016. "Women in National Parliaments: Situation as of 1st December
2016." August 2021. http://archive.ipu.org/wmn-e/arc/classif01
1216.htm

IPU. 2021. "Women in Politics: 2021." July 2021. https://eca.unwomen.org
/sites/default/files/Headquarters/Attachments/Sections/Library/Pub
lications/2021/Women-in-politics-2021-en.pdf

IPU. 2022a. "Global and Regional Averages of Women in National Parliaments. Averages as of 1st September 2022." October 2022. https://
data.ipu.org/women-averages

IPU. 2022b. "Monthly Ranking of Women in National Parliaments. Ranking as of 1st September 2022." October 2022. https://data.ipu.org
/women-ranking?month=9&year=2022

IPU. n.d. "Women's Suffrage. A World Chronology of the Recognition of
Women's Rights to Vote and to Stand for Election." July 2021.
http://archive.ipu.org/wmn-e/suffrage.htm

Jecks, Nikki. 2009."I Was Iran's Last Woman Minister." *BBC News*, August
19, 2009. http://news.bbc.co.uk/2/hi/middle_east/8207371.stm

Kasapoglu, Aytul, and Necmettin Ozerkmen. 2011. "Gender Imbalance:
The Case of Women's Political Participation in Turkey." *Journal of
International Women's Studies* 12 (4): 97–107.

Kharroub, Tamara. 2015. "Five Things You Need to Know about Women in Islam: Implications for Advancing Women's Rights in the Middle East." Arab Center Washington, DC, October 4, 2015. https:// arabcenterdc.org/resource/five-things-you-need-to-know-about -women-in-islam-implications-for-advancing-womens-rights-in -the-middle-east/

Leake, Adam. 2012. "A Brief History of the Feminist Movements in Turkey." E-International Relations, August 29, 2012. https://www.e-ir.info /2012/08/29/a-brief-history-of-the-feminist-movements-in-turkey/

Lomazzi, Vera. 2020. "Women's Rights and Shari'a Law in the MENA Region." In *Migrants and Religion: Paths, Issues and Lenses*, edited by Laura Zanfrini, 231–250. Leiden, Netherlands: Brill.

Masad, Razan. 2020. "The Struggle for Women in Politics Continues." United Nations Development Programme, March 13, 2020. https:// www.undp.org/content/undp/en/home/blog/2020/the-struggle-for -women-in-politics-continues.html

Mcloughlin, Claire. 2013. "Women's Economic Role in the Middle East and North Africa (MENA)." GSDRC Helpdesk Research Report. Birmingham, UK: Governance and Social Development Resource Centre, University of Birmingham. http://gsdrc.org/docs/open/hdq 889.pdf

Middle East Monitor. 2021. "Tunisia MP Repeatedly Slaps Female Colleague in Parliament." July 1, 2021. https://www.middleeastmonitor .com/20210701-tunisia-mp-repeatedly-slaps-female-colleague-in -parliament/

Nasser, Afrah. 2019. "Yemen: Women, War & Political Marginalization." Atlantic Council, January 25, 2019. https://www.atlanticcouncil .org/blogs/menasource/yemen-women-war-political-marginaliza tion/

Nazra for Feminist Studies. n.d. "About Us." https://nazra.org/en/about-us

NDI (National Democratic Institute). 2021. "It's a Woman's World: Change-Makers in the MENA Region." March 10, 2021. https://www.ndi .org/our-stories/it-s-woman-s-world-change-makers-mena-region

The New Arab. 2021. "Tunisian Parliament Bars 2 Deputies for Attacking Female Colleague." July 6, 2021. https://english.alaraby.co.uk/news /tunisian-parliament-bars-2-deputies-who-attacked-mp

Ohman, Magnus. 2016. "Political Finance and the Equal Participation of Women in Tunisia: A Situation Analysis." Stockholm and The Hague: International IDEA and the Netherlands Institute for Multiparty Democracy. https://www.idea.int/sites/default/files/publica

tions/political-finance-and-the-equal-participation-of-women-in
-tunisia.pdf

Osman, Ahmed Zaki. 2013. "This Week in 1958: An Advocate of Creative
Theater and Free Press Dies." *Egypt Independent*, April 11, 2013.
https://www.egyptindependent.com/week-1958-advocate-creative
-theater-and-free-press-dies/

Raghd. 2021. "The Maximum Punishment Awaits the Aggressors against
Abeer Moussa." Middle East in 24, July 5, 2021. https://middleeast
.in-24.com/world/53143.html

Right Livelihood. 2016. "2016 Laureate: Mozn Hassan/Nazra for Feminist
Studies." https://rightlivelihood.org/news/2016-laureate-mozn-has
san-nazra-for-feminist-studies/

Robbins, Michael, and Kathrin Thomas. 2018. "Women in the Middle
East and North Africa: A Divide between Rights and Roles." Arab
Barometer, October 2018. https://www.arabbarometer.org/wp-con
tent/uploads/AB_WomenFinal-version05122018.pdf

Shojaei, Seyedeh Nasrat, Ku Hasnita Ku Samsu, and Hossein Asayeseh.
2010. "Women in Politics: A Case Study of Iran." *Journal of Politics and Law* 3 (2): 257–268.

Tetreault, Mary Ann. 2001. "A State of Two Minds: States, Cultures,
Women and Political Participation in the Gulf." *International Journal of Middle East Studies* 8 (1): 203–220.

Transitional Governance Project. 2015. http://gld.gu.se/en/projects/related
-projects/transitional-governance/

UNDP Lebanese Elections Assistance Project. 2018. "2018 Lebanese Parliamentary Elections: Results and Figures." https://aceproject.org
/ero-en/regions/mideast/LB/lebanon-2018-lebanese-parliamen
tary-elections/view

United Arab Emirates: The Cabinet. 2021. "Her Excellency Shamma bint
Suhail Faris Al Mazrui." https://uaecabinet.ae/en/details/cabinet
-members/her-excellency-shamma-bint-suhail-faris-al-mazrui

The Voice of Libyan Women. n.d. "About VLW." http://www.vlwlibya.org/#

Young, Iris Marion. 2003. "The Logic of Masculinist Protection: Reflections on the Current Security State." *Journal of Women in Culture
and Society* 29: 1–25.

FIVE

Sub-Saharan Africa

Martha C. Johnson and Melanie L. Phillips

The region of sub-Saharan Africa includes forty-nine countries on the African continent and in nearby waters. It stretches from the Sahara Desert in the northern hemisphere to the Cape of Good Hope in the southern hemisphere and includes both massive countries, such as the Democratic Republic of the Congo, the eleventh-largest country in the world, and small island nations. Almost all countries in the region were colonized by the late 1800s and gained their independence between the 1950s and 1970s.

Women in sub-Saharan Africa have a rich history of political participation as leaders, activists, and citizens. Despite the erosion of women's political status during colonialism and decades of authoritarian rule following independence, the region has seen significant women's political mobilization and expanded women's representation since the 1990s. As of 2021, women made up more than 40 percent of the legislature in Rwanda, Senegal, Mozambique, South Africa, and Namibia (IPU 2021). Women presidents have become more common (although only one has become president via competitive elections), as have women ministers, who hold an increasingly diverse set of ministerial portfolios. Not only are there more women in political office but more women are also voting. Gender gaps in voter turnout are generally low and shrinking (Coffe and Bolzendahl 2011). Nonetheless, across Africa, women continue to face significant barriers to political participation. Gender gaps in other forms of political participation, like attending public meetings and contacting elected officials, remain common. And women seeking public office face numerous party, economic, and social barriers. To overcome these challenges, women activists, political parties, governments, and regional and international organizations need to pursue innovative strategies for women's political empowerment that go beyond the electoral quota systems that have helped African countries increase women's legislative representation in recent decades.

Sex and political power were not as closely tied in precolonial African societies as they became under colonialism and after independence. Political power was generally masculine, but women could and did access leadership positions in many societies. Examples include Abla Pokou, founder and monarch of the Baulé people in the Ivory Coast; Queen Njinga Mbandi, who ruled much of what would become Angola in the seventeenth century and resisted Portuguese efforts to colonize her people; and Labotsibeni Mdluli, the queen mother of Swaziland, who used her authority to resist European incursions into the area in the 1800s (UNESCO n.d.). In addition to women monarchs, many African women during the precolonial period served as chiefs in parallel chieftaincy systems in which women governed alongside men and were responsible for regulating specific sectors, like market activities (Sudarkasa 1986).

As European powers built their colonial states in sub-Saharan Africa, they incorporated a very different vision of gender and political power that conceived of women's proper roles as wives and mothers only being responsible for the private realm. In so doing, European colonizers generally ignored or condemned the various public and political roles that women had played in Africa, creating administrative structures and laws that relegated women to drastically reduced social and political roles (Tamanaha 2021). For example, in much of southern Africa, colonial authorities reinforced and enhanced the formal powers of male chiefs and husbands, giving them the right to dictate when women could leave their village or move to the city (Berger and White 1999). Gendered access to school, employment, land, and the legal system also meant that African women had fewer opportunities to generate material and educational resources or build political networks than their male counterparts (Jefremovas 1991). Many women contested these infringements on their rights, particularly when they undermined their economic interests, and women eventually became important forces in the push for independence in Africa. They protested, engaged in strikes and supported male strikers, spoke out for independence, backed independence leaders, and often took up arms for the cause (Fallon 2010).

Unfortunately, women's role in securing independence did not translate into significant political representation in the early days of African statehood. Although women were granted the right to vote at independence in almost all countries, few women ran for or were elected to public office, and even fewer were appointed to executive cabinets. Moreover, in many countries, elections were suspended or greatly restricted, such that women's voting rights mattered little. With political opening and the reemergence of autonomous women's movements in the 1990s, often after periods of civil war, women's political participation in Africa entered a new era. This era has seen dramatic increases in the proportion of women elected and appointed to political office in many African countries, including in democracies such as South Africa and Senegal, and in more authoritarian countries, like Rwanda and Uganda. This chapter focuses on this contemporary era of political participation and considers the opportunities and constraints facing women as they seek to further expand their presence in politics.

WOMEN AS VOTERS

Almost all African countries established universal suffrage at independence (see table 5.1). Liberia, which was never an official colony, granted women the right to vote in 1946, and Ethiopia, which was occupied by Italian forces during World War II but is generally considered to have never been colonized, granted women the right to vote in 1955. During this same period, many colonial powers also began to grant women the right to vote in their colonies. In Senegal, for example, African women who had French citizenship by virtue of their residence in one of the colony's special *quatres communes*, the four oldest colonial towns in French West Africa, gained the right to vote in 1945 after vigorously and publicly protesting their exclusion from France's initial plan to expand the vote in its colonies (Lord Fransee 2016). In 1956, under a new framework for France's relationships with its colonies called the *Loi Cadre*, suffrage was granted to all women in France's African colonies. The franchise granted women a say in electing local government representatives as well as African representatives to the French National Assembly. In British colonies, as well, including Ghana, Kenya, and Uganda, women were allowed to vote (and run) in elections for colonial legislatures in the mid-1950s before independence (Willis, Lynch, and Cheeseman 2018).

In Southern Africa, suffrage followed a different path in the context of white racial domination. When the British recognized South Africa's

Table 5.1   Independence and Women's Suffrage in Sub-Saharan Africa

Year of Independence*	Women's Suffrage	Country
1910	1930/1984/1994	South Africa**
1957	1957	Ghana
1958	1958	Guinea
1960	1960	Burkina Faso
	1960	Chad
	1960	Madagascar
	1960	Benin
	1960	Congo, Republic
	1960	Côte d'Ivoire
	1960	Gabon
	1960	Mali
	1960	Niger
	1960	Nigeria
	1960	Senegal
	1960	Togo
	1967	Democratic Republic of the Congo
	1986	Central African Republic
1961	1961	Sierra Leone
	1961	United Republic of Tanzania
1962	1962	Rwanda
	1962	Burundi
	1962	Uganda
1964	1964	Zambia
	1964	Malawi
1965	1965	Gambia (The)
1966	1966	Botswana
	1966	Lesotho
1968	1968	Equatorial Guinea
	1968	Eswatini

Table 5.1 (*Continued*)

Year of Independence*	Women's Suffrage	Country
	1968	Mauritius
1974	1974	Guinea-Bissau
1975	1975	Angola
	1975	Comoros
	1975	Mozambique
	1975	Sao Tome and Principe
1975	1975/1989	Cabo Verde**
1976	1976	Seychelles
1977	1977	Djibouti
1990	1989	Namibia**
1941/1993	1993	Eritrea
1960	1960	Cameroon
1965/1980	1957/1980	Zimbabwe**
NA	1946	Liberia
NA	1955	Ethiopia

* Although women were allowed to vote in some colonial-era elections, their governments were not independent; therefore, we have chosen to instead report when women were granted the right to vote by independent African governments.

** South Africa granted white women the right to vote in 1930, followed by voting rights for mixed-race (known as "Colored") women in 1984, and finally all women in 1994. Cabo Verde granted women the right to vote in national elections in 1975 at independence and extended full suffrage to local elections in 1989. Namibia adopted universal suffrage for the 1989 election to select the government that would take over in 1990, when it became fully independent from South Africa. Zimbabwe became a fully independent country with multiracial elections in 1980 in which all women could vote. In 1957, white settlers had held elections in which all white women could vote in defiance of British colonial claims to the area (then known as Southern Rhodesia), and in 1965, the settlers declared Southern Rhodesia independent, though the British did not accept that declaration.

independence in 1910, all women—as well as almost all Black men—were denied the right to vote. In 1930, in an effort to bolster support for his reelection, Prime Minister Herzog allied with the movement for white women's suffrage. Subsequently, he helped push voting rights for white women through parliament. However, this victory was conditional on the denial of Black men's right to vote in the Cape Province, the only province in which they had been granted the vote in 1910 (SAHO n.d.). Black women only gained the right to vote in 1994 with the end of **apartheid** following years of women's activism in the anti-apartheid movement. Likewise, in Southern Rhodesia, which would become Zimbabwe, white women gained the right to vote in 1957 before Black women, who were fully enfranchised with the creation of an independent, majority-ruled Zimbabwe in 1980.

Although women gained the right to vote across Africa with independence, in many cases, women (as well as men) did not exercise this right for long. Across the region, weakly institutionalized democratic systems gave way to authoritarian regimes in the form of military governments, personal dictatorships, and **one-party rule** by the 1970s in almost all African states (Botswana and Mauritius were exceptions). Although some African governments, like Senegal, Tanzania, and Kenya, continued to allow elections in the 1970s and 1980s, voter choice was highly constrained, often limited to candidates from the governing party. Women's political participation was channeled into women's wings of the ruling party, and women leaders were charged with mobilizing other women, who were in turn expected to turn out for the ruling party. As Geisler (2004) argues, "From Ghana to Zimbabwe, which gained independence in 1957 and 1980 respectively, women were not represented in legislatures, party hierarchies and government positions, but were instead dressed in party colours singing and dancing praise songs for the male leadership, raising money and support" (24).

In the 1990s, however, many African countries saw the rise of influential women's movements outside the ruling party and government. Independent women's movements in countries as diverse as South Africa, Uganda, and Kenya played a role in both advocating for political liberalization and taking advantage of political openings to defend women's interests and increase their political participation. Many of the parliamentary and executive improvements discussed in this chapter are due in part to these movements (Tripp et al. 2008). Yet, even as elections have become more common and more competitive in most African countries since the mid-1990s, women (as well as men) continue to face important limits on their electoral freedom. In 2021, at least nineteen sub-Saharan African countries continued to highly restrict political rights and civil liberties according to Freedom House measures (Freedom House 2021).

Women's Political Participation

On the whole, **Afrobarometer** survey results suggest that women in African countries turn out to vote at roughly the same rate as men, although there is important variation across the region (Kuenzi and Lambright 2005). At the lower end, in some countries, like Nigeria and Kenya, men are 10–15 percent more likely to vote than women. However, in six countries (Botswana, Cape Verde, South Africa, Senegal, Lesotho, and Malawi), surveys suggest women are actually more likely to vote than men (Isaksson, Kotsadam, and Nerman 2013). These results are somewhat surprising given that gender gaps in education, literacy, and wealth remain high in most African countries.

Despite women's propensity to vote, surveys indicate considerable gender gaps in political participation between elections. For example, women are significantly less likely to "join others to raise an issue" than men in all the African democracies covered by the Afrobarometer survey. Some studies suggest lower educational and informational levels among women largely explain their relative lack of engagement with elected officials beyond the ballot box (Isaksson, Kotsadam, and Nerman 2013), but others emphasize that women's relative poverty may also play an important role in their inability to allocate the time and resources needed to participate in politics between elections (Isaksson 2014).

Beyond gender gaps in women's likelihood to vote and participate in politics, research suggests differences in voter preference by gender in some parts of Africa. In countries where women's formal labor force participation is limited, for example, men are more likely than women to prioritize investments in infrastructure. And across African countries, women are more likely than men to prioritize poverty alleviation policies. Unfortunately, scholars find that in those countries where men and women's policy preferences diverge the most, the gap between women and men's voting is also most pronounced (Gottlieb, Grossman, and Robinson 2016). This finding suggests African women are less likely to vote precisely where they have unique policy preferences that need to be heard.

In addition to gender differences in policy preferences, scholars suggest that women value different forms of political campaigning than men. For example, Tripp (2001) contends that because women have historically been excluded from **patronage politics**, they are less attracted to patronage appeals and are more supportive of policy-oriented and cross-ethnic campaigns. An experiment in which actual candidates altered their campaign platforms in Benin lends support to this argument. Women voters proved to be more responsive than men to public policy appeals and less responsive to appeals that emphasized individual patronage rewards for voting (Wantchekon 2003).

WOMEN AS MEMBERS OF PARLIAMENT

Across the continent, we have seen tremendous growth in women's representation at the legislative level. Largely fueled by electoral gender quotas, women have gained access to positions of political power thanks to political party action and voter demand. The increase in women's legislative presence since independence is not exclusive to democratic states but has occurred in both democratic and authoritarian states (Johnson and Phillips 2019). Therefore, despite trends of **democratic backsliding** in recent years, women's representation at the legislative level has continued to rise in many sub-Saharan African countries, as illustrated in figure 5.1.

As a region, sub-Saharan Africa ranks near the global average for women in legislative office. On average, in 2021, 25.9 percent of seats in lower houses of parliament were held by women in the region, on par with the global average. Only Europe and the Americas had higher averages, at 29.9 and 30.8 percent, respectively. In 2021, the regions of Asia (20.1 percent), the Middle East and North Africa (16.9 percent), and the Pacific (16.6 percent) all fell below the African average (IPU Parline n.d.). The sub-Saharan African average, while below 50 percent parity, is near what scholars refer to as the critical mass threshold. *Critical mass* refers to a proportion beyond which women, though in the minority, may still have enough voice and influence to shape a political body (Dahlerup 1988). While there are many debates on whether critical masses are necessary or sufficient for women legislators to have an impact (Childs and Krook 2009), the critical mass argument does suggest that even if women are still in the minority in African legislatures, they may still be able to achieve change if they are a sizable minority.

Although Africa's average may place it in the middle of other regions in terms of women's legislative representation, the region also boasts some of the highest and lowest percentages of women legislators in specific

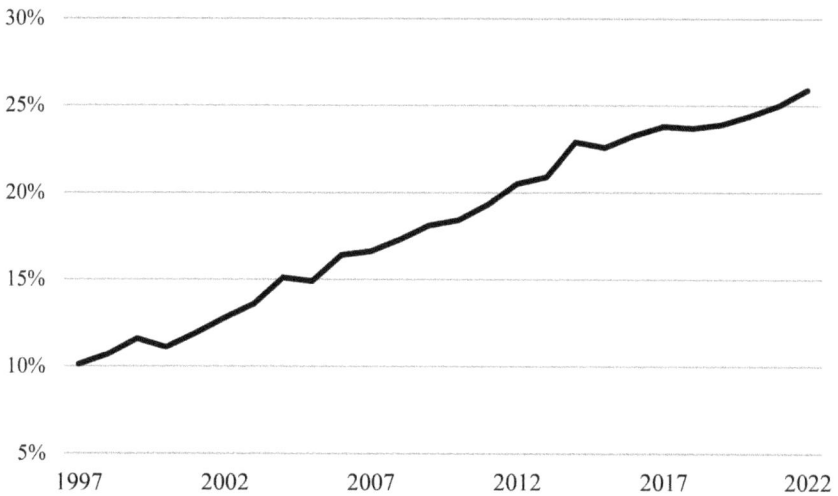

Figure 5.1 Average Proportion of Women in the Lower Houses of Sub-Saharan African Legislatures, 1997–2022 (Inter-Parliamentary Union: Parline database on national parliaments, July 31, 2021).

countries. The countries of East Africa hold the highest average, with 32.4 percent of the region's legislative seats held by women, followed by Southern Africa with 30.6 percent. On the lower end, women occupy only 22.1 percent of legislative seats in the countries of Central Africa and only 16.3 percent of seats in West African legislatures (IPU Parline n.d.). Despite the low percentages in Central and West Africa, the overall trend in Africa is toward expanded women's representation, and averages have all increased since 2019, showing continued growth in women's presence. This growth is more notable in the context of COVID-19. Although women faced a disproportionate burden from the disease and efforts to prevent its spread, these burdens do not seem to have undermined women's political representation in the legislature.

As noted, in the early days of African democracies, women were generally sidelined in electoral politics. Despite being active leaders and participants in African independence movements, relatively few women were elected into newly established legislatures at independence (Mama 1998; Ibrahim 2004). In 1960, only three countries had any women in parliament: Cameroon (1 percent), Ghana (9.8 percent), and South Africa (3.7 percent).

Over the next decade, the number grew slowly. Many of the women who entered legislative politics in the 1960s were educated abroad and participated in independence movements, which allowed them to build political ties to the men who would become presidents after independence. For example, Mabel Dove Danquah, who was the first woman elected to Ghana's postcolonial parliament in 1954, was an influential journalist and is considered one of Africa's first literary feminists. Before running for parliament, she worked with soon-to-be president Kwame Nkrumah to push for an end to colonial rule (Chinbuah 2007). In a later example, Grace Onyango, a teacher and widowed mother of six in Kenya, repeatedly broke gender barriers as the first woman to run for election for her local council, the first to serve as an elected mayor in Kenya, and the first to serve in parliament in 1969. She was an avid advocate for women in politics, advocating a policy of allowing widows to assume their husbands positions upon their death, for example (Mbenywe 2018).

While women were allowed to run for office in most African countries at independence, this right was not universal. In South Africa, South West Africa (which would gain its independence from South Africa in 1990 as Namibia), and Southern Rhodesia (which would become Zimbabwe in 1980), racial hierarchies limited women's options. In all three countries, the white minority dominated parliamentary elections. While South Africa was technically the first African nation to grant women the right to stand for election in 1930, this right was restricted to white women (Walker 1990). It would take sixty-four more years for Black women in South Africa to be granted the right to contest political elections. Southern Rhodesia and South West Africa followed a similar pattern.

When South Africa and Namibia emerged as multiracial democracies in 1994 and 1989, respectively, they ushered in a new period of rapid expansion of women's legislative representation in Africa. In 1985, women only made up 7.8 percent of legislators in sub-Saharan Africa (Arriola and Johnson 2014). By 1995, that number had reached 10 percent, and it was 15 percent by 2005. Indeed, sub-Saharan Africa saw the fastest growth rates of women in parliament of any world region in the second half of the twentieth century (Tripp 2019). In South Africa, women made up 29.8 percent of the national legislature by the end of the 1990s. In Namibia, they made up 25 percent. In African countries, as well, the proportion of women in the legislature was among the world's highest by 2000: Mozambique at 30 percent, Rwanda at 25.7, and Uganda at 17.8.

As shown in figure 5.1, this pattern of expanded legislative presence has continued into the twenty-first century. As a result, many African countries lead the world in terms of women's legislative presence. Rwanda holds the global record, with over 60 percent of the seats in their parliament held by women. Rwanda is joined at the top of the global list by South Africa (tenth on the global list with 46.4 percent of its parliamentary seats held by women), Namibia (eleventh with 44.2 percent), Senegal (nineteenth with 43 percent), and Mozambique (twenty-first with 42.2 percent) (IPU Parline 2022a). As demonstrated in table 5.2, there is still significant variation across Africa, but in many countries, women have achieved significant descriptive representation.

Improvements in women's legislative representation since the 1990s in sub-Saharan Africa parallel a pattern of political opening in many countries, although democratization is not the best predictor of women's legislative representation. Most scholars agree that competitive elections on their own have not significantly increased the number of women legislators in the region. Rather, it is political opening, in the sense of greater freedoms of association and speech, that has helped women expand their political role. As governments began to allow more space for independent civil society organizing in the 1990s, women's movements took advantage of (and helped push for) this space, using it to call for new tools to ensure women's representation in politics (Fallon 2010).

Electoral quotas were among the most important of these tools. Scholars widely agree that gender quotas have been the single strongest factor in increasing women's representation in the legislature in Africa (Tripp and Kang 2008; Dahlerup and Freidenvall 2005). Gender quotas fall largely into three categories: reserved seats, legislated candidate quotas, and voluntary party quotas. Reserved seats, which allow only women to compete for specific seats in the legislature, generally have the largest impact on women's presence in the legislature because they guarantee that a certain percentage of the legislature will be made up of women. While they are the least common form of electoral quota globally, they are significantly more common in African countries (Dahlerup 2005).

Quotas were adopted in sub-Saharan Africa in two waves. The first wave of quota adoption primarily occurred in postconflict countries in eastern and southern Africa in the 1990s and early 2000s. Globally, the end of conflict and increases in women's descriptive representation are correlated (Hughes 2009). This relationship is especially strong in sub-Saharan

Table 5.2   Proportion of Women in Parliament and Quota Systems in Sub-Saharan Africa, 2021

Country	Percentage of Women in Parliament	Type of Quota
Angola	29.6	Legislated candidate quotas
Benin	7.4	Reserved seats
Botswana	11.1	Voluntary party quotas
Burkina Faso	6.3	Legislated candidate quotas
Burundi	38.2	Reserved seats
Cameroon	33.9	Voluntary party quotas (major party)
Cape Verde	38.9	Legislated candidate quotas
Central African Republic	12.9	Legislated candidate quotas
Chad	31.2	Legislated candidate quotas
Comoro Islands	16.7	No quota system
Congo, Democratic Republic of	12.8	Legislated candidate quotas (no penalty)
Congo, Republic of	11.3	Legislated candidate quotas
Cote d'Ivoire	14.2	Voluntary party quotas
Djibouti	26.2	Reserved seats
Equatorial Guinea	22	Voluntary party quotas
Eritrea	22	Legislated candidate quotas
Ethiopia	41.5	Legislated candidate quotas
Gabon	15.4	No quota system
Gambia	10.3	No quota system
Ghana	14.6	No quota system
Guinea	16.7	Legislated candidate quotas
Guinea-Bissau	13.7	Legislated candidate quotas
Kenya	21.4	Reserved seats
Lesotho	24.4	Legislated candidate quotas
Liberia	11	Legislated candidate quotas

Table 5.2   (*Continued*)

Country	Percentage of Women in Parliament	Type of Quota
Madagascar	18.5	No quota system
Malawi	22.9	No quota system
Mali	26.5	Legislated candidate quotas
Mauritania	20.3	Legislated candidate quotas
Mauritius	20	No quota system
Mozambique	42.4	No quota system
Namibia	44.2	Voluntary party quotas (major party)
Niger	25.9	Reserved seats
Nigeria	3.6	No quota system
Rwanda	61.3	Reserved seats and legislated candidate quotas
Sao Tome and Principe	23.6	Legislated candidate quotas
Senegal	42.7	Legislated candidate quotas
Seychelles	22.9	Voluntary party quotas (major party)
Sierra Leone	12.3	No quota system
Somalia	24	Reserved seats
South Africa	46.7	Voluntary party quotas (major party)
South Sudan	32.4	Legislated candidate quotas
Sudan	NA	Reserved seats
Swaziland	42.5	Reserved seats
Tanzania	36.9	Reserved seats
Togo	18.7	Legislated candidate quotas
Uganda	33.85	Reserved seats
Zambia	15.1	No quota system
Zimbabwe	30.6	Reserved seats

Source: IDEA (n.d.).

HOW RWANDA ACHIEVED LEGISLATIVE PARITY

Following elections in September 2018, Rwanda was the first country in the world where women held more than 50 percent of the seats in the legislature. Sixty-one percent of the seats in their Chamber of Deputies are currently held by women. Two elements appear to have been key to this success: ruling party commitment and the use of quotas. Even before coming to power in Rwanda in 1994, the Rwandan Patriotic Front (RPF) prioritized women's inclusion in party structures and leadership. Following the Rwandan genocide and the creation of a transitional government, the RPF appointed women to high-profile political positions and created a Ministry of Gender, Family, and Social Affairs, which later held elections for newly created women's councils throughout the country. These councils elected the first women to Rwanda's transitional parliament. By 1999, the RPF had approved the appointment of enough women to the transitional parliament that women came to occupy a quarter of the body's seats (Burnet 2008).

When the governing RPF instituted elections for local office in 2001, it further expanded women's presence by reserving a portion of local seats for women. In 2006, it adapted how local elections were conducted, requiring that voters complete three ballots: one ballot that can include candidates of any gender, one ballot that includes only women, and one ballot that includes only youth. As a result, women came to occupy, at a minimum, one-third of local elected positions (Powley 2008). Then, in a new constitution adopted in 2003, the country adopted a reserved seat system for its national parliament in which twenty-four seats are reserved for women. Moreover, it legislated a party quota for the remaining seats, which are allocated to party candidate lists in a proportional representation system. The quota requires that party lists include at least 30 percent women. In combination, these two quota systems pushed Rwanda to the world's highest rate of legislative representation for women.

Africa. Postconflict transitions provide an ideal context for the adoption of quotas because they provide political openings that women can use to influence political structures, including new constitutions and electoral systems. In Africa, women often played an important role in movements for the end of white rule, peace, and postconflict reconstruction. As such, women were well organized to push for their interests in postconflict politics in Rwanda, South Africa, Namibia, Mozambique, Tanzania, Uganda, and Burundi. Women in all of these countries capitalized on postconflict political opening to demand quotas, thereby ensuring their presence in new legislatures (Tripp 2015).

Governments in Africa were also influenced by international forces in adopting quotas. Women's activism across borders and international women's rights agendas helped reinforce domestic movements' calls for quotas. For example, the Fourth World Conference on Women in Beijing in 1995, which promoted the global adoption of gender quotas, was directly followed by an uptick in quota adoption in Africa and Latin America (Ballington 2004). In Africa, governments are often especially concerned with external perceptions of domestic governance. Because many African governments rely on the financial support of Western governments, they may be particularly attuned to shifting international gender norms. Quota adoption and the related increase in women's political representation may help these governments cultivate a positive image among potential allies and financial donors (Edgell 2017).

These international factors, plus regional diffusion, whereby a country is influenced by developments in neighboring countries, may help explain why a second wave of quota adoption occurred in the 2010s in African countries that had not experienced conflict. Over the course of the 2010s, quotas became more common in southern and eastern Africa, as countries like Zimbabwe, Lesotho, Kenya, Somalia, Sudan, and South Sudan adopted them. In western Africa, as well, Senegal, Cameroon, Cape Verde, and Benin all adopted quotas in the 2010s.

By 2021, twenty-three countries in sub-Saharan Africa had some form of gender quota in place at the parliamentary level. Twelve countries use a legislated candidate quota that stipulates that political party lists for election must include a certain threshold of women. For example, in Togo, political party lists for parliamentary election must include at least one-third (33 percent) women. The remaining eleven countries use a reserved seat quota, where specific elected seats are only contestable by women. Reserved seats, in Uganda, for example, stipulate that all of the 112 districts must have at least one woman representative.

Africa's second wave of quota adoption was, like its first, driven by pressure from domestic women's organizations in conjunction with pressure from regional and international organizations (Bauer 2015). The Southern African Development Committee (SADC), an economic and political association that brings together sixteen Southern African states, has been particularly important in this regard. It adopted a gender and development protocol in 2008 that specifically calls on member states to ensure women's political representation: "States Parties shall endeavor that, by 2015, at least fifty percent of decision-making positions in the public and private sectors are held by women including the use of affirmative action measures," including but not limited to electoral quotas. Although few member states have met the parity goal, many have embraced the protocol, adopting quotas and producing notable improvements in women's representation. As of 2019, the SADC region had the highest levels of proportion of seats held by women in parliament in the world (Mlambo, Kapingura, and Meissner 2019).

As women have made great strides toward parity in African legislatures, they have begun to also hold more prominent legislative roles, including the role of Speaker. As the presiding officer of a legislative body, the **Speaker of the House** largely determines which issues are discussed in the body, when, and by whom. Moreover, in most presidential countries, House Speakers are in the line of succession for the presidency. As such, women in this position can have both a substantive impact on policy through their control of the legislative process and a symbolic impact on women's political status, as they offer a visible representation of women's growing political importance. Remarkably, 23.5 percent of Speakership positions in sub-Saharan Africa are held by women. This is the third-highest regional average; only Europe (28.6 percent) and the Americas (37 percent) have more women Speakers (IPU Parline 2022b). In total, sixteen African countries have had or currently have a woman as Speaker. South Africa was a leader in this regard. Its first multiracial, democratic legislature was led by journalist and politician Frene Ginwala for ten years, and only one of her five successors has been men.

As table 5.2 illustrates, despite the growing prevalence and influence of women in many African parliaments, countries without electoral quotas remain far from gender parity. In Ghana, one of the region's most democratic countries, for example, women hold only 14.1 percent of the seats in parliament. Nearby Nigeria, despite being one of the region's largest economies, has even fewer women in parliament (3.6 percent of seats). Governments and nongovernmental organizations (NGOs) have attempted nonquota strategies to increase women's representation, such as helping women finance their candidacies and training potential women candidates, but the results have generally been modest. In Malawi, a joint effort by government, international donors, and NGOs called the "50/50" campaign tried using financial assistance to increase the proportion of women elected in 2009 and 2014. While it seemed successful in 2009, the number of women legislators dropped in 2014, suggesting the modest amount of money women received was not enough to ensure their electoral success (Wang et al. 2019).

WOMEN AS LEADERS

Despite improvements in women's political participation and parliamentary representation, women remain rare in positions of executive leadership across sub-Saharan Africa. Only one woman, Ellen Johnson Sirleaf of Liberia, has ever been directly elected as president. Other women have served as a **ceremonial head of state** in the region's parliamentary systems. Others have been appointed to the presidency following the death of their predecessor, and others have been appointed as interim or acting president following periods of political instability. However, none of the women who came to office through appointment have translated that experience into a successful electoral campaign for the position of chief executive (table 5.3).

Except for President Sirleaf in Liberia, African women have acceded to their countries' highest political office only through appointment or constitutional succession. Two women, Joyce Banda, the president of Malawi from 2012 to 2014, and Samia Suluhu Hassan, the president of Tanzania at the time of this writing, became president following their predecessors' death. Banda was elected as the country's first woman vice president on the Democratic Progressive Party (DPP) ticket with running mate Bingu wa Mutharika in 2009. She was then sworn in after Mutharika died suddenly in 2012. Many DPP leaders opposed her assumption of the presidency, despite its clear constitutional basis, because she had been expelled from the party in 2010 over disputes about who should run for president in the next election. Although Banda was initially popular, she was soon tarnished by a major corruption scandal and lost her 2014 electoral campaign to remain president (Dulani et al. 2021). Suluhu Hassan is also an experienced politician who served as vice president before assuming the remainder of her predecessor's five-year term upon his death. Whether she will run for reelection and her prospects if she does remain to be seen.

In addition to Banda and Suluhu Hassan, two other women have served as acting or interim presidents following their predecessor's death. (Banda and Suluhu Hassan did not have the terms *acting* or *interim* in their title.) Burundian prime minister Sylvie Kiningi served as acting president for seven months in 1983 after the president's assassination, and Rose

Table 5.3   Women Executives in Sub-Saharan Africa

Country	Name	Role	Period
Burundi	Sylvie Kinigi	Prime minister	1993–1994
Central African Republic	Elisabeth Domitien	Prime minister	1975–1976
	Catherine Samba Panza	Interim president	2014–2016
Ethiopia	Sahle-Work Zewde	President	2018–present
Gabon	Rose Christiane Raponda	Prime minister	2020–present
Liberia	Ellen Sirleaf Johnson	President	2006–2018
Malawi	Joyce Banda	President	2012–2014
Mali	Cissé Mariam Kaïdama Sidibé	Prime minister	2011-2012
Mauritius	Ameenah Gurib-Fakim	President	2015–2018
Mozambique	Louisa Dias Diogo	Prime minister	2004–2010
Namibia	Saara Kuugongelwa-Amadhila	Prime minister	2015–present
Rwanda	Agathe Uwilingiyimana	Prime minister	1993–1994
São Tomé e Principé	Maria das Neves Ceita Batista de Sousa	Prime minister	2002–2003 2003–2004
	Maria do Carmo Silveira	Prime minister	2005–2007
Senegal	Mame Madior Boye	Prime minister	2001–2002
	Aminata Touré	Prime minister	2013-2014
Tanzania	Samia Suluhu Hassan	President(inherited)	2021–present
Togo	Victoire Tomegah Dogbé	Prime minister	2020–present

Source: Data courtesy of Farida Jalalzai (excludes interim or appointed leaders).

Francine Rogombé, the president of the Gabonese Senate, served as acting president for five months following the death of longtime president Omar Bongo in 2009.

Finally, three women, Carmen Pereira (Guinea-Bissau), Ruth Sando Perry (Liberia), and Catherine Samba Panza (Central Africa Republic), became interim presidents by appointment. Pereira led the country for just three days in 1984 during a constitutional transition, but Perry and Samba Panza were in power closer to a year. Both were charged with overseeing elections as part of tenuous peace-making processes and eventually stepped down to allow a newly elected male president to take office. Samba Panza, who was barred from running in the 2016 election she helped organize, eventually ran for president in the 2020 elections but was easily defeated, earning only 0.9 percent of the vote. These electoral defeats do not negate women's accomplishment in being appointed

Mauritian President Ameenah Gurib-Fakim (2015–2018). (Tarikh Jumeer | Dreamstime.com)

president. Unlike in Asia and Latin America, none of the women who have occupied executive leadership positions in sub-Saharan Africa were close relatives of powerful men. Their individual reputations and political acumen rather than family connections explain their political rise.

Overall, as with women in parliament, women have been more likely to assume leadership roles in African countries that have experienced violent conflict. For example, Ellen Johnson Sirleaf was elected after nearly ten years of civil war in Liberia. Her success built on a highly influential women's movement for peace. In another example, Sylvie Kinigi came to office when Burundi's hopes of democracy faltered following an assassination, a coup attempt, and increasing political violence. Her time in office was short lived, as she was not able to quell the violence and soon fled the country (Kamau 2021). Similarly, the Central African Republic's transitional council selected Samba Panza following a year of political crisis and widespread communal violence. She was seen as a neutral arbitrator who could guide the country through competitive elections, which she did in 2016 (Smith 2014). Looking at women's appointment to secondary executive positions as well, like those of prime minister in semipresidential systems and vice president in presidential ones, postconflict countries predominate (Adams 2008).

Although moments of instability and change have created openings for women to access the presidency in Africa, the electoral path to leadership has remained exceptionally difficult. Samba Panza is not alone in struggling to secure the popular vote. For example, Kenyan politician Martha Karua also had excellent name recognition and significant experience in government when she decided to run for president in the 2013 elections. Polls suggested she could garner at least 16 percent of the vote; yet, on election day, she received less than 1 percent of the vote. Overall, "among the women who have sought the presidency in African countries between 1992 and 2017, only six of 47 received more than 1 percent of the vote" (Gichohi 2021, 117).

While women have struggled to win presidential elections in Africa, they have increasingly entered the executive branch via ministerial appointments. Since the 1990s, the overall percentage of women ministers has increased in most African states as well as the diversity of portfolios allocated to them. Figure 5.2 illustrates women's growing presence in African cabinets since 1990, when many African countries began to democratize.

Women have not only become more common in ministerial cabinets, but they are also responsible for an increasingly diverse set of cabinet portfolios. Generally, the first women ministers in Africa were in ministries related to family, children, or women's affairs, including areas such as education and health care. Gender and women's affairs ministries, in particular, tend to be held almost exclusively by women and often have less prestige and fewer resources than other ministries (Bauer and Okpotor 2013). However, other social welfare ministries, like health and education, are among the largest ministries in African countries in terms of personnel and resource consumption (Adams 2008). As such, women's leadership in those areas can be impactful.

Over time, women's roles in the executive cabinet have shifted considerably in Africa. In 1980, nearly 90 percent of women cabinet ministers were concentrated in sectors related to social welfare. However, by 2005, that proportion had dropped to just over half of all women ministers (Arriola and Johnson 2015). By the late 2000s, women had increasingly moved into ministries related to economic activity and been named to lead ministries of justice, foreign affairs, and even finance. Moreover, leaders in countries as diverse as South Africa, Guinea-Bissau, and Ethiopia have

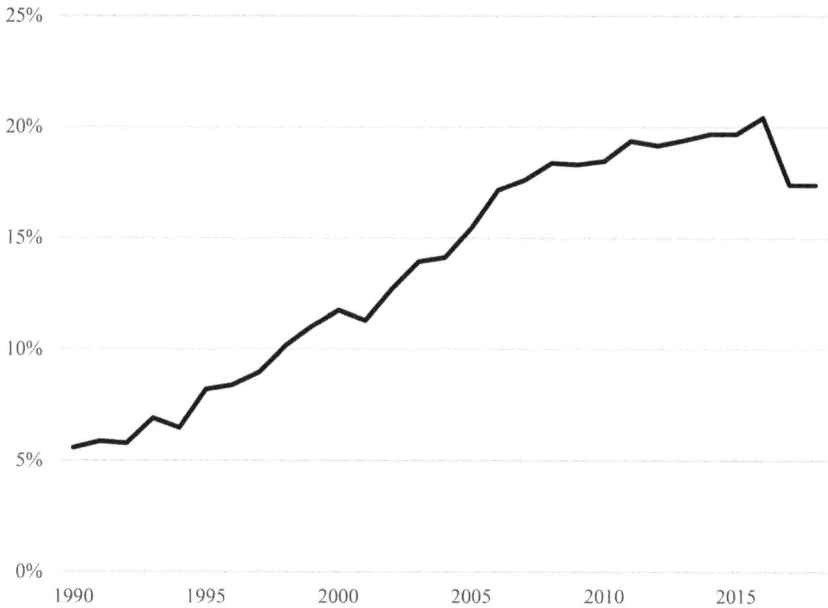

Figure 5.2 Average Proportion of Women Cabinet Ministers in Sub-Saharan Africa, 1990–2018 (WhoGov dataset. https://politicscentre.nuffield.ox.ac.uk/whogov-dataset/).

appointed women to lead the traditionally masculine ministry of defense. Among the most notable women to be appointed to a high-status ministry in Africa is Ngozi Okonjo-Iweala, who led Nigeria's Ministry of Finance from 2011 to 2015 before becoming director general of the World Trade Organization in 2021.

BARRIERS TO POLITICAL PARITY

Women in sub-Saharan Africa today enjoy many new political opportunities, yet numerous barriers to full participation and parity persist. These barriers largely fall into three groups: (1) political party bias that limits women selection as candidates, (2) socioeconomic constraints that make it difficult for women to participate and compete in politics, and (3) cultural norms that perpetuate hostile political environments.

Political parties are among the most significant gatekeepers in determining whether women enter politics in Africa. They act as a filter in the political pipeline, excluding a portion of potential women candidates interested in contesting political office through their role in candidate selection. Party members, through both formal and informal processes, determine which candidates are placed on the election ballot and, in some cases, where in the party's list of candidates they appear. For example, in closed-list proportional representation systems, where the party predetermines a list of ranked candidates for voters, only those near the top of that list are likely to win seats in the election. Numerous studies from around the world have indicated that these party processes tend to be biased against women (Hinojosa 2012; Bauer and Darkwah 2021; Kenny 2013).

In Africa, as in many parts of the world, party structures are dominated by men, and men fill most leadership positions. As a result, women are rarely in the room when party leaders finalize candidate selection. Only a small minority of African political parties hold primaries where voters can select their candidates. As a result, most women must pass through the party rather than public primaries to become candidates (Ichino and Nathan 2012). Sometimes even political quotas are not enough to overcome party bias in candidate selection. When quotas are not paired with meaningful punishments for parties that fail to comply, gender biases among male party leaders and stiff competition from men seeking party nominations can prevent women from securing their party's nominations.

In addition to engaging in biased candidate selection, political parties may also create or condone organizational environments that are hostile toward women. In Africa, members of parties traditionally dominated by men may actively dissuade women from politics in both overt and less obvious ways. For example, male politicians may threaten women, as they did in Sierra Leone, where women reported facing threats of violence when attempting to secure party nominations during the 2008 local elections (Abdullah 2014). Or they may adopt party practices, like late night meetings or backroom negotiations, that exclude women with familial obligations and who face social stigma for interacting with men at inappropriate times or places.

Although women in Africa face many of the same party barriers to political representation as women in other parts of the world, research suggests they may face less resistance in the media. In much of the world, the media limits women's political ambitions through less or unfavorable coverage (Kittilson and Fridkin 2008). Gender bias in the media in Africa, however, appears to be less pronounced (Adams 2016; Anderson, Diabah, and Afrakoma hMensa 2011; Mudavadi 2020). Analyzing the coverage of

President Ellen Johnson Sirleaf, the president of Liberia, for example, Adams finds no gender bias. In fact, Sirleaf received more coverage than the men competing against her, and, more importantly, this coverage did not perpetuate any potentially harmful gender stereotypes. Research in Ghana and Nigeria further found that women candidates receive more coverage than men, to their benefit. This is not to say that no media coverage in Africa portrays women politicians in gendered frames (Osei-Appiah 2019), but the barrier in Africa is not as prominent as it is in other countries (Coffie and Medie 2021).

Large persistent gender gaps in women's social and economic status in sub-Saharan Africa must also be considered when explaining women's persistent underrepresentation in African politics. One way in which women's economic status is linked to women's political options is through campaign finance. In most African countries, candidates are expected to self-finance their campaigns. They receive little support from their parties, and donating to campaigns is not widely popular (Kramon 2016). At the same time, relative to per capita income, African elections are notoriously expensive, and that cost appears to increase with every electoral cycle (Lindberg 2003; Koter 2017).

The expectation of self-financing amid rising campaign costs creates inequality in access to politics because women in Africa have significantly less opportunity to accumulate financial resources than men. Women in Africa have a more difficult time entering the formal job market than men (Dieterich, Huang, and Thomas 2016), are less likely to inherit family resources or land (Cooper 2012), and are even prevented from holding bank accounts or obtaining credit in some cases (Arriola and Johnson 2015). As such, they are more likely to experience poverty than men and are less likely to be able to use family resources for political aims.

Furthering the economic divide and potentially contributing to inequality in politics is the gender gap in access to education in sub-Saharan Africa. According to UNESCO statistics as of 2019, 72.2 percent of adult men in the region were literate, while the share among women was only 58.9 percent. In secondary school, there were nine girls in school for every ten boys on average. Yet, on average, "far fewer girls than boys complete this level in sub-Saharan Africa (36 percent for girls and 42 percent for boys)" (Guyatt 2019). Although Yoon (2004) finds no statistical correlation between women's educational attainment and women's descriptive representation in African legislatures, it is reasonable to assume that women's relative lack of education may impede political candidacy. This exclusion may be directly related to education if candidates are required to demonstrate literacy or specific educational criteria either by law or by party practice. However, the impact may be less direct as well, with uneducated women perhaps choosing not to run or, if they do run, facing potential bias because they are less educated than the men with whom they must compete. At least one study from Zambia indicates that women candidates may in fact have lower levels of education than men (Arriola, Phillips, and Rakner 2021).

A key contributor to gender inequity in secondary education in Africa is the high prevalence of child marriage. Child marriage disproportionately affects girl children because it is most often the case that underage girls are being married to older men. In sub-Saharan Africa, 40 percent of girls are married before the age of eighteen (Human Rights Watch 2017). Child marriage most often ends girls' education, as they must take on household responsibilities and may become pregnant. Until recently, many African countries formally barred pregnant girls from attending school. For example, until the appointment of Tanzania's first woman president in 2021, girls in Tanzania who become pregnant were immediately expelled from school. Fortunately, these policies have begun to change. In the past several years, numerous countries have changed their laws. "At least 30 African countries now protect the educational rights of pregnant girls and young mothers, according to Human Rights Watch (HRW)" (*The Economist* 2022).

The challenges facing teenage wives and mothers are not unique. Patriarchal norms are strong in many African countries and often dictate individuals' beliefs on what women should or should not do. In Afrobarometer surveys from 2016, 37.9 percent of respondents across nine African countries agreed that "when jobs are scarce, men should have more right to a job than women." An additional 49.7 percent agreed that it "is better for a family if a woman has the main responsibility for taking care of the home and children rather than a man" (Johnson and Phillips 2019). These types of beliefs can limit women's political participation both by reinforcing women's duties in the home and by decreasing voters' and party leaders' interest in women candidates. Political careers and candidacies require significant time commitments away from the home, yet a sizable minority of African voters question whether public commitments and obligations outside the home are appropriate. As such, it is not surprising that many women politicians have been viewed as bad mothers, unfaithful wives, or even prostitutes (Tamale 1999).

Because women politicians challenge social norms and threaten men's long-standing hold on politics, many women who aspire to or hold political office are subject to verbal harassment and both threats of and actual physical violence in sub-Saharan Africa. Recent research on women in politics in Africa suggests that violence shapes women's political options in several ways. In Zambia, for example, women's concerns with violence on the campaign trail lead them to engage in fewer large public events (Arriola, Phillips, and Rakner 2021). In Ghana, sexual harassment undermines women's ability to fundraise, for fear of being alone in the room with an aggressor, and online social media slander has reduced women's ability to use modern technology to their advantage (Bauer and Darkwah 2021; Coffie and Medie 2021). The threat of violence against women politicians persists after they are elected. In fact, a recent Inter-Parliamentary Union (IPU) study indicates that the main perpetrators of violence against women members of parliament are their male colleagues. As one journalist covering the study writes, "Female MPs in Africa have a lot to fear with 80 percent of them having experienced psychological violence in parliament, 67 percent having been subjected to sexist behavior or remarks and 39 percent of them having faced sexual violence. Disturbingly, the main perpetrators of this violence are their male counterparts" (Betteridge-Moes 2021). Such harassment and violence may dissuade women from running for and remaining in office.

Finally, among the barriers to women's political participation that may be somewhat unique to Africa is the interaction between patriarchal norms and ethnic politics. In many African countries, politicians heavily rely on the support of their ethnic community and are expected to serve as "patrons" for their community, helping channel public resources and special favors to members of their ethnic group. For the most part, the role of ethnic patron tends to be fulfilled by men, who have more financial resources and a longer history in politics (Arriola and Johnson 2014). Women who try to represent their ethnic group may face serious resistance from ethnic elders and existing politicians who resent their challenge to existing gender hierarchies. As a result, they will find it difficult to mobilize voter support. To compensate, women candidates may choose to campaign on policy issues. Yet, as Gichohi (2021) shows in a study of Martha Karua's campaign for the presidency in Kenya, women candidates suffer without the support of their coethnics. With fewer resources and no specific voter base, it is more difficult for them to run a successful campaign.

ACHIEVING POLITICAL PARITY—A WAY FORWARD FOR SUB-SAHARAN AFRICA

To date, sub-Saharan Africa has been the global leader in using quotas to achieve greater political representation for women. Yet, several African countries have not yet adopted quotas, and even among those that have, most have not achieved actual parity. Moreover, women's legislative successes have not been matched by equal presidential successes. Cabinet appointments for women have expanded but continue to vary greatly across the region. Women are active as voters, and concerns about voting gaps are muted; however, there are still important gender gaps in nonvoting political participation. In other words, significant room for improvement in women's political status in the region remains.

Electoral quotas are not likely to offer an easy solution for future parity. In part, there is little reason to believe that countries that resisted the first and second waves of quota adoption will now choose to adopt quotas. In addition, among quota countries, continued growth in women's legislative representation may be slowing. Moreover, quotas for ministerial cabinets are rare, and it is difficult to imagine a scenario in which the presidency would ever be reserved for a woman.

As a result, African countries need new paths for gender parity. History suggests that organized women's movements autonomous from the government must play a central role in any efforts to improve women's political representation. For the most part, their efforts at present focus on the core socioeconomic inequalities facing their societies. For example, women's movements—often in collaboration with women in parliament—have helped change inheritance and marriage laws, improve women's land rights, and increase funding for health and education, such that women and girls have more opportunities to become educated, accumulate resources, and potentially pursue political careers. For example, in Rwanda, women parliamentarians and women activists secured new legislation that gave women the right to inherit land, seek employment, and sign contracts (Burnet 2011). These types of changes are key to ensuring fundamental shifts in the gendered balance of power in the region moving forward.

These socioeconomic strategies need to be paired with explicitly political ones that address the party biases, resource constraints, and threats of harassment and violence that limit women's entry into politics. Unfortunately, there are no easy solutions for these problems. Women's leadership can be important for overcoming party biases, as in South Africa, where women are represented at the highest levels of the African National Congress party. Yet, it is not clear how to improve women's party leadership. Many parties formed by women struggle to gain broad support, although exceptions exist. For example, Rosine Soglo, the former first lady of Benin, proved a more skilled politician than her husband and created one of Benin's longest-lasting and most prominent political parties. In addition, both governments and parties have tried to limit the financial barriers facing women candidates by eliminating filing fees, that is, the money candidates must pay to register their candidacy for public office (Bauer and Darkwah 2021). In some countries, like Malawi, governments have also worked with international organizations to provide additional funding for women. Public campaign finance, though costly, may offer an important alternative for women considering running for office. Similarly, governments and parties can potentially combat party bias by introducing public primaries and establishing clear and transparent candidate selection processes (Bauer and Darkwah 2021).

Regional actors also have a role to play in improving women's political access in sub-Saharan Africa. As the example of the SADC illustrates, African governments can influence the priorities of neighboring states through regional organizations and some research suggests simply through example or by raising the political bar. One important path forward is for other regional organizations, like the Economic Community of West African States, to adopt similar gender parity protocols and for the African Union to update its protocol on women's rights to include a specific call for parity via affirmative measures like those found in the SADC protocol.

Organizations originating outside Africa, as well as foreign governments allocating aid to the region, can support all of the above efforts by embracing women's political rights at the international level and setting ambitious goals in international forums. As previously noted, many African governments have been responsive to shifts in international expectations about women's political rights. Many international programs have focused on training women candidates and increasing women's political ambition in the past; however, they are increasingly coming to terms with the role of parties and violence in preventing even ambitious women from successfully entering politics. In Kenya, the United Kingdom financed the Deepening Democracy Programme to specifically engage party leaders to improve women's representation. And the National Democratic Institute, financed by the United States, has engaged in a #NotTheCost campaign, which seeks to assess political violence against women and develop tools for women and governments to mitigate it (Arriola, Johnson, and Phillips 2021, 236). It is too early to know whether these strategies will work, but they are at least focused on some of the most important barriers that women face when seeking office.

Overall, there are many reasons to be optimistic about the possibilities for women in politics in sub-Saharan Africa. Women are voting, running for office, being appointed to cabinets, and exercising political influence at rates unseen since the start of colonialism. They have been important forces for change in movements for racial equality, peace, political opening, and legal reform. Though women continue to face important barriers in politics, potential solutions exist, and African women's movements will undoubtedly continue to advocate for many of them.

REFERENCES

Abdullah, Hussaina. 2014. "Independent Candidacy: An Alternative Political Pathway for Women in Sierra Leone?" In *Women in Politics: Gender, Power and Development*, edited by Mariz Tadros, 233–258. New York: Zed Books.

Adams, Melinda. 2008. "Liberia's Election of Ellen Johnson-Sirleaf and Women's Executive Leadership in Africa." *Politics & Gender* 4 (3): 475–484. https://doi.org/10.1017/S1743923X0800038X

Adams, Melinda. 2016. "Context and Media Frames: The Case of Liberia." *Politics & Gender* 12 (2): 275–295.

Anderson, Jemima Asabea, Grace Diabah, and Patience Afrakoma hMensa. 2011. "Powerful Women in Powerless Language: Media Misrepresentation of African Women in Politics (the Case of Liberia)." *Journal of Pragmatics* 43 (10): 2509–2518. https://doi.org/10.1016/j.pragma.2011.02.004

Arriola, Leonardo R., and Martha C. Johnson. 2014. "Ethnic Politics and Women's Empowerment in Africa: Ministerial Appointments to Executive Cabinets." *American Journal of Political Science* 58 (2): 495–510. https://doi.org/10.1111/ajps.12075

Arriola, Leonardo R., and Martha C. Johnson. 2015. "Economic Rights and Women's Policy Influence in Africa." Working Paper. http://cpd.berkeley.edu/wp-content/uploads/2015/02/Arriola_Johnson_Portfolios.pdf

Arriola, Leonardo R., Martha C. Johnson, and Melanie L. Phillips. 2021. "Conclusion." In *Women and Power in Africa: Aspiring, Campaigning, and Governing*, edited by Leonardo R. Arriola, Martha C. Johnson, and Melanie L. Phillips, 213–244. New York: Oxford University Press.

Arriola, Leonardo R., Melanie L. Phillips, and Lise Rakner. 2021. "Same Rules, Higher Costs." In *Women and Power in Africa: Aspiring, Campaigning, and Governing*, edited by Leonardo R. Arriola, Martha C. Johnson, and Melanie L. Phillips, 39–60. New York: Oxford University Press.

Ballington, Julie, ed. 2004. *The Implementation of Quotas: African Experiences Quota Report Series*. Stockholm: International IDEA.

Bauer, Gretchen. 2015. "'A Lot of Head Wraps': African Contributions to the Third Wave of Electoral Gender Quotas." *Politics, Groups, and Identities* 4 (2): 196–213. https://doi.org/10.1080/21565503.2015.1112293

Bauer, Gretchen, and Akosua K. Darkwah. 2021. "Party Primaries and Women's Representation in Ghana: How Can More Women Aspirants Win?" In *Women and Power in Africa: Aspiring, Campaigning, and Governing*, edited by Leonardo R. Arriola, Martha C. Johnson, and Melanie L. Phillips, 61–84. New York: Oxford University Press.

Bauer, Gretchen, and Faith Okpotor. 2013. "'Her Excellency': An Exploratory Overview of Women Cabinet Ministers in Africa." *Africa Today* 60 (1): 76–97.

Berger, Iris, and E. Frances White. 1999. *Women in Sub-Saharan Africa: Restoring Women to History*. Bloomington: Indiana University Press.

Betteridge-Moes, Maxine. 2021. "The Main Perpetrators of Violence against Female MPs in Africa Are Male MPs." *Quartz Africa*, November 30, 2021. https://qz.com/africa/2096344/study-reveals-prevalence-of-violence-against-africas-female-mps/

Burnet, Jennie E. 2008. "Gender Balance and the Meanings of Women in Governance in Post-Genocide Rwanda." *African Affairs* 107 (428): 361–386.

Burnet, Jennie E. 2011. "Women Have Found Respect: Gender Quotas, Symbolic Representation, and Female Empowerment in Rwanda." *Politics & Gender* 7 (3): 303–334.

Childs, Sarah, and Mona Lena Krook. 2009. "Analysing Women's Substantive Representation: From Critical Mass to Critical Actors." *Government and Opposition* 44 (2): 125–145.

Chinbuah, A. B. 2007. "Heroes of Our Time—Ms Mabel Ellen Dove." *Daily Graphic*, April 13, 2007. https://www.modernghana.com/news/133915/1/heroes-of-our-time-ms-mabel-ellen-dove.html

Coffe, Hilde, and Catherine Bolzendahl. 2011. "Gender Gaps in Political Participation across Sub-Saharan African Nations." *Social Indicators Research* 102 (2): 245–264. https://doi.org/10.1007/s11205-010-9676-6

Coffie, Amanda, and Peace A. Medie. 2021. "Media Representation of Women Parliamentary Candidates in Africa: A Study of the Daily Graphic Newspaper and Ghana's 2016 Election." In *Women and Power in Africa: Aspiring, Campaigning, and Governing*, edited by Leonardo R. Arriola, Martha C. Johnson, and Melanie L. Phillips, 141–160. New York: Oxford University Press.

Cooper, Elizabeth. 2012. "Women and Inheritance in Sub-Saharan Africa: What Can Change?" *Development Policy Review* 30 (5): 641–657. https://doi.org/10.1111/j.1467-7679.2012.00592.x

Dahlerup, Drude. 1988. "From a Small to a Large Minority: Women in Scandinavian Politics." *Scandinavian Political Studies* 11 (4): 275–298.

Dahlerup, Drude. 2005. "Increasing Women's Political Representation: New Trends in Gender Quotas." In *Women in Parliament: Beyond Numbers*, edited by Julie Ballington and Azza Karam, 141–186. Stockholm: International IDEA.

Dahlerup, Drude, and Lenita Freidenvall. 2005. "Quotas as a 'Fast Track' to Equal Representation for Women." *International Feminist Journal of Politics* 7 (1): 26–48. https://doi.org/10.1080/1461674042000324673

Dieterich, Christine, Anni Huang, and Alun Thomas. 2016. *Women's Opportunities and Challenges in Sub-Saharan African Job Markets*. IMF Working Paper. Washington, DC: International Monetary Fund.

Dulani, Boniface, Lise Rakner, Lindsay Benstead, and Vibeke Wang. 2021. "Do Women Face a Different Standard? The Interplay of Gender and Corruption in the 2014 Presidential Elections in Malawi." *Women's Studies International Forum* 88. https://doi.org/10.1016/j.wsif.2021.102501

The Economist. 2022. "More African Countries Are Letting Pregnant Girls Stay at School." February 12, 2022. https://www.economist.com/middle-east-and-africa/2022/02/12/more-african-countries-are-letting-pregnant-girls-stay-at-school

Edgell, Amanda B. 2017. "Foreign Aid, Democracy, and Gender Quota Laws." *Democratization* 24 (6): 1103–1141. https://doi.org/10.1080 /13510347.2016.1278209

Fallon, Kathleen M. 2010. *Democracy and the Rise of Women's Movements in Sub-Saharan Africa*. Baltimore, MD: Johns Hopkins University Press.

Freedom House. 2021. "Freedom in the World Data." Freedom House International. https://freedomhouse.org/report/freedom-world/2021 /democracy-under-siege/countries-and-regions

Geisler, Gisela G. 2004. *Women and the Remaking of Politics in Southern Africa: Negotiating Autonomy, Incorporation, and Representation*. Uppsala: Nordic Africa Institute.

Gichohi, Matthew. 2021. "With Hands Tied: A Kenyan Woman's Presidential Bid." In *Women and Power in Africa: Aspiring, Campaigning, and Governing*, edited by Leonardo R. Arriola, Martha C. Johnson, and Melanie L. Phillips, 117–140. New York: Oxford University Press.

Gottlieb, Jessica, Guy Grossman, and Amanda Lea Robinson. 2016. "Do Men and Women Have Different Policy Preferences in Africa? Determinants and Implications of Gender Gaps in Policy Prioritization." *British Journal of Political Science* 48 (3): 611–636. https://doi.org/10.1017/s0007123416000053

Guyatt, Tanya. 2019. "Millions of Girls Are out of School—But Data Show That Gender Alone Is Not the Main Culprit." UNESCO Institute for Statistics, May 3, 2019. http://uis.unesco.org/en/blog/millions -girls-are-out-school-data-show-gender-alone-not-main-culprit

Hinojosa, Magda. 2012. *Selecting Women, Electing Women: Political Representation and Candidate Selection in Latin America*. Philadelphia: Temple University Press.

Hughes, Melanie M. 2009. "Armed Conflict, International Linkages, and Women's Parliamentary Representation in Developing Nations." *Social Problems* 56 (1): 174–204. https://doi.org/10.1525/sp.2009.56 .1.174

Human Rights Watch. 2017. "Africa: Make Girls' Access to Education a Reality: End Exclusion from School for Married, Pregnant Students." June 16, 2017. https://www.hrw.org/news/2017/06/16/africa -make-girls-access-education-reality#

Ibrahim, Jibrin. 2004. "The First Lady Syndrome and the Marginalisation of Women from Power: Opportunities or Compromises for Gender Equality?" *Feminist Africa* 3 (2004): 48–69.

Ichino, Nahomi, and Noah L Nathan. 2012. "Primaries on Demand? Intra-Party Politics and Nominations in Ghana." *British Journal of Political Science* 42 (4): 769–791.

IDEA. n.d. "Gender Quotas Database." https://www.idea.int/data-tools/data /gender-quotas

IPU (Inter-Parliamentary Union). 2021. *Women in Politics 2021 Map.* New York: IPU and UN Women.

IPU Parline. 2022a. "Monthly Ranking of Women in National Parliaments." https://data.ipu.org/women-ranking?month=1&year=2022

IPU Parline. 2022b. "Women Speakers: Global and Regional Percentages." https://data.ipu.org/speakers-percentages

IPU Parline. n.d. "Global and Regional Averages of Women in National Parliaments." https://data.ipu.org/women-averages

Isaksson, Ann-Sofie. 2014. "Political Participation in Africa: The Role of Individual Resources." *Electoral Studies* 34: 244–260. https://doi .org/10.1016/j.electstud.2013.09.008

Isaksson, Ann-Sofie, Andreas Kotsadam, and Måns Nerman. 2013. "The Gender Gap in African Political Participation: Testing Theories of Individual and Contextual Determinants." *Journal of Development Studies* 50 (2): 302–318. https://doi.org/10.1080/00220388 .2013.833321

Jefremovas, Villia. 1991. "Loose Women, Virtuous Wives, and Timid Virgins: Gender and the Control of Resources in Rwanda." *Canadian Journal of African Studies/Revue Canadienne des Études Africaines* 25 (3): 378–395. https://doi.org/10.2307/485975

Johnson, Martha C., and Melanie L. Phillips. 2019. "Gender Politics." In *Routledge Handbook of Democratization in Africa*, edited by Gabrielle Lynch and Peter VonDeopp, 302–316. New York: Routledge.

Kamau, John. 2021. "The Forgotten Sylvie Kinigi." *Nation*, March 18, 2021. https://nation.africa/kenya/news/africa/the-forgotten-sylvie -kinigi-east-africa-s-first-female-president-3327018?view=html amp

Kenny, Meryl. 2013. *Gender and Political Recruitment: Theorizing Institutional Change.* New York: Palgrave Macmillan.

Kittilson, Miki Caul, and Kim Fridkin. 2008. "Gender, Candidate Portrayals and Election Campaigns: A Comparative Perspective." *Politics & Gender* 4 (3): 371–392.

Koter, Dominika. 2017. "Costly Electoral Campaigns and the Changing Composition and Quality of Parliament: Evidence from Benin."

African Affairs 116 (465): 573–596. https://doi.org/10.1093/afraf /adx022

Kramon, Eric. 2016. "Electoral Handouts as Information: Explaining Unmonitored Vote Buying." *World Politics* 68 (3): 454–498.

Kuenzi, Michelle, and Gina Lambright. 2005. "Who Votes in Africa? An Examination of Electoral Turnout in 10 African Countries." Afrobarometer Working Papers no. 51. East Lansing: Afrobarometer. https://gsdrc.org/document-library/who-votes-in-africa-an-ex amination-of-electoral-turnout-in-10-african-countries/

Lindberg, Staffan I. 2003. "'It's Our Time to 'Chop': Do Elections in Africa Feed Neo-Patrimonialism Rather Than Counter-Act It?" *Democratization* 10 (2). https://doi.org/10.1080/714000118

Lord Fransee, Emily. 2016. "Senegal: Gender and Colonial Legacy." *Perspectives on History* (September). https://www.historians.org /research-and-publications/perspectives-on-history/september -2016/senegal-gender-and-colonial-legacy

Mama, Amina. 1998. "Khaki in the Family: Gender Discourses and Militarism in Nigeria." *African Studies Review* 41: 1–18.

Mbenywe, Mactilda. 2018. "Grace Onyango: I Stood against 158 Male MPs and Beat Them All in Debate." *The Standard.* https://www .standardmedia.co.ke/politics/article/2001289000/grace-onyango -i-stood-against-158-male-mps-and-beat-them-all-in-debate

Mlambo, Courage, Forget Kapingura, and Richard Meissner. 2019. "Factors Influencing Women Political Participation: The Case of the Sadc Region." *Cogent Social Sciences* 5 (1). https://doi.org/10.1080 /23311886.2019.1681048

Mudavadi, K. C. 2020. "Patriarchy and Print Media Coverage in Kenya: An Analysis of Newspaper Framing of Women Politicians in Pre-and-Post 2017 General Election." In *Challenging Patriarchy: The Role of Patriarchy in the Roll-Back of Democracy*, edited by C. Kioko, R. Kagumire, and M. Matandela, 101–115. Nairobi, Kenya: Heinrich Böll Stiftung.

Osei-Appiah, Sally. 2019. "Media Representations of Women Politicians: The Cases of Ghana and Nigeria." PhD diss., University of Leeds.

Powley, Elizabeth. 2008. *Engendering Rwanda's Decentralization: Supporting Women Candidates for Local Office.* Washington, DC: Inclusive Security.

SAHO (South African History Online). n.d. "White Women Achieve Suffrage in South Africa." https://www.sahistory.org.za/dated-event /white-women-achieve-suffrage-south-africa

Smith, David. 2014. "Can Catherine Samba-Panza Save the Central African Republic?" *The Guardian*, March 2, 2014. https://www.theguardian.com/world/2014/mar/02/catherine-samba-panza-central-african-republic

Sudarkasa, Niara. 1986. "'The Status of Women' in Indigenous African Societies." *Feminist Studies* 12 (1): 91–103. https://doi.org/10.2307/3177985

Tamale, Sylvia. 1999. *When Hens Begin to Crow: Gender and Parliamentary Politics in Uganda*. Boulder, CO: Westview Press.

Tamanaha, Brian Z. 2021. "Legal Pluralism across the Global South: Colonial Origins and Contemporary Consequences." *Journal of Legal Pluralism and Unofficial Law* 53 (2): 168–205.

Tripp, Aili. 2001. "Women's Movements and Challenges to Neopatrimonial Rule: Preliminary Observations from Africa." *Development and Change* 32 (1): 33–54. https://doi.org/10.1111/1467-7660.00195

Tripp, Aili Mari. 2015. *Women and Power in Postconflict Africa*. Cambridge Studies in Gender and Politics. New York: Cambridge University Press.

Tripp, Aili Mari. 2019. "New Trends in Women and Politics in Africa." In *The Palgrave Handbook of African Women's Studies*, edited by Olajumoke Yacob-Haliso and Toyin Falola, 1–21. Cham, Switzerland: Springer International Publishing.

Tripp, Aili Mari, Isabel Casimiro, Joy Kwesiga, and Alice Mungwa. 2008. *African Women's Movements: Transforming Political Landscapes*. New York: Cambridge University Press.

Tripp, Aili Mari, and Alice Kang. 2008. "The Global Impact of Quotas on the Fast Track to Increased Female Legislative Representation." *Comparative Political Studies* 41 (3): 338–361. https://doi.org/10.1177/0010414006297342

UNESCO. n.d. "Women in African History." https://en.unesco.org/womeninafrica/

Walker, C. 1990. *Women and Gender in Southern Africa to 1945*. Claremont: David Philips Publishers.

Wang, Vibeke, Happy M. Kayuni, Asiyati Chiweza, and Samantha Soyiyo. 2019. "Relieving Women's Costs of Standing for Election: Malawi's 50:50 Campaigns." In *Gendered Electoral Financing: Money, Power and Representation in Comparative Perspective*, edited by Ragnhild L. Muriaas, Vibeke Wang and Rainbow Murray, 114–132. New York: Routledge.

Wantchekon, Leonard. 2003. "Clientelism and Voting Behavior: Evidence from a Field Experiment in Benin." *World Politics* 55 (3): 399–422. https://doi.org/10.1353/wp.2003.0018

Willis, Justin, Gabrielle Lynch, and Nic Cheeseman. 2018. "Voting, Nationhood, and Citizenship in Late-Colonial Africa." *The Historical Journal* 61 (4): 1113–1135. https://doi.org/10.1017/S0018246X18000158

Yoon, Mi Yung. 2004. "Explaining Women's Legislative Representation in Sub-Saharan Africa." *Legislative Studies Quarterly* 29 (3): 447–468.

SIX

Central and East Asia

Chang-Ling Huang and Esther Somfalvy

Central and East Asia is a vast and diverse region not only geographically but also based on cultural traditions, economic situation, and political histories. Central Asia comprises five countries: Kazakhstan, Kyrgyz Republic, Tajikistan, Turkmenistan, and Uzbekistan. Situated in the heart of the Eurasian continent, these Muslim-majority countries share a history as part of the Russian Empire and the Soviet Union (Keller 2019). East Asia includes China, Hong Kong, Taiwan, Japan, South Korea, and North Korea, who equally share a common history and cultural and religious roots. Because East and Central Asia are distinct subregions that share similar histories, cultures, and politics, the chapter will discuss each subregion separately. In the first part, Esther Somfalvy provides an overview of women in politics, highlighting how the Soviet legacy still shapes women's political participation today. In the second part, Chang-Ling Huang turns her attention to East Asia and how the process of democratization has influenced and guided women's participation in politics.

WOMEN IN CENTRAL ASIAN POLITICS

Central Asian Women as Voters

On March 8, 2020, people gathered in the center of Kyrgyzstan's capital, Bishkek, to commemorate International Women's Day. The march, which a court had initially forbidden due to fears of the unfolding COVID-19 pandemic then permitted on short notice, was intended to draw attention to the many issues faced by Kyrgyzstan's women: domestic violence and forced marriages (Djanibekova 2020). Before the march could begin, as the organizers started handing out banners, the protestors were attacked and beaten by a group of young men (*dzhigit*) in traditional felt hats (*ak kalpak*)—a beloved national symbol once worn by elders and recognized as a UNESCO intangible cultural heritage that has become associated with Kyrgyz nationalist vigilante groups (Djanibekova 2020). When the police arrived on the scene, they detained the participants of the march, not the attackers.

This episode, which is not an isolated incident in a heated political environment, shows that Central Asian women still run into obstacles when they want to make their voices heard. In the following section, I outline the state of women's political participation and representation across Central Asia. I discuss how women's place in society has changed since the Central Asian countries gained their independence from the Soviet Union and how the imaginations of tradition play a role in shaping it.

Important for the development of women's political participation today is the fact that belonging to the Soviet Union left the countries a similar institutional structure at independence as well as a common narrative centered around gender equality, progress, and an emphasis on the education of girls. Lenin and other early **Bolshevik** leaders saw women as some form of oppressed **surrogate proletariat** and therefore as a potential ally in their struggle for building communism (Massell 1974). Already the first

Table 6.1   Introduction of Universal Suffrage in Central Asia

Country	Year
Kazakhstan	1924
Kyrgyzstan	1924
Tajikistan	1924
Turkmenistan	1927
Uzbekistan	1938

Source: Graph compiled by the author based on data from the Inter-Parliamentary Union (IPU) Parline database (for Kazakhstan, Kyrgyzstan, Tajikistan, and Turkmenistan—"Notes" section of historical data on women) and IPU Women in Politics, "Women's Suffrage," http://archive.ipu.org/wmn-e/suffrage.htm (Uzbekistan).

Soviet constitution of 1918 had declared the equality of all Soviet citizens and established the right of women to be elected to the **Soviets**. At the latest, women's suffrage was established in the Central Asian Republics with their incorporation into the Soviet Union. But some states granted women suffrage as early as 1924 (Kazakhstan, Kyrgyzstan, and Tajikistan), 1927 (Turkmenistan), and 1938 (Uzbekistan). It is noteworthy that the formal rights did translate into representation, with women making up over 40 percent of the Soviet Union's representatives at all levels (Friedgut 1979; Hough and Fainsod 1979). Unfortunately, we do not know much about women's participation beyond voting, as data on voter turnout do not exist in the region (table 6.1).

Central Asian Women as Members of Parliament

Although the formal rights of women were confirmed in the constitutions of the newly independent states after the collapse of the Soviet Union, in many respects the 1990s constituted a step back in regard to women's political participation in the region. Amid attempts of state and nation building, it was often the roles and values that were deemed traditional that governments reverted to in an attempt to distance from or rupture with the Soviet past, and these included gender norms (Cleuziou and Direnberger 2016, 196). Scholars have identified three pivotal elements of how nation building and gender norms are intertwined in Central Asia: (1) a division between public (masculine) and private (feminine) societal spheres, (2) the equation of womanhood with motherhood, and (3) the restriction of women's political participation in the name of "traditions, authenticity or nature" (Cleuziou and Direnberger 2016, 196–197). These resulted, for example, in the policing of women's appearance and in pressure on women to get married. Although these elements are present in the narratives of all countries after independence, differences are also noteworthy. On the one hand, these are based on different gender roles rooted in religious traditions and historically different lifestyles. Women in nomadic Kazakh and Kyrgyz participated in herding and riding, while the sedentary Uzbek and Tajik women were less visible and mixed little with men. These different local lifestyles had interacted with the official Soviet model and amounted to distinct real-world practices of political participation on the ground (Kamp 2006; Peshkova 2013).

Today, most Central Asian parliaments have a higher share of women members of parliament (MPs) than in the executives. For the lower chambers, it ranges from 19 percent (Kyrgyzstan) to 32 percent (Uzbeki-stan), with Tajikistan's 24 percent, Turkmenistan's 25 percent, and Kazakh-stan's 30 percent in-between (IPU 2022). Both the country with the lowest (Kyrgyzstan) and highest (Uzbekistan) shares of women MPs have an electoral system that prescribes a 30 percent legislated candidate quota. That the same type of quota leads to very different outcomes in terms of representation draws attention to the long-term effects of quota designs over the legislature's term (table 6.2).

Kazakhstan has seen a rise in the share of women in politics from 16 percent in 2007 to 24 percent in 2012 and 26 percent of women MPs in 2021 (convocations). There are differences between the parties, with the small faction (parliamentary group) of the Ak Zhol Democratic Party in the lead: three out of its eight (2012) or seven (2016) MPs in both parlia-ments elected in 2012 (37.5 percent) and 2016 (42.8 percent) were women (IPU 2022, analysis in Somfalvy 2020, 87). Until very recently, Kazakh-stan chose to approach women's representation informally, only introduc-ing a legislated candidate quota of 30 percent in the spring of 2020. This makes the 2021 legislative elections the first one where a quota was in effect. When asked about their opinion on quotas, interview partners of the author said that the fact that the share of women was already higher than in many countries that had quotas showed that their introduction was not necessary, as "the Kazakhstani woman is educated and competitive" (personal communication, see Somfalvy 2020, 87).

Although party officials rejected the need to introduce quotas for a long time, they nevertheless agreed that gender was a concern when drawing up party lists, as parties wanted to appear likable to the over 50 percent of women voters (personal communication, see Somfalvy 2020, 87). The wording of the new quota provision within the electoral law, however, sug-gests a weak quota, stating that candidate lists should be at least 30 percent women (and young people under the age of twenty-nine) without spelling out any sanctions in case the quota is not met (Constitutional Law on Elec-tions, Art. 89.6-4). After the elections, it became evident that the quota did not make for a large difference in women MPs when compared to the pre-vious parliament.

In the Kyrgyz legislature, the share of women after independence was initially low, with both the parliaments elected in 1995 and 2000 being a mere 5 percent women MPs. Kyrgyzstan introduced an electoral gender quota in 2007, simultaneously with the adoption of proportional represen-tation, after the previous 2005 elections had led to the creation of a

Table 6.2 Share of Women in Parliament in Central Asia

Country	Parliament	Unicameral Legislature or Lower Chamber (No. of Seats)	Share of Women (2021 in Percentage)	Quota	Year Introduced
Kazakhstan	Parliament	Mazhilis (107)	30	Legislated candidate quota	2020
Kyrgyzstan	Jogorku Kenesh	Jogorku Kenesh (120)	19	30% legislated candidate quota	2007
Tajikistan	Majlisi Oli	Majlisi namoyandogon (63)	24	No	
Turkmenistan	Milli Gengesh (National Council)	Mejlis (125)	25	No	
Uzbekistan	Oliy Majlis	Qonunchilik palatasi (150)	32	30% legislated candidate quota	2004

Sources: Author's table based on IPU Database. https://data.ipu.org/women-ranking?month=9&year=2022).

parliament without a single woman representative. The quota mandates that parties need to ensure that at least 30 percent of the underrepresented gender are nominated at the time of registration (Electoral Law, Art. 60.3). Additionally, the quota is ranked, meaning that no more than three subsequent candidates on the list may be of the same gender. This gives women positions high up on the list, making sure they win seats. This ranked quota is more effective in guaranteeing representation than a quota merely prescribing a share among the candidates, where parties can fill up their lists with candidates to meet the quotas on positions so low that winning a seat is unlikely. This practice has been criticized in connection to the 15 percent minority quota that has failed to elevate the share of representatives from ethnic minorities (OSCE ODIHR 2013, 17). Contrasting the situations before and after the introduction of quotas clearly shows that quotas did contribute to women's empowerment (Zakharchenko 2015): the share of women sharply increased to 28 percent (2007) and remained at 20 percent for 2010 and 2015 (Turdalieva and Tiulegenov 2018, 141). Again, the share of women among the ranks for MPs varies strongly between parties. For example, parties represented in the 2010 parliament had between 14 percent (Ata Zhurt, which also held the highest number of seats, namely twenty-eight) and nearly 30 percent (SDPK, twenty-six seats) (Zakharchenko 2015, 8). The Annual Reports of the Speaker reveal that there is a party (Bir Bol) without any women members in 2018 or 2019 (Annual Report of the Speaker of the Jogorku Kenesh 2018, 2019).

Interestingly, there are discrepancies between the share of women at the time of election and after. In 2010, over 27 percent of newly elected MPs were women, while their share had dropped to 20 percent by 2014 (Tiulegenov and Tursunkulova 2015). Experts attribute this to dropouts and transfers of elected women MPs to administrative positions. Under the rules about ranked quotas, a woman candidate is usually followed by several male candidates on the party lists. If she drops out, the next person on the list takes the mandate. Hence, parties could replace up to three women dropouts with men, revealing weaknesses in the original quota design. After both the Venice Commission and several prominent women MPs advocated for improvements to the quota design, a provision was introduced to the electoral law in June 2017 that requires replacements for dropouts be made by candidates of the same gender (European Commission for Democracy thorough Law/ODIHR 2014, 15; Turdalieva and Tiulegenov 2018, 146). Their long-term effects would have become visible after the 2020 parliamentary elections, where the provisions first applied;

however, the protests in the aftermath of the election and subsequent regime change prevented that.

In Tajikistan, the share of women holding elected office was at 24 percent in parliament, the *Majilis namoyandogon*, in 2020. Previous legislatures had seen 19 percent of women elected (both 2010 and 2015), 17 percent (2005), and 15 percent (2000) (IPU 2022). The early elections after independence in 1990 and 1995 only led to 3 percent of women winning a mandate (IPU 2022). There are no quotas in Tajikistan. Power in Turkmenistan is centered around the president, currently Gurbanguly Berdymukhamedov, while the parliament has little autonomy. Since 2018, the Majilis has 25 percent women among its 125 representatives. The share of women had been similar for the parliament elected in the previous legislative period (2013–2018) and was a large increase from the 16 percent before (elected in 2004 and 2008). With 32 percent women MPs, the 2020 parliament (*Qonunchilik palatasi*) of Uzbekistan has the highest share of women representatives in Central Asia (IPU 2022). Although the candidate quota for women was first introduced in 2004, it was met for the first time during the 2019 parliamentary elections (Electoral Law, Art. 22). Previous legislatures remained below the target of 30 percent women: 22 percent in 2009 and 17 percent in 2014 (IPU 2022; figure 6.1).

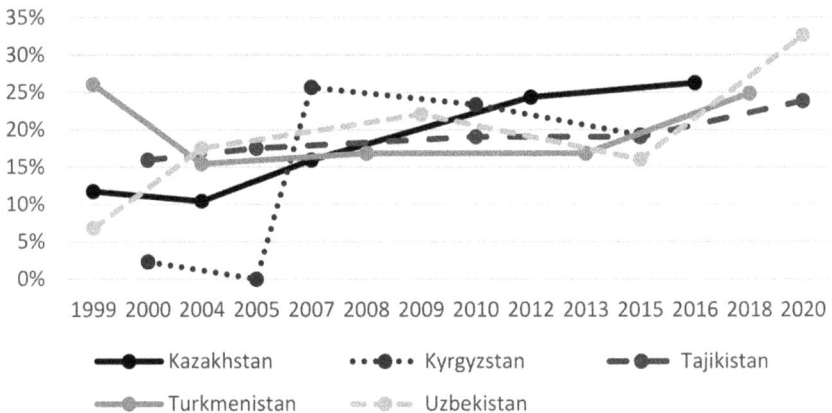

Figure 6.1 Share of Women MPs in Parliaments of Central Asia, 1999–2020 (https://data.ipu.org/women-ranking?month=9&year=2022; http://archive.ipu.org/wmn-e/classif-arc.htm).

ROZA OTUNBAYEVA—CENTRAL ASIA'S ONLY WOMAN HEAD OF STATE

Roza Isakovna Otunbayeva (b. 1950) is a long-serving diplomat and politician in Kyrgyzstan. In 2010–2011, she served as interim president, making her Central Asia's only woman head of state. She is also a member of the high-level group of mediation advisers to the UN secretary-general and a recipient of the International Women of Courage Award.

In the 1980s, Otunbayeva started to rise in the ranks of the Communist Party and the Soviet foreign ministry. After independence, she was named Kyrgyzstan's first minister of foreign affairs and deputy prime minister, until she became the ambassador to the United States in 1992. She also served in other diplomatic positions during the presidency of Askar Akayev.

In 2004, Otunbayeva broke with Akayev, accusing the president of being corrupt and increasingly autocratic. She was the cofounder of a public movement *Ata Zhurt* ("fatherland"), which later became a party by the same name. When the revolution broke out that led to the ouster of President Akayev (which would soon be labeled the "Tulip Revolution"), she was one of its leaders. Otunbayeva served as acting foreign minister in the interim government but was subsequently sidelined by her former ally Kurmanbek Bakiyev, who became president.

Otunbayeva, running for the Social Democratic Party of Kyrgyzstan, was elected into Kyrgyzstan's parliament, the Jogorku Kenesh, in 2007. When in spring 2010 another popular uprising swept Bakiyev from office, she was made acting head of the interim government and later declared she would serve as its interim president until regular elections were organized. Since her term as interim president ended, Otunbayeva has continued to influence public life through her fund, the Roza Otunbayeva Initiative, that was established in 2012.

Sources: European Parliament (n.d.); Carnegie Endowment for International Peace (2012); Roza Otunbayeva Initiative (n.d.).

Central Asian Women as Leaders

No woman has ever been elected to executive leader in Central Asia. However, Roza Otunbayeva did become interim president of Kyrgyzstan after the overthrow of President Bakiyev in 2010, the first and so far only woman in Central Asia to hold the highest office. Her tenure was short: she only governed from May 2010 to December 2011.

The number of women cabinet members in all Central Asian countries remains low, with women holding from one to three of the twenty-two to thirty-one top executive positions. While it is not possible to compile a full list of cabinet members due to governments in the region being characterized by frequent cabinet reshuffles, it is possible to say that the number of women in government remains low.

In Kazakhstan, two members of the government with twenty-three cabinet positions are women in 2021, namely the minister for information and social development and the minister for culture and sports. When writing about women in power, it is impossible not to mention Dariga Nazarbayeva, the daughter of Kazakhstan's first president with political ambitions of her own. The founder of a political party that was incorporated into the presidential party Nur Otan in 2006, Nazarbayeva served as a member of parliament between 2004 and 2007 and again in 2012–2015 and was vice speaker of the Majilis from 2014 until she was appointed deputy prime minister in 2015. She was appointed to the Senate in 2016. The same day her father stepped down as president, Nazarbayeva was elected chairperson of the Senate, succeeding Kassy-Zhomart Tokayev, who became acting president. This move triggered speculations about her being groomed as a potential successor to the presidency. Apart from the issue of dynastic succession, this possibility was often discussed in terms of "Is Kazakhstan ready to have a woman leader?" Asked about this possibility in 2015, a successful women entrepreneur said, "I would generally prefer a man myself. . . . To me, men are more analytical, and they are more pragmatic" (Lillis 2015).

In the Kyrgyz Republic, two out of twenty-two cabinet positions were filled with women. One deputy prime minister, Alla Ismailova, and the minister of finance are women. In Tajikistan, three of twenty-two cabinet positions are occupied by women in 2021 (President of the Republic of Tajikistan 2021). There is little information on Turkmenistan due to the largely centralized press, limitations on the work of international organizations and nongovernmental organizations (NGOs), and few researchers with expertise. Consequently, reporting on Turkmenistan often highlights curious anecdotes, such as the fact that the president published a book in 2018 with the title *Worshipping Mother: Worshipping a Sacred Person* (Akhal-Teke 2018). The book is devoted to the "role of motherhood in forming national and spiritual values" (Akhal-Teke 2018), which is a common theme in Central Asia. Such anecdotes should be understood in their context of the lack of more substantive information on the country's opaque politics. As of 2021, there was one woman deputy prime minister in the cabinet, Mahrijemal Mammedova, who is responsible for issues related to media and culture. In Uzbekistan, one woman is a member of a cabinet with thirty-one senior positions, the minister of preschool education, Agrippina Shin. A further three women are deputies to a minister.

Achieving Political Parity—A Way Forward for Central Asia

Before independence, all Central Asian states had relatively good conditions for women's political participation. Yet, these conditions deteriorated in the 1990s. The rejection of Soviet values and the reemergence of gender stereotypes deemed traditional led to the sidelining of women in many spheres of political life. The marginalization of women is most visible when looking at the composition of the executives: across Central Asia, there are no more than three women in cabinets. The representation of women is better in the legislative bodies, as most countries work toward an improvement in this sphere, for example, with the introduction of quotas. It is apparent that consistent and high-level commitment does indeed improve the number of women in parliament. A further factor that allows for optimism is the fact that governments and civil societies alike have started to pay more attention to the underlying issues within the societies that have hindered women's political participation in the past years.

WOMEN IN EAST ASIAN POLITICS

This section tells the story of women and politics in East Asia by illustrating three important points. First, Japan was the only democracy in this region until the late 1980s and early 1990s, when South Korea, Taiwan, and Mongolia embarked on democratization as well. Therefore, when most East Asian women gained suffrage rights, they received the same political rights as their fellow male citizens or residents, but those rights were limited under authoritarian rules. In today's East Asia, Japan, South Korea, Taiwan, and Mongolia are democracies, but China, Hong Kong, and North Korea are not. Second, as the most advanced economy and the earliest democracy in the region, Japan has always had the lowest level of women's political representation in its parliament. The current percentage of women in Japan's lower house is only 9.9 percent. The contrast between Taiwan and Japan, or generally the entire variation of women's representation in East Asia, at least numerically, could largely be explained by whether, when, and how gender quotas have been adopted and implemented in each country. Third, the number of women holding executive positions in governments in East Asia remains small, though there have been women presidents, women premiers, and women ministers in conventionally male-dominated fields, such as defense and diplomacy. While the patriarchal culture no doubt affects women's chances to hold executive power, institutional designs, such as constitutional structures, could be another reason as well.

Women as Voters in East Asia

Women in East Asia primarily gained suffrage in the 1940s after World War II, with Mongolia and Hong Kong being the exceptions. Mongolian women gained suffrage the earliest and Hong Kong women the latest. The timing was related to Chinese history. In the twentieth century, China experienced three regimes: Imperial Qing China (1636–1911), Republican China (1911–1949), and Communist China (1949–present). Mongolia was under the control of Imperial China until 1911, when a republican revolution took place. Mongolia took advantage of the opportunity and declared its independence in 1912. However, Mongolian independence was not recognized by the newly established Republican China until 1921. Once Mongolia secured its independence, the government enacted its first constitution and granted women and men the same rights. That constitution made Mongolian women the first in the region to gain suffrage. In 1924, Mongolian women exercised their rights to vote and to be elected for the first time.

Hong Kong was ceded to Britain by Imperial China in 1842 after a war and, a century and a half later, was returned to Communist China in 1997. Under British rule, Hong Kongers enjoyed civil liberties such as freedom of expression and assembly but had no political rights. In 1981, the British colonial government released the White Paper on District Administration in Hong Kong and granted anyone who had lived in Hong Kong for seven years the right to vote for district boards, which are Hong Kong's local councils. Hong Kong women therefore gained suffrage in 1981, though these rights were only able to be exercised for local affairs. Hong Kongers did not get to directly elect representatives for Hong Kong's Legislative Council until 1991, and some seats remained appointed until 1995. Today's Hong Kong theoretically has all its legislative council members elected by Hong Kong voters, but about half of them—those elected through functional groups such as professional associations and occupational groups—are elected by only a small number of people.

Women in China, Japan, Taiwan, and the two Koreas all gained suffrage in the late 1940s, after Japan's defeat in World War II and the struggle between capitalist and socialist forces in this region, manifested by the Chinese Civil War and the Korean division. After its 1911 republican revolution, China had its first experience of a parliamentary election in 1912. However, only men who owned property and had an elementary school education were granted voting rights. Women were disappointed and angry, especially those who had participated in the republican revolution. They had fought fiercely for suffrage in the early 1910s, with no success (Edwards 2008). It was not until 1946, in the middle of the Chinese Civil War, when the Republic of China's government enacted its constitution, that Chinese women finally got suffrage. The 1946 Republic of China Constitution affected both Chinese women and Taiwanese women, because at that time both China and Taiwan were under the rule of the Republic of China.

Taiwan was a province of Imperial China before 1895, when Japan defeated China in a war. Imperial China subsequently ceded Taiwan to Japan, and Taiwan became a Japanese colony until 1945, when Japan was defeated in World War II and Taiwan was returned to Republican China. However, immediately following the end of World War II, the Chinese Civil War broke out, which lasted for four years. In 1949, the Chinese Communist Party won the civil war and established the People's Republic of China, or Communist China. The defeated Chinese Nationalist Party moved its national government to Taiwan, and up until today, Taiwan's official country name is still the Republic of China. In other words, the only time in which Taiwan and China were one country was between 1945 and 1949, under the government of the Republic of China. That short time span later had important impacts on women's political rights and representation in both China and Taiwan. On the one hand, as previously mentioned, both Chinese and Taiwanese women gained suffrage because of the 1946 Republic of China Constitution. However, in that constitution, there was a very important clause regarding women's reserved seats, and that made Taiwan one of the earliest countries in the world to implement gender quotas in elections. I will return to this point in the next section.

After Taiwanese and Chinese women received suffrage from the 1946 Republic of China Constitution, the first election during which they could exercise their voting rights was held in 1947. In 1949, when the Chinese Communist Party won the Chinese Civil War and established the People's Republic of China, the new regime granted women the same political right as that of men, though the political rights were always limited under China's authoritarian rule. In today's China, the only direct election is for council members of the most basic level of government. Representatives of all governments above the basic level are elected indirectly.

The year 1947 was also when Japanese women would cast their votes for the first time. Since the 1890s, Japan had held parliamentary elections, and only men who owned property had voting rights. In 1925, Japan enacted the Voters Rights Act, but that act only ensured male suffrage. In 1931, a women's suffrage bill, sponsored by the prime minister, was defeated in the parliament over suffragists' rejections to the bill. That bill allowed Japanese women to vote for local elections only, and if they were married, it required them to obtain their husband's permission to run for offices (Nolte 1986). Despite the great mobilization efforts of Japanese women during the interwar years, Japanese women did not gain suffrage until 1947—after Japan was defeated in World War II—when a new constitution was written under the occupying force of the United States.

Korea was a tributary state to Imperial China, and after China ceded Taiwan to Japan, China's control over Korea also declined after 1895. In 1910, Japan finally annexed Korea and designated it as a colony of Japan. After World War II, because of the competition between socialist and capitalist forces on the Korean Peninsula, Korea was eventually divided in 1948. Both the Republic of Korea (South Korea) and the Democratic People's Republic of Korea (North Korea) were established, and women were granted suffrage rights in that same year.

Overall, East Asian women have primarily gained suffrage because of wars and revolutions that usually led to the creation of new regimes or the reform of old regimes. The expansion of women's rights is known to be related to governments' efforts in enhancing their legitimacy, whether these governments are old or new, authoritarian or democratic (Tripp 2019; Clayton, O'Brien, and Piscopo 2019). By the time that the United Nations, itself a product of the end of World War II, had the Convention on the Political Rights of Women approved by its assembly in 1952, East Asian women had largely all gained suffrage rights, as shown in Table 6.3.

East Asian Women's Political Engagement

East Asian women voters participated in politics as much as or even more than men. Women's voter turnout rates have been found to be higher than that of men's in recent years in Mongolia, South Korea, and Taiwan

Table 6.3   Year of Universal Suffrage in East Asia

Country/Area	Suffrage Year
China	1947
Hong Kong	1991
Japan	1945
Mongolia	1924
South Korea	1948
Taiwan	1947

Sources: Hong Kong Legislative Council (n.d.); IPU (2021); Taiwan Legislative Yuan (n.d.).

(Taiwan Central Election Commission 2017; Koo 2019; Barras 2020). In Japan's 2017 lower house election, voter turnout for women was 53 percent, almost the same as men's 54 percent (Japanese Ministry of Internal Affairs and Communications 2017). Women's higher voter turnout rate has been attributed to the expansion of education and women's changing social roles and status. Such changes gave women, when still facing a patriarchal social structure, more incentives to be actively engaged in politics. Though women as voters participate in politics as much or more than men do, they still encounter more challenges when they seek to run for political offices and remain minorities in leadership roles, as the next section illustrates.

East Asian Women as Members of Parliament

Gender quotas have become a prevailing institution over the past two decades to enhance women's representation in politics (Hughes, Paxton, and Krook 2017). What gender studies scholars already know, but which is not yet popularly perceived, is that women's political representation is more related to institutional variables such as gender quotas and electoral systems than to socioeconomic variables such as GDP per capita or women's education attainment. The variation of women's political representation in East Asia is quite obviously related to institutional factors. Countries in this region have shared cultural heritages and historical legacies, so sociocultural variables could hardly explain their differences in women's political representation.

Figure 6.2 shows the trend of women's representation across East Asia's parliament since the early 1990s. It is clear from the figure that more women became members of parliament in Taiwan than in its neighboring countries or territories. The gap between Taiwan and others has become increasingly greater since the late 2000s. Japan is consistently lagging. The difference between Taiwan and Japan, and to a greater extent between Taiwan and all the other countries in this region, can be attributed to Taiwan's early and comprehensive adoption of gender quotas.

Table 6.4 shows the current level of women's representation in each of the East Asian countries/territories as well as whether, when, and how they adopted and implemented gender quotas.

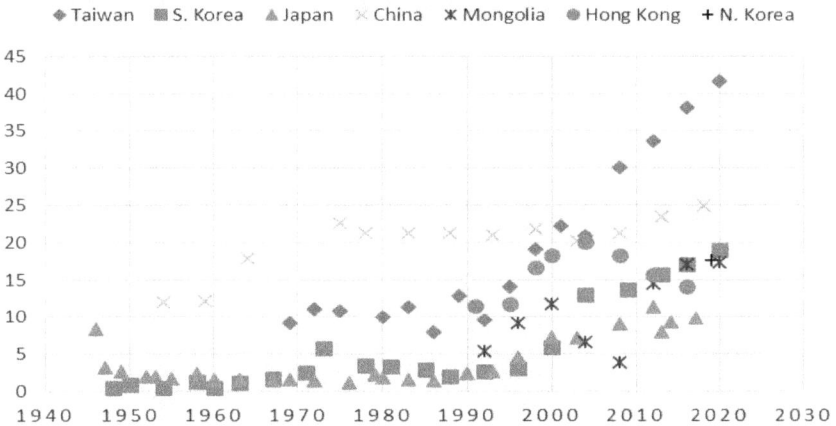

Figure 6.2 Women's Share in East Asian Parliaments (Data compiled by author from database in the following websites or online publication, accessed between October 10 and October 20, 2020:

Central Election Commission of Taiwan: https://db.cec.gov.tw/

National Election Commission of Republic of Korea: http://info.nec.go.kr/

Ministry of Internal Affairs and Communications of Japan: https://www.soumu.go.jp/senkyo/senkyo_s/data/shugiin/ichiran.html

National Bureau of Statistics of China: http://www.stats.gov.cn/tjsj/ndsj/2019/indexch.htm

Mongolian Statistical Information Service http://www.1212.mn/stat.aspx?LIST_ID=976_L02

Legislative Council Secretariat of Hong Kong: https://www.legco.gov.hk/research-publications/english/1819issf02-womens-participation-in-public-affairs-in-hong-kong-20181016-e.pdf).

Table 6.4 Women's Share, Electoral System, and Gender Quota Adoption in East Asia

Country/ Territory	Women in Parliament (%) as of 2021**	Electoral System	First Quota Adoption Year	Current Quota Regulation for Parliament
China	25	Indirect election	N/A	No law; Quota practice through directives
Hong Kong*	14	Proportional representation and functional groups	N/A	None
Japan	10	Mixed-member majoritarian	N/A	None
South Korea	19	Mixed-member majoritarian	2000	Proportional representation: legislative quota of 50% of candidatesSingle-member districts; Legislative quota of 30% of candidates
North Korea	18	N/A		None
Mongolia	17	Block vote	Before 1990	Legislative quota of 20% of candidates
Taiwan	42	Mixed-member majoritarian	1946	Proportional representation only; 50% reserved seats

*Hong Kong's Legislative Council has seventy seats, and after the 2016 election, some members were disqualified.

**The number is for lower house only.

Source: Data compiled by author through websites and online publications cited in figure 6.1.

Taiwan's level of women's political representation has two groups of women's movement activists to thank. The first group is women's movement activists in Republican China in the 1930s and 1940s, and the second group is women's movement activists in Taiwan in the 1990s and 2000s. The former made the adoption of gender quotas, in the form of women's reserved seats, a constitutional practice that later had a lasting impact in Taiwan, and the latter pushed for quota reform and made the gender quotas a more meaningful institution in terms of enhancing women's political participation and representation. As previously mentioned, when the Republic of China enacted its constitution in 1946, both China and Taiwan were under the same government. Article 134 of that constitution stipulated that there should be women's reserved seats in all elections. In 1949, because of the Chinese Civil War, the Republic of China's national government was moved to Taiwan, and since then, the Republic of China has virtually become the equivalent of Taiwan. Women's reserved seats were implemented in elections in postwar Taiwan, though those elections were not democratic elections until the late 1980s. The early adoption of gender quotas had some important impacts on women's political representation, the most important of which was probably the fact that this institution enjoyed an advantage of already existing when the international trend of quota adoption emerged in the 1990s.

Taiwan went through a series of quota reforms between the mid-1990s and 2000s (Huang 2016). The literature about gender quotas usually discusses three quota types: reserved seat, legislative candidate quotas, and voluntary political party quotas. By the mid-2000s, Taiwan had all of these. Though not every political party voluntarily adopted gender quotas for its candidate selection and party offices, the large and major political parties did. The reserved seat requirement for the national parliament ensured that political parties needed to place enough women on their party lists, so it also had the effect of creating an electoral candidate quota.

For the national parliament, Taiwan, South Korea, and Japan have similar mixed-member electoral systems. Under this electoral system, members of parliament are elected through two tiers: single-member districts and party lists. Voters cast two votes, one for a candidate in the district and one for a party list. Single-member district candidates win their seats by getting the largest number of votes in an electoral district, while party list candidates win their seats when their parties win enough votes. In all three countries, seat distribution between the two tiers is unbalanced, and most of the members of these parliaments are elected through single-member districts. Such an unbalanced seat distribution mitigated the effects of gender quotas. As shown in table 6.4, though both Taiwan and South Korea adopted a 50 percent gender quota for their party list seats, because of the smaller number of party list seats, the real quota levels are 15 percent and 8 percent for the total seats.

Japan has never adopted gender quotas, though activists and scholars have advocated for quota adoption (Miura 2018; Stores 2020). In 2018, the Japanese parliament enacted the Gender Parity Act, which was not actually a quota law because it did not specify a quota level. The law merely stipulated that political parties should do their best to select an equal number of male and women candidates in elections, but there is no penalty if they do not comply with the act. Quotas are encouraged but not required. As a result, the percentage of women in Japanese parliament has remained low (Miura 2019).

South Korea shared Japan's experience of having very low levels of women's political representation for decades, until the early 2000s, when South Korea finally adopted gender quotas. When gender quotas were first implemented, the enforcement mechanism was weak. Women's movement activists went through rounds of reforms to strengthen the enforcement, and the quota effects became more effective (Lee and Shin 2016). South Korea has implemented gender quotas for both single-member districts and party lists. Because of that, some South Korean women politicians have succeeded in running in single-member districts after they finished their term through the party lists (Shin 2014).

Mongolia's experience with gender quotas is especially telling. Mongolia used to have 25 percent gender quotas for parliamentary representation, but in the process of democratic transition and reform, the quota system was subsequently abolished. This led to a sharp decline of women's share in parliament in the 1992 election, from 23 percent to 3.9 percent (Burn and Oidov 2001, 53–54). After the reintroduction of a 20 percent candidate quota in 2012, the women's share climbed back up to 13 percent. As of 2020, the women's representation stood at 17 percent which is still lower than before the transition to democracy (Burn and Oidov 2001, 55).

After the establishment of the People's Republic of China in 1949, China never enacted any gender quota law but always has quota policies intended to include less-represented social groups. China's national parliament, the National People's Congress, has members who are both elected and selected. Ever since the 1990s, it has been well known that the Chinese government has made efforts to include those who are nonparty members, intellectuals, ethnic minorities, and women. There were quotas for those who belong to the previously mentioned groups, but the quota levels were never clear for any of these groups. However, the attention paid to including women has allowed the National People's Congress to always have at least 20 percent of women representation since the 1960s, but over the past half a century, that number has never exceeded 25 percent. In Hong Kong's Legislative Council, neither the district tier nor the party list has gender quotas. The percentages of women in Hong Kong's Legislative Council have been between 15 percent and 20 percent since Hong Kong came under Chinese rule, which is higher than the average 12 percent under British rule (Women's Commission 2019).

Women's representation in legislative bodies in East Asia illustrates the fact that democracies without gender quotas do not have higher levels of women's political representation and that authoritarian regimes with socialist ideologies tend to ensure at least some level of women's representation. While most countries in the region have about 20 percent of women representation in their parliaments, Japan and Taiwan are both the exceptions.

East Asian Women as Leaders

When it comes to the situation of women leaders, an examination of the context of East Asia shows interesting and paradoxical patterns. On the one hand, this region has had more than one popularly elected woman head of government and some women ministers in charge of traditionally male-dominated policy realms. On the other hand, the number of women cabinet members remains small, even in countries that have elected women heads of government.

There was no woman head of government in East Asia until the 2010s. South Korea elected Park Geun-hye in 2012, and she was the first popularly elected woman president in this region. Taiwan elected Tsai Ing-wen in 2016, and she was reelected in 2020. Hong Kong's chief executive, Carrie Lam, is arguably also a head of government, although she was appointed, and not elected, to that position in 2017. All three women leaders are highly educated, and only Park had a family background in politics.

As the daughter of former authoritarian leader Park Chung-hee, Park's life has been full of political drama. She lost both her mother and father in political assassinations, and her victory in the 2012 presidential election for South Korea's conservative camp was both an electoral victory and a validation of her father's memory. However, her impeachment over charges of corruption and abuse of power in 2017 also made her the first president to be impeached in South Korean history.

When Taiwan's Tsai Ing-wen won the presidential election in 2016, she broke a very important pattern in Asia regarding women in political leadership, as she did not come from a political family. Unlike many women political leaders in Southeast Asia or South Asia, no one in her family had ever been a politician before she herself became one.

Hong Kong's Carrie Lam, though not popularly elected, was a ranking member of the Hong Kong government for many years before she became the chief executive. While Carrie Lam was not popularly elected, and Hong Kong's degree of autonomy in recent years has declined, more women hold executive positions in the Hong Kong government under Chinese rule than under British rule (table 6.5).

When South Korean president Moon Jae-in was running for president, he made the promise that his cabinet would be at least 30 percent women. He not only kept his promise but also appointed the country's first woman minister of diplomacy and first woman minister of veteran affairs. In contrast, although Park and Tsai were the first women presidents of their respective countries, their records on promoting women in politics have both been disappointing. Park's cabinet only had four women among its more than forty members when she was inaugurated in 2017. One might attribute Park's gender-unbalanced cabinet to her coming from the conservative camp, but the same could not apply to Tsai, since she represents Taiwan's progressive camp. The first cabinet of the Tsai government, with only 10 percent of its members being women, frustrated and angered women's organizations, and they subsequently protested. Four years later, when Tsai began her second term in early 2020, the percentage of women

Table 6.5   Women Executives in East Asia

Country/Area	Women Executive Leader
Taiwan	President Ying-wen Tsai (2016–)
South Korea	Prime Minister Myeong-Sook Han (2006–2007)
	President Geun-hye Park (2013–2017)
Hong Kong	Carrie Lam (2017)

Source: Data courtesy of Farida Jalalzai (excludes interim or appointed leaders).

went down further, to just 5 percent. Tsai's record on the gender ratio of cabinets has been significantly worse than her male predecessors. The gender-unbalanced cabinets under her presidency interrupted the trend of increasing the number of women in cabinets when new presidents were inaugurated since Taiwan's democratization.

How could Taiwan in 2020 have a parliament composed of more than 40 percent women but a cabinet of only 5 percent? Why did women presidents in both South Korea and Tai-

First woman South Korean President Geunhye Park. (2013–2017) (Odemll | Dreamstime.com)

wan appoint such gender-unbalanced cabinets? There could be two possible answers. One is about the gender value or gender equality track records of these two women presidents, and the other is about the constitutional structure. In their previous career tracks, neither Park nor Tsai had any connection to the women's movement, and neither had demonstrated any particular care in regard to any specific women's issue before becoming president. Though Park did appoint fewer women than her male predecessors, the difference was not that significant (Lee and Jalalzai 2017).

Park's and Tsai's failures to appoint more women cabinet members could also be related to the institutional disconnection between the presidency and cabinet appointments. In a parliamentary system, the cabinet is usually filled by members of parliament, but in a presidential system, cabinet members do not necessarily need to be elected members of parliament. South Korea and Taiwan are semipresidential systems, which means they have a popularly elected president and a premier in charge of the government's operation. When there is no requirement for cabinet members to be members of parliament first, cabinet member appointment can easily separate from parliament, and thus the increase of women in parliament does not automatically translate into cabinet appointments.

PI WOO-JIN

Pi Woo-jin is South Korea's first woman minister of veteran affairs; she was appointed by progressive president Moon Jae-in in 2017. She was the first woman helicopter pilot in the South Korean army and had a military career for thirty years before entering politics. In 1988, when South Korea was at its initial stage of democratization, she was a captain and declined a request from senior officers to send women soldiers to their drinking session, as the request came with an instruction for the women soldiers to "dress nicely, not in uniform." She eventually sent women soldiers in combat uniform. She was diagnosed with breast cancer during her military career, and she subsequently had a mastectomy. The army discharged her after her surgery, citing the regulation that whoever has lost a body part can no longer serve in the army. She sued the Ministry of Defense because of the decision and was later reinstated.

Sources: Choi (2017); Jung (2017).

Japan's Inada Tomomi has also captured international attention, partially because she was groomed by Japan's former prime minister Shinzo Abe to be a likely candidate to succeed him in office. Inada was Japan's second woman minister of defense, and the first served for less than two months. She is a stalwart of Japan's conservative camp and a hard-liner over political disputes that Japan has had with neighboring China and South Korea, especially over issues concerning Japan's role during World War II. Though she is politically ultraconservative, Inada was audacious in performing her job responsibilities. When she was entrusted by Abe to develop strategies promoting Japanese culture and fashion, she sometimes dressed like a cosplayer, wearing costumes and fashion accessories to represent a comic or animation character (Fifield 2016). In 2020, when Prime Minister Suga Yoshihide appointed only two women in his twenty-one-member cabinet, Inada openly commented that Japan is "a democracy without women" (McCurry 2020).

Not all East Asian democracies have elected or appointed women political leaders. Mongolia is the only democracy in the region that has had no high-level woman political executive, though there were women ministers and heads of local governments appointed by the authoritarian government before the democratic transition. Socialist authoritarian countries such as China and North Korea share one thing in common: there were never any women members in these two countries' most

---

TANG FENG (AUDREY TANG)

Though women ministers are few in East Asia, their appointments are sometimes gender landmarks in their countries as well as East Asia as a whole. Tang Feng (Audrey Tang), Taiwan's minister without a portfolio in the Tsai government since 2016, is the first transgender minister in Taiwan, in East Asia, and probably in the entire world, too. Born a biological male, Tang started her own company when she was nineteen years old, changed her name when she was twenty-five, and became a minister when she was thirty-five. She has overseen Taiwan's information and communication technology (ICT) policies and has been praised by the media for creating an alliance between the private sector and the government to help Taiwan more effectively using technology to deal with the COVID-19 pandemic. Wearing long hair and always dressed in a gender-neutral way, she declared no gender in her government personnel data sheet. Not accepting the gender binary, she said during an interview that she did not "change sex"; she has simply just been herself (Chiu 2020).

---

powerful decision-making bodies—the Standing Committee of the Politburo. China has had policies designed to increase and enhance women's political leadership, but women usually face the glass ceiling when they reach positions as deputy leaders. Though China has no women in the Standing Committee of the Politburo, a very small number of women did become members of the Politburo. Among the current twenty-five members, there is only one woman, and there have never been more than two women in the Politburo. North Korea has not only never had any woman member in the Presidium, the equivalent of the Standing Committee of the Politburo, but it has also never had any member in the Politburo. Kim Yo-jung, North Korean leader Kim Jong-un's younger sister who is speculated by the foreign media to possibly be Kim Jong-un's successor if something were to happen to him, is only an alternate member of the Politburo.

Achieving Political Parity—A Way Forward for East Asia

A recent survey of members of the parliament in the three East Asian democracies, Taiwan, South Korea, and Japan, showed that women were less likely to propose their own candidacy and had more concerns about work and family balance in their decisions to run for office as compared to men (Yang, Miura, and Kwon 2019). The World Value Surveys also revealed that Japan has the strongest gendered division between the public and private spheres and that Taiwan has the lowest level in terms of harboring gender stereotypes. Acceptance of women political leaders in Korea has been polarizing, with people either showing strong support or strong opposition (Yang, Miura, and Kwon 2019). These survey results have demonstrated both similarities and differences among these three countries. On the one hand, social norms regarding gender roles remain a major barrier for women to enter politics. On the other hand, we do see a connection between levels of women's political representation and citizens' values regarding gender-related issues.

While social and cultural values no doubt affect the formation of policies and institutions, the East Asian experience illustrates the loop between culture and institutions. Japan's lack of gender quotas makes the early modernizer in this region now seem very far behind regarding gender equality. Gender quotas certainly are not the cure-all solution, but as an important institution, they do help to change people's values by having more women holding political positions; their effects sometimes take time to be visible. Taiwan having a woman president who is not from a political family, a transgender minister, and approximately 30 percent women heads of local governments could be regarded as the long-term impacts of gender quotas. President Tsai entered parliament through the party list, and her party had quotas in its nomination rule at that time. All the current women heads of local governments in Taiwan, when they first entered the political realm many years ago, chose to run in districts that had women's reserved seats, though none of them ever actually got elected by invoking these reserved seats (Huang 2019).

The evidence from East Asia's experience is clear in terms of showing that the path to gender equality in politics is through establishing proper institutions. Besides gender quotas that have been discussed in this chapter, there could be others as well, such as women-friendly electoral systems, political finance regulations that target women's recruitment, or public policies such as good childcare or long-term care policies. Whenever the patriarchal culture or values are cited by political parties or governments as a reason not to recruit more women into politics, it is important for whoever supports gender equality to remind these parties and governments that cultural or value changes could also be shaped by institutions, and decisions regarding whether to adopt or create these institutions is a strong testament to these parties' or governments' commitment to gender equality.

REFERENCES

Akhal-Teke. 2018. "Turkmenistan's Mommy Issues. The President's Attempts to Make Public Conversation about Bicycles and His Mom Cannot Paper over a Broken Economy." Eurasianet, June 12, 2018. https://eurasianet.org/turkmenistans-mommy-issues

Annual Report of the Speaker of the Jogorku Kenesh. 2018. "Otchet o deiatel'nosti Zhogorku Kenesha za sessionnyi period (1 sentiabria 2017–1 iunia 2018). IV sosyv 4 sessia." [Report on the Activities of the Jogorku Kenesh for the Session (1 September 2017–1 June 2018). IV convocation, 4th session]. Bishkek: Jogorku Kenesh.

Annual Report of the Speaker of the Jogorku Kenesh. 2019. "Report on the Activities of the Jogorku Kenesh for the Session (1 September 2018–1 June 2019)." [Otchet o deiatel'nosti Zhogorku Kenesha za sessionnyi period (1 sentiabria 2018–1 iunia 2019). IV sosyv 5 sessia]. IV convocation, 5th session. Bishkek: Jogorku Kenesh.

Barras, Camille. 2020. "Women's Voter Turnout: Substantial Reverse Gender Gap." Mongolia Focus, June 15, 2020. http://blogs.ubc.ca /mongolia/2020/guest-post-womens-turnout-reverse-gender-gap/

Burn, Nalini, and Oyuntsetseg Oidov. 2001. *Women in Mongolia: Mapping Progress under Transition*. New York: United Nations Development Fund for Women.

Carnegie Endowment for International Peace. 2012. "Background on Ata Jurt Party." January 13, 2012. https://carnegieendowment.org/2012 /01/13/background-on-ata-jurt-party-pub-46468

Chiu, Iris. 2020. "Digital Minister Audrey Tang: Taiwan's 'Genius' and Her Unique Past." Nippon.com, April 10, 2020. https://www.nippon .com/en/japan-topics/g00837/digital-minister-audrey-tang-taiwan %E2%80%99s-genius-and-her-unique-past.html

Choi, Jieun. 2017. "Moon Jae-in's Road to Gender Equal Cabinet." Korean Expose, May 22, 2017. https://www.koreaexpose.com/moon-jae-in -road-to-gender-equal-cabinet/

Clayton, Amanda, Diana Z. O'Brien, and Jennifer M. Piscopo. 2019. "All Male Panels? Representation and Democratic Legitimacy." *American Journal of Political Science* 63 (1): 113–129.

Cleuziou, Juliette, and Lucia Direnberger. 2016. "Gender and Nation in Post-Soviet Central Asia: From National Narratives to Women's Practices." *Nationalities Papers* 44 (2): 195–206.

Djanibekova, Nurjamal. 2020. "Kyrgyzstan: Women's March against Male Violence Attacked by Masked Men. Police Detained Marchers, but

Not Attackers." Eurasianet.org, March 8, 2020. https://eurasianet
.org/kyrgyzstan-womens-march-against-male-violence-attacked
-by-masked-men

Edwards, Louise P. 2008. *Gender, Politics, and Democracy: Women's Suffrage in China*. Stanford, CA: Stanford University Press.

European Parliament. n.d. "Roza Otunbayeva (Unofficial CV)." https://
www.europarl.europa.eu/meetdocs/2009_2014/documents/afet/dv
/201/201103/20110301otunbayeva_cv_en.pdf

Fifield, Anna. 2016. "Japan's Prime Minister-in-Waiting to Make Her Debut in Washington." *Washington Post*, September 13, 2016.

Friedgut, Theodore H. 1979. *Political Participation in the USSR*. Princeton, NJ: Princeton University Press.

Hong Kong Legislative Council. n.d. "History, Art and Architecture." https://www.legco.gov.hk/general/english/intro/hist_lc.htm

Hough, Jerry F., and Merle Fainsod. 1979. *How the Soviet Union Is Governed*. Cambridge, MA, and London: Harvard University Press.

Huang, Chang-Ling. 2016. "Reserved for Whom? The Electoral Impact of Gender Quotas in Taiwan." *Pacific Affairs* 89 (2): 325–343.

Huang, Chang-Ling. 2019. "Gender Quotas and Women's Increasing Political Competitiveness." *Taiwan Journal of Democracy* 15 (1): 25–40.

Hughes, Melanie M., Pamela Paxton, and Mona Lena Krook. 2017. "Gender Quotas for Legislatures and Corporate Boards." *Annual Review of Sociology* 43: 331–352.

IPU (Inter-Parliamentary Union) 2022. "Data on Women." https://data.ipu
.org/women-ranking?month=9&year=2022 China: https://data.ipu
.org/node/36/data-on-women?chamber_id=13.364. Japan: https://
data.ipu.org/node/85/data-on-women?chamber_id=13432.   South
Korea: https://data.ipu.org/node/138/data-on-women?chamber_
id=13500. Mongolia: https://data.ipu.org/node/113/data-on-women
?chamber_id=13468:

Japanese Ministry of Internal Affairs and Communications. 2017. https://
www.soumu.go.jp/senkyo/senkyo_s/data/shugiin48/index.html

Jung, In-hwan. 2017. "S. Korea's First-Ever Female Helicopter Pilot Appointed Minister of Veterans Affairs." Hankyoreh, May 18, 2017. https://english.hani.co.kr/arti/english_edition/e_national/795336
.html

Kamp, Marianne. 2006. *The New Woman in Uzbekistan: Islam, Modernity and Unveiling under Communism*. Seattle and London: Washington University Press.

Keller, Shoshana. 2019. *Russia and Central Asia. Coexistence, Conquest, Convergence.* Toronto: University of Toronto Press.

Koo, Bon Sang. 2019. "Traditional Gender Gap in a Modernized Society: Gender Dynamics in Voter Turnout in Korea." *Asian Women* 35 (1): 19–45.

Lee, H., and K. Y. Shin. 2016. "Gender Quotas and Candidate Selection Processes in South Korean Political Parties." *Pacific Affairs* 89 (2): 345–368. https://doi.org/10.5509/2016892345

Lee, Young-Im, and Farida Jalalzai. 2017. "President Park Geun-Hye of South Korea: A Woman President without Women?" *Politics & Gender* 13: 597–617.

Lillis, Joanna. 2015. "'Slowly, Change Is Coming': Life for Women in the Post-Soviet World." Eurasianet.org, March 8, 2015. https://eurasianet.org/slowly-change-is-coming-life-for-women-in-the-post-soviet-world

Massell, Gregory J. 1974. *The Surrogate Proletariat: Moslem Women and Revolutionary Strategies in Soviet Central Asia 1919–1929.* Princeton, NJ: Princeton University Press.

McCurry, Justin. 2020. "Japan Is a 'Democracy without Women,' Says Ruling Party MP." *The Guardian*, September 23, 2020.

Miura, Mari. 2018. "Interview with Mari Miura. The Gender Parity Law in Japan: The Potential to Change Women's Under-Representation." *Journal of Gender Studies* 21: 87–99.

Miura, Mari. 2019. "Japan's Leader Wants to Empower Women. Just Not in His Party." *New York Times*, July 26, 2019.

Nolte, Sharon. 1986. "Women's Rights and Society's Needs: Japan's 1931 Suffrage Bill." *Comparative Studies in Society and History* 28 (4): 690–714.

OSCE Office for Democratic Institutions and Human Rights (ODIHR). 2013. *A Comparative Study of Structures for Women MPs in the OSCE Region.* Drafted by Sonia Palmieri. Warsaw: ODIHR.

Peshkova, Svetlana. 2013. "A Post-Soviet Subject in Uzbekistan: Islam, Rights, Gender and Other Desires." *Women's Studies* 42 (6): 667–695.

President of the Republic of Tajikistan. 2021. "Composition of the Government of the Republic of Tajikistan." [Sostav pravitel'stva Respubliki Tadzhikistan]. http://www.prezident.tj/ru/taxonomy/term/5/136

Shin, K. Y. 2014. "Women's Sustainable Representation and the Spillover Effect of Electoral Gender Quotas in South Korea." *International Political Science Review* 35 (1): 80–92.

Somfalvy, E. 2020. *Parliamentary Representation in Central Asia: MPs Between Representing their Voters and Serving an Authoritarian Regime*. London and New York: Routledge.

Stores, Nick. 2020. "In Japan's Post-Abe Era, Addressing Political Gender Inequality Is Essential: A More Uncertain and Competitive Political Climate Could Lead to Urgently Needed Quota Legislation for Female Politicians." *The Diplomat*, September 17, 2020. https://thediplomat.com/2020/09/in-japans-post-abe-era-addressing-polit ical-gender-inequality-is-essential/

Taiwan Central Election Commission. 2017. "Research on the Reform of Gender Statistics on Voters Turnout." Press Release, January 17.

Taiwan Legislative Yuan. n.d. "Brief History." https://www.ly.gov.tw/Pages /Detail.aspx?nodeid=157&pid=6

Tiulegenov, Medet, and Bermet Tursunkulova. 2015. "Parlamentarizm na elektoralnom rynke Kyrgyzstana. Do I posle 2010 g." [Parliamentarianism on the Electoral Market of Kyrgyzstan. To and from the Year 2010]. ICP Policy Research Paper no. 1. Bishkek: American University of Central Asia, International and Comparative Politics Department (AUCA/ICP).

Tripp, Aili Mari. 2019. *Seeking Legitimacy: Whey Arab Autocracies Adopt Women's Rights*. Cambridge: Cambridge University Press.

Turdalieva, Cholpon, and Medet Tiulegenov. 2018. "Women, the Parliament and Political Participation in Post-Soviet Kyrgyzstan." *Central Asian Affairs* 5 (2): 134–159.

Women's Commission. 2019. *Hong Kong Women in Figures 2019*. Hong Kong: Labour and Welfare Bureau.

Yang, Wan-Ying, Mari Miura, and Soo Hyun Kwon. 2019. "Women's Candidacy and Gender Norms in Japan, South Korea, and Taiwan." Paper delivered in the European Conference on Politics and Gender, Amsterdam, July 6–8.

Zakharchenko, Natalia. 2015. "Quotes on Quotas? Political Representation of Women in Kyrgyzstan in the 2007 and 2010 Convocations." In *Kyrgyzstan beyond "Democracy Island" and "Failing State,"* edited by Marlene Laruelle and Johann Engvall, 7–15. Lanham, MD: Rowman & Littlefield.

SEVEN

South and Southeast Asia

Zainab Alam and Ryan Goehrung

South and Southeast Asia is an incredibly diverse region of the world. Home to a wide array of religions (e.g., Islam, Buddhism, Hinduism, Confucianism, and Jainism), varied languages and vibrant cultures, and many different forms of government. Numerous democratic, monarchic, communist, and authoritarian states exist and evolve within the region, making it difficult to generalize about any aspect of South and Southeast Asian politics. The study of women in politics is no exception to this complexity and diversity. Geographically, South Asia consists of the sub-Himalayan countries of Afghanistan, Bangladesh, Bhutan, India, the Maldives, Myanmar, Nepal, Pakistan, and Sri Lanka. While the area below China and toward the east of the Indian Ocean, known as Southeast Asia, is composed of Brunei, Cambodia, East Timor, Indonesia, Laos, Malaysia, Philippines, Singapore, Thailand, and Vietnam.

Within these nineteen countries, collectively home to over two and a half billion people, women's political participation and leadership is just as varied, challenging assumptions about the oft-generalized Global South. For instance, in South Asia, although about half of the population is impacted by various forms of **multidimensional poverty**, the region has witnessed an unusually high number of women heads of state and government (Alkire et al. 2014; UNDP 2019). Paradoxically, the gender gap in South Asia is the second worst in the world, suggesting economic participation and opportunity is not always a precursor to political empowerment (World Economic Forum 2020).

Southeast Asia fairs slightly better than South Asia in terms of both gender parity and levels of development (World Economic Forum 2020; UNDP 2019). However, like South Asia, there is a remarkable amount of variation in both respects. For instance, the Philippines has had two women presidents, has more women in parliament than many industrialized Western nations, and routinely ranks in the top twenty of most gender equitable countries in the world (World Economic Forum 2020). At the same time, both Brunei and Myanmar rank in the lowest twenty countries in the world in terms of women's political empowerment (World Economic Forum 2020). The diversity in regime types also complicates the issue of women's representation in Southeast Asia. The governments of these ten countries range from fairly established democracies (Philippines and Indonesia) to authoritarian-leaning regimes (Singapore and Brunei) and include both communist-led governments (Cambodia, Laos, and Vietnam) and very newly established democracies (Timor-Leste, Myanmar, and Bhutan). This diversity in regime types leads to some unique outcomes regarding women in politics. For instance, Halimah Yacob became president of Singapore in 2017, but hers was the only name on the ballot, suggesting that the country's political electoral institutions may not always support truly competitive elections. So the success of women candidates in this context may not be indicative of trends in other countries of the region (Rodan 2018).

In both South and Southeast Asia, more traditional views on women and gender roles have paradoxically both improved and impeded women's role in politics. For instance, women politicians have at times used traditional views on gender to their advantage, portraying themselves as more honest, modest, or religious than their male counterparts to their electoral advantage (Derichs, Fleschenberg, and Hüstebeck 2006). Strong associations of women with moral purity have also helped propel some women politicians in the region to being successful leaders of anticorruption and prodemocracy movements, like Aung San Suu Kyi (Myanmar) and Megawati Soekarnoputri (Indonesia). At the same time, adherence to traditional gender roles has often led women to engage less in politics (a typically male-dominated sphere), often voting less, running less frequently as candidates, and being relegated to support roles for men politicians (Loring 2018). Similarly, many women leaders in the region hail from dynastic political families, which sometimes raises questions about whether they are viewed as placeholders for male relatives rather than self-motivated, independent women leaders (Choi 2019). To better understand these complexities and the contemporary state of women in politics in this part of the world, a look at the region's history is warranted.

Although the study of women in politics typically focuses on modern states that have democratized and developed institutions to support civil liberties such as voting, in the case of South and Southeast Asia, it is important to first understand the legacy of colonialism in shaping modern governance structures in the region. Throughout the wave of Western imperialism that began in the sixteenth century, South and Southeast Asia were mostly agrarian societies in which population densities and literacy rates were fairly low (Kamat 1976). A diverse range of ethnic and linguistic groups meant that many countries in the region were made up of smaller units of government administered by provincial royals or local leaders of tribal/familial groups. In the archipelagic nations of the Philippines and Indonesia, which are made up of thousands of islands, there were hundreds of distinct ethnic and linguistic groups that largely governed themselves prior to colonization by European powers. Other areas, encompassing modern-day India and Pakistan, were united by larger empires, like the Maurya (322 BCE), Gupta (300 BCE), or Mughal (1526 BCE), which provided more centralized forms of government. In these cases, political power was often monocratic, concentrated in the hands of a single leader, nearly all of whom were men.

There were, however, some notable exceptions. In Sri Lanka, Queen Anula of Anuradhapura led as head of state for about four years around 48 BC, and queens like Lilvati and Sugala led their kingdoms in battle around the twelfth century BCE (Jayathilake 2016; Jayawardena 2016). In historical India, of which present-day Pakistan, Bangladesh, and Myanmar were also a part, queens had been rulers and military commanders of various states and dynasties since at least the fourth century BCE (Altekar 1956). Later, starting in 1819, four generations of Muslim queens ruled the state of Bhopal, in India, for over a hundred years, the last of whom was a particularly active social reformer (Hurley 1998). Additionally, between 1300 and 1800 BCE Southeast Asia had a remarkably large number of women political rulers in the islands of present-day Indonesia and Timor-Leste, with at least 168 women sovereigns documented during this time (Amirell 2015).

In the sixteenth century, certain European powers began to claim many parts of South and Southeast Asia as their colonies—sometimes through manipulative trading practices and often with military force. In many areas, native rulers coexisted alongside varying levels of colonial presence.

Every country in South and Southeast Asia, except Thailand, eventually came under the influence of Western colonialism, which greatly impacted women's struggle for rights and political participation. Colonial governments set social policies, created laws, and drafted early constitutions that shaped the development trajectories of states after independence and influenced women's opportunities for political participation, upon which many states continued after independence. In addition, many women who participated in preindependence nationalist struggles subsequently became important political figures in their newly independent states.

The status of women varied in precolonial South and Southeast Asia according to cultural, class, and religious norms. Perhaps surprisingly, in some contexts, women enjoyed greater social and political freedoms before colonization. Certain policies aiming to civilize the colonies imposed European gender norms that sometimes severely limited women's rights (Chitnis and Wright 2007). However, native women were not merely passive recipients of colonial policy. Women negotiated financial transactions, pushed for legal privileges, and expressed cultural and religious identities despite the influence of Christian missionaries and colonial leaders (Ghosh 2006). For example, in the late nineteenth and early twentieth centuries, Indian women pushed for the right to inherit property and divorce as part of the struggle for full citizenship (Sturman 2012). And some royal woman in India—such as Bhima Bai Holkar, Keladi Chennamma, Avanti Bai, Baiza Bai, Rani Abbaka Chowta, Rani Lakhsmi Bai, and Begam Hazrat Mahal—became revolutionaries by resisting British rule (Ganie and Sisodia 2020).

While colonialism had many negative consequences for native populations, ranging from the erasure or suppression of local languages, religions, and customs to extraction of natural resources and forced exploitation of labor, colonial powers often also established the first centralized government systems resembling modern states. This infrastructure included judicial and education systems to help support the colonial project. As a result, toward the latter half of the nineteenth century, literacy rates in South and Southeast Asia drastically improved, and a small emerging class of literate, largely urban upper- and middle-class women began to join various nationalist struggles for independence throughout the region (Eichenwald 2016). For instance, in colonial Indonesia, a radical women's movement promoting independence from Dutch imperialism and women's suffrage called *Isteri Sedar* ("Conscious Women") formed in the 1930s, inspiring another group of elite women activists in neighboring colonial

Malaysia, called *Angkatan Wanita Sedar* or "Generation of Conscious Women," to form a resistance to British occupation (Aljunied 2013).

WOMEN AS VOTERS

As the Indonesian and Malaysian examples illustrate, women were often vital members of their countries' independence movements, which frequently formed the foundation for postcolonial governments and opened some important pathways for women's political participation in the modern era. For instance, women were able to join the preindependence parties of the Indian National Congress (1885) and Muslim League (1906), and these women sometimes took on political roles after Pakistan and India became independent. Similarly, in the Philippines, during the 350-year period of Spanish colonialism, several women rose to prominence as anticolonial revolutionaries by leading political movements and even armed struggles against Spanish forces, including Gabriela Silang, Melchora Aquino, and Teresa Magbanua (Rallonza 2009). Then, after Spain ceded colonial control of the Philippines to the United States in 1898, Filipino women organized a large political movement calling for democracy, independence, and the right to vote. They succeeded in winning women's suffrage in 1937, though the Philippines did not become formally independent until 1946 (Rallonza 2009).

Women's movements in Sri Lanka, India, and Burma (now Myanmar) also succeeded in mobilizing for and achieving the right to vote in elections while still under British occupation. In the case of Sri Lanka, this victory required a persistent suffrage movement that began in 1919, only to finally succeed in 1931 (deAlwis and Kodikara 2019). Though Indian and Burmese women secured the right to vote in the 1920s, colonial policy in Burma dictated that women could not run for political office. In response to these restrictions, the nationalist Burmese Women's Association protested in 1927, forcing the colonial government to change this policy and making it possible for Hnin Mya to become the first woman elected to the Burmese Legislative Council in 1929 (Minoletti 2019).

Colonial policies, thus, not only mediated the degree to which women could engage in formal politics prior to their independence but also helped shape the type of political systems that emerged in their wake. Although most countries in the region eventually became republics, the years in which women gained the right to vote or to hold political office vary (see table 7.1). In most cases, women were only granted suffrage in the first

Table 7.1   Women's Right to Suffrage in South and Southeast Asia

Country	Year Women Achieved Suffrage Rights
South Asia	
Afghanistan	1964
Bangladesh	1972
Bhutan	1953
India	1950
Maldives	1932
Myanmar	1947
Nepal	1951
Pakistan	1947
Sri Lanka	1931
Southeast Asia	
Brunei	1983
Cambodia	1953
Timor-Leste	2002
Indonesia	1945
Laos	1953
Malaysia	1957
Philippines	1937
Singapore	1947
Thailand	1932
Vietnam	1946

Source: IPU Parline (2021).

postindependence constitutions—typically in the 1930s–1950s—and often in partial recognition of their contributions to nationalist struggles. In both Indonesia and Malaysia, for example, women gained suffrage at the time of independence, in 1945 and 1957, respectively, due in part to their involvement in anticolonial political movements (Mustafa 1999; Graham Davies 2005). However, in other cases, it was decades after formal independence that countries established their own democratic governments and enshrined the right to vote for women. The Maldives, for instance, only became an independent republic in 1968, over thirty years after independence.

In many cases, a long history of colonial exploitation followed by U.S. and Soviet meddling in the region throughout the Cold War era left behind scars of violence, institutional dysfunction, and underdevelopment that have taken decades to heal. While every country in South and Southeast Asia has at least once held an election at some point in its history, many have been plagued by unstable regimes. Some are more appropriately categorized as authoritarian governments rather than democracies, and others have simply not had the opportunity to develop democratic norms and well-functioning electoral institutions. The island nation of Timor-Leste (formerly East Timor), for example, only became independent in 2002— after 300 years of colonial rule by Portugal and another quarter century of military occupation by Indonesia. Many other countries in the region, including Thailand, Myanmar, Pakistan, Afghanistan, Indonesia, and Malaysia, have suffered decades of political turmoil, the roots of which can usually be traced to the legacy of colonialism, including frequent regime changes as well as internal and external military conflicts. This political instability and the long shadow of colonialism have had implications for women's participation in formal politics in many countries throughout South and Southeast Asia.

Voting is the most fundamental form of political participation in democracies, but even this basic right for women in South and Southeast Asia has been influenced by the history of colonialism. The opportunities for women's political participation in the modern era, including when and how women achieved the right to vote, often heavily depend on the government systems that were established in the postcolonial era and the relative stability (or lack thereof) of these regimes. Women commonly gained the right to vote when their countries became independent, but in some cases, this right was revoked, discouraged, or made ineffectual by subsequent regimes, even though it often continued to exist on paper. In Indonesia, for example, the postcolonial government established in 1946 only lasted twenty years before it was overthrown by General Suharto in a violent **coup**, who then ruled as an authoritarian leader until 1998 (Graham Davies 2005). During this time the militaristic Suharto regime largely barred women from political participation and publicly promoted the idea that women's primary role in society was in the household as wives and mothers rather than in politics (Graham Davies 2005). Similarly, after gaining independence in 1948, Myanmar underwent fifty years of insular military rule that effectively barred women from formal politics until 2011 (Minoletti 2019).

Myanmar is not the only case in which women enjoyed periods of universal suffrage only to have it stripped away by foreign powers or due to internal regime changes. For instance, Afghanistan's King Amanullah supported women's suffrage in 1919 and extended several political and social rights to women during his reign (Amnesty International UK 2022). However, King Amanullah was driven from power in 1929, and most of the political rights for women were overturned. The right to vote was only regranted to women in 1964. After the country was entangled in the U.S.-supported fight against the Soviets, the subsequent **Taliban** government again prevented women's access to the public sphere in 1994, and voting was prohibited until 2004 (Nijat and Murtazashvili 2015).

Similarly, in Thailand, women were legally guaranteed the right to vote in village elections in 1897, making it the second country in the entire world to grant universal women's suffrage (Bowie 2010). After a constitutional monarchy was installed in 1932, women also gained the right to vote in national elections (Bowie 2010). However, the next eighty years were so politically tumultuous that women had little opportunity to establish their role in any given regime before it changed hands. More than twenty military coup attempts have occurred in Thailand since 1932, the most recent being in 2014, and the country has had seventeen different constitutions throughout that period.

Women's Political Engagement

Still, the hard-fought battles for political independence and women's suffrage may have helped to create a strong tradition of women's political participation in the region, even in the face of political turmoil. In contrast to many non-Western regions of the world, such as Latin America and sub-Saharan Africa, where women typically engage in formal political activities less than men, this is not the case in Southeast Asia (Liu 2020). Not only do women and men vote at roughly equal rates throughout this region, but in some instances, they also participate more than men. For example, in the Philippines, women turned out to vote in higher numbers than men in twenty out of twenty-six elections between the 1940s and 1970s (Rallonza 2009). Likewise, in Sri Lanka, a majority of registered voters are women, a fact that has helped women's movements in the country successfully demand governmental reforms to bring political attention to women's issues (Kamdar 2020).

In most South Asian countries, a gender gap in voting persists, suggesting that these examples from Southeast Asia are indeed exceptions to the general rule. In Afghanistan, for example, women voters face a disproportionate threat of violence for engaging in politics and therefore make up only 34 percent of the registered voters (Ahmadi 2018). In Pakistan's 2018 elections, eleven million more men voted than women (Cheema et al. 2019). Interestingly, while gender gaps in voting around the world tend to manifest because women in rural areas of those countries vote at lower rates than men, in Pakistan, this gender gap was found to be larger in urban areas—despite some rural women being culturally barred from voting (Cheema et al. 2019). At the same time, a strong women's movement in Pakistan is encouraging gender justice and pushing against some of the cultural norms regarding women's participation in public life, including voting (Chughtai 2020; Alam 2021). Similarly, in India, efforts to reduce the gender gap in voting have successfully reduced this participation gap to less than 2 percent over the past decade.

One other important case in the region bears mentioning: Brunei Darussalam. Brunei, which makes up a small portion of the larger island of Borneo, is a sultanate, meaning it is ruled by a hereditary monarch, and thus neither men nor women have any rights to democratic political representation. Though Brunei still has a parliament that advises the sultan, its members are appointed rather than elected (True et al. 2014). As of 2022, women made up only 9.1 percent of the appointed parliament (IPU Parline 2022). This low level of women's representation in the sultanate and a lack of political rights for women (and men) make it the least inclusive government in Southeast Asia.

WOMEN AS MEMBERS OF PARLIAMENT

As the case of Brunei suggests, there is considerable variation in South and Southeast when it comes to the levels of women's political representation in local and national legislatures (see table 7.2), depending not only on the type of government in place but also the political stability of their respective regimes. For instance, persistent and ongoing political instability in Thailand, Myanmar, and Malaysia has limited the ability of women to gain significant levels of representation in their parliaments. Thai women have participated in popular movements to protest particularly

Table 7.2   Current Number of Women in Parliament in the Lower House for Each Country

Country	Number of Women in Lower House of Parliament (as of 2022)	Total Seats	Percent of Seats Held by Women (%)
Afghanistan	–	–	–
Bangladesh	73	350	20.9
Bhutan	8	46	17.4
India	81	541	14.9
Maldives	4	84	4.8
Myanmar	–	–	–
Nepal	91	271	33.6
Pakistan	70	342	20.5
Sri Lanka	12	225	5.3
Brunei	3	33	9.1
Cambodia	26	125	20.8
East Timor	26	65	40.0
Indonesia	126	575	21.9
Laos	36	164	22.0
Malaysia	33	220	15.0
Philippines	85	311	27.3
Singapore	30	103	29.1
Thailand	77	489	15.8
Vietnam	151	499	30.3

Source: IPU Parline (2022).

repressive regimes, such as the Black May protests in 1992, and have occasionally run for elected political office. Yet, their presence in parliament remains negligible (Neher 1995). Though the first woman was elected to the Thai parliament in 1949 and five more were elected in the 1950s (Iwanaga and Suriyamongkol 2008), women still account for only 15.8 percent of parliament as of 2022. Similarly, although the 2015 elections tripled the number of women in Myanmar's parliament, their presence in elected political office was still low, accounting for only 15.3 percent of parliamentarians that year. Women in Malaysia also remain highly underrepresented in national government, accounting for only 5 percent of parliament on average in the 1980s and 1990s (Mustafa 1999). Though these numbers have notably improved more recently, women continue to make up only a small portion of Malaysia's national government, accounting for less than 15 percent of parliament as of 2022.

In contrast, despite contending with some history of political turmoil, including a two-decade-long autocratic regime under Ferdinand Marcos, the Philippines stands out as being one of the most equal countries in the region when it comes to gender parity in politics. Women have a long history of political organizing in the Philippines, and the country is now among the best in the world when it comes to women's political representation (Labonne, Parsa, and Querubin 2019). Although women comprised only 9 percent of the national legislature during the Marcos dictatorship, women's organizations were instrumental in the success of the People Power movement, which nonviolently overthrew the Marcos regime and restored a democratic system of government in 1986 (Labonne, Parsa, and Querubin 2019). Women's engagement in this political movement helped them gain more formal representation in parliament in the post-Marcos era. Filipino women now hold nearly 30 percent of seats in the national legislature, and more than 20 percent of municipalities are headed by women in mayoral roles (Labonne, Parsa, and Querubin 2019). Even in regard to top political leadership positions such as cabinet members, parliamentary committee chairs, and Supreme Court justices, the Philippines is a regional leader (Joshi and Goehrung 2018).

As a final example of the ways in which history has profoundly influenced the current status of women in parliaments throughout the region, it is useful to look at Vietnam, Laos, and Cambodia, a unique set of countries due to the role of communism. All three were French colonies that after regaining their independence briefly became constitutional monarchies. However, in the 1960s, communist factions developed and quickly grew with the encouragement of Mao Zedong's Chinese communist government. With Chinese support in the form of training and supplies, Marxist insurgent groups successfully overthrew the postcolonial governments of all three countries in the 1970s and established one-party socialist states. In Vietnam and Cambodia, in particular, the transition to a socialist government was long and bloody, resulting in the deaths of tens of thousands of citizens. In Cambodia, the Marxist rebel group known as the

Khmer Rouge murdered thousands of its own citizens in an effort to wipe out political opposition (Jacobsen 2008). In Vietnam, U.S. forces intervened to support South Vietnam's democratic government, drawing out a conflict with the Northern Vietnamese communist government for years before the United States admitted defeat and a socialist state was established.

In all three of these cases, the history of socialism has important implications for women's representation. Women's groups were actively involved in Marxist insurgencies, and the ideology of these groups supported the basic premise of gender equality. As a result, these newly installed socialist governments attempted to institutionalize some aspects of gender parity by creating a women's branch of the state's political party and encouraging equal participation in the economy, military, and government. However, the results did not always live up to the rhetoric of gender equality in practice (Hoang 2020). Women still account for less than 30 percent of parliament in all three countries, and though their participation in the labor force is high and nearly equal to that of men, socially women are still far from equal in practice (True et al. 2014). However, there is some evidence that women's political participation in Laos and Vietnam may be improving. In 2011, the People's Revolutionary Party, the only political party allowed in Laos, established a goal of having 30 percent women's representation in its national parliament (True et al. 2014). And in 2015, Vietnam's single national party established a 35 percent candidate quota for women (Hughes et al. 2019).

Though the above examples illustrate the weight of history in shaping women's current political representation levels, there are other countries that, like Vietnam, have attempted to pave a new path forward by introducing gender quotas into their national parliaments to promote greater equity in representation. In South Asia, all the countries have legislated gender quotas at a subnational or national level, except for Bhutan, the Maldives, and Myanmar. Four of the five highest-ranked countries in Southeast Asia with regard to women's representation (the Philippines, Timor-Leste, Laos, and Vietnam) all have quota systems that guarantee representation of women in parliament (Loring 2018). These quotas are typically attributed with increasing women's legislative participation over time (figure 7.1). Some of the countries establishing gender quotas are newly established democracies and thus have written these provisions into their constitutions. For example, after gaining independence in 2002, Timor-Leste's newly drafted constitution included many important provisions

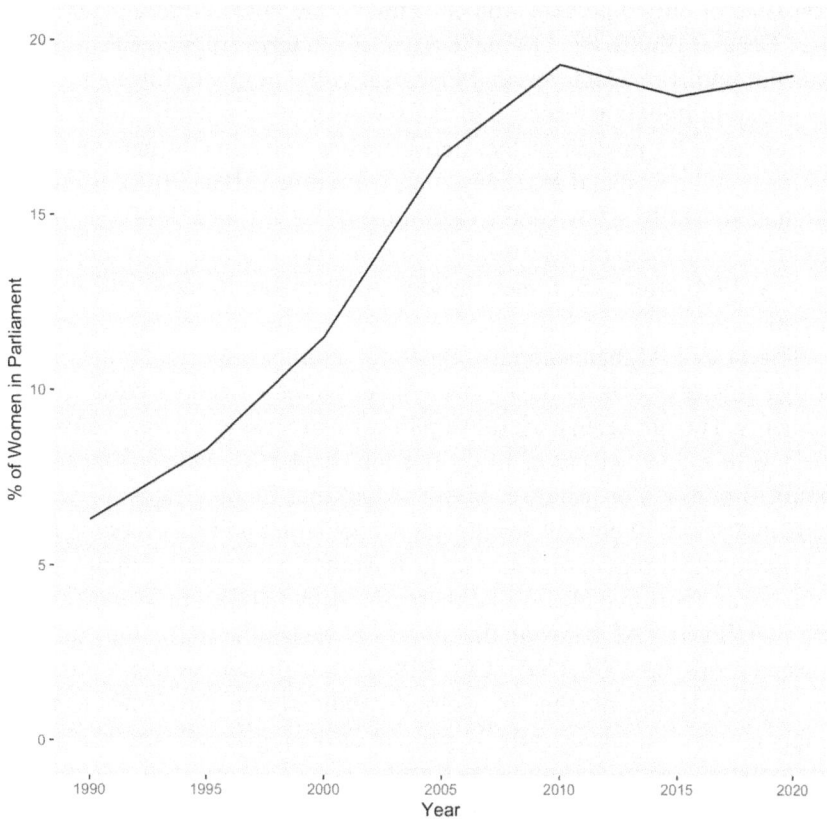

Figure 7.1 Percentage of Women in Parliament: Regional Average over Time (Inter-Parliamentary Union: Parline database on national parliaments, July 31, 2021).

supporting gender equality and encouraging women's representation in politics, including gender quotas mandating that one in four candidates for political office be women (Mulder 2019). As a result, Timor-Leste has the highest rate of women's representation in the region and is ranked fifteenth in the world as of 2022 with 40 percent of its parliament members being women (IPU Parline 2022).

In other cases, moments of political disruption have created opportunities for gender quotas or similar provisions to be introduced at the national level. For instance, almost half of Pakistan's existence has been under military rule, and throughout the twentieth century, its national legislature consisted of only 3 percent women. Though the twice-elected prime minister Benazir Bhutto tried to make advances in terms of women's rights, it was not until President Pervez Musharraf came to power through a military coup in 1999 that reserved seats for women were successfully instated, setting aside 33 percent of local government seats and 17 percent of the national and provincial assembly seats for women (Bari 2010). Similarly, Afghanistan only established a requirement that 27 percent of seats in the national parliament be reserved for women when drafting its new constitution in 2004, after U.S. forces invaded Afghanistan to topple the Taliban regime.

The case of Afghanistan also illustrates another important point, which is that gender quotas alone are not a silver bullet for gender parity in parliaments. Though often a useful step toward increasing women's presence, even with quotas in place, other barriers hold back women's access to political power. For instance, both the fact that literacy rates for women remain around 30 percent for the adult population and that there is a disproportionate threat of violence against women who exercise their right to vote or run for office means that there are many barriers to women engaging in politics in Afghanistan that quotas alone cannot overcome (Ballington and Dahlerup 2006; UNESCO 2018). Although there were, promisingly, an unprecedented number of women candidates in the 2018 elections, Afghan women made up only 34 percent of the registered voters and have yet to exceed the minimum quota threshold of 27 percent representation in parliament (Ahmadi 2018). It remains to be seen what the future holds for Afghan women in politics after the American troop withdrawal in 2021.

As the above examples suggest, not all quota systems are the same, and not all are equally as effective. The strongest form of gender quotas are reserved seats, which mandate a specific percentage of seats in parliament that must be filled by women. While these quotas are effective at maintaining a minimum level of women in parliament, if systemic efforts are not made to support gender equality, this minimum level also often becomes the ceiling. A weaker form of quota is a legislative candidate quota, which requires that political parties must put forth a minimum number of women candidates. This is effective at getting women on the ballot but does not always mean that women are elected in higher numbers. In 2003, Indonesia adopted a gender quota mandating that 30 percent of political candidates must be women, which almost immediately increased women's presence in the national parliament to 18 percent (Rhoads 2012). However, subsequent elections in Indonesia have not seen the percent of women parliamentarians increase beyond this point, and women's representation in local governments remains considerably lower, suggesting that there is still much work to be done to improve gender parity in Indonesian politics (Rhoads 2012).

In other cases, gender quotas have helped spark greater levels of women's representation that have exceeded the minimum threshold outlined in the law. For example, though Bangladesh has a 14 percent quota for women, the current parliament in Bangladesh is composed of 20.9 percent women (Paasilinna 2016). In Nepal, as well, after passing a 30 percent candidate quota in 2007, the 2008 Constituent Assembly exceeded this minimum by electing women to 33 percent of the total seats (Yadav 2018). Importantly, in the case of Nepal, these gender quotas were supported by a cultural change, as Nepalese women were instrumental in the armed conflict against a repressive state from 1996 to 2006, which opened the door for more formal public roles in elected office (Gautam, Banskota, and Manchanda 2011). However, the Constituent Assembly was dissolved, and in the 2013 and 2017 elections, the number of officeholding women dropped with the change in electoral system (Uprety 2018).

Table 7.3 outlines the different quota systems adopted in South and Southeast Asia and can usefully be compared to the previous table depicting the current percent of women in politics to help get a sense of how effective these systems have been. Though some countries, like the Philippines, have successfully integrated a considerable number of women into parliament even without a national gender quota, many countries in the region have only seen notable increases in women's representation since adopting some form of gender quota. Also, it is worth noting that some countries have adopted gender quotas at the local level but not yet the national level with mixed effects. For instance, Indian law mandates that one-third of all councils at the village, subdistrict, and district levels be filled by women, which has ensured that women have considerable influence in local politics (Jensenius 2019). Yet, in 2019, less than 15 percent of national parliamentary candidates were women, despite a record number of women coming to the polls in this election.

Women as Leaders

Though South and Southeast Asia have a mixed record of women's representation in national parliaments, this region stands out for having a remarkably high number of women in executive office compared to most

Table 7.3   Regional Gender Quota Adoption

Country	Year Current National Gender Quota Adopted	Type of Quota	Percent Mandated by Quota (%)
South Asia			
Afghanistan	2004	Reserved seats	27
Bangladesh	2004	Reserved seats	13
Bhutan	NA	None	NA
India	NA	Reserved seats only at subnational level	33
Maldives	NA	None	NA
Myanmar	NA	None	NA
Nepal	2007	Candidate	30
Pakistan	2002	Reserved seats	17.5
Sri Lanka	NA	Reserved seats only at subnational level	25
Southeast Asia			
Brunei	NA	None	NA
Cambodia	NA	None	NA
East Timor	2011	Candidate	30
Indonesia	2003	Candidate	30
Laos	2011	Party quota	30
Malaysia	NA	Voluntary party quota*	30
Philippines	NA	Voluntary party quota*	25–30
Singapore	NA	None	NA
Thailand	NA	Voluntary party quota*	30
Vietnam	2015	Candidate	35

* At least one major political party established voluntary gender quotas established in the country.

Source: Hughes et al. (2019).

other parts of the world. As table 7.4 illustrates, out of the nineteen countries in this region, eleven have had at least one woman leader in recent history (IPU Parline 2021). In total, South and Southeast Asia boast fifteen women heads of state in the last half century, many of whom have made history for their groundbreaking achievements. Perhaps most notably, Sirimavo Bandaranaike of Sri Lanka was the first elected woman head of government in the world. In 1994, her daughter, Chandrika Kumaratunga, also became both prime minister and president (Kodikara 2009).

Pakistan's Benazir Bhutto made global headlines when she became the first Muslim women to hold executive office in 1988. This said, the **symbolic representation** of women politicians has existed since Pakistan's 1947 independence from the British. Soon afterward, Fatima Jinnah, the sister of the country's founder, ran for president in 1965 with the support of the most influential Islamic party, and though she did not ultimately become president, she won the popular vote and greatly encouraged women's political participation in subsequent elections (Ali 2000). The example of Pakistani prime minister Benazir Bhutto, the daughter of former prime minister Zulfikar Ali Bhutto, is a parallel for dynastic politics in Bangladesh, which gained independence from Pakistan in 1971 after a devastating War of Liberation. Since the country turned toward democracy in 1990, both Sheikh Hasina Wazed, the daughter of Bangladesh's first president, and Begum Khaleda Zia, the wife of a former Bangladeshi president, have alternated holding the role of prime minister in the country (Ahmed 2013). Dynastic politics also played a role in the success of Indian National Congress president Sonia Gandhi, who was the wife of former prime minister Rajiv Gandhi, and for the twice-elected prime minister Indira Gandhi, who was the daughter of former prime minister Jawaharlal Nehru.

As these examples illustrate, dynastic ties are an important aspect of politics in South and Southeast Asia and have frequently been a factor in influencing the rise of women to positions of executive leadership. This does not undermine the significant achievements of these individual women leaders and their remarkable political skills, but it is important for explaining the fact that this region has boasted so many women in the executive role, even though women's political representation more broadly has been relatively modest and traditional gender roles in much of the region remain quite strong. In many cases these dynastic women leaders came to power during times of political upheaval and violence, when their countries were trying to recover from corrupt or violent male-led regimes. At such times,

Table 7.4   Women Heads of State and Government in South and Southeast Asia

Country	Function	Name	Period
Bangladesh	Prime minister	Khaleda Zia	1991–1996
			2001–2006
		Sheikh Hasina	1996–2001
			2009–present
India	Prime minister	Indira Gandhi	1966–1977
			1980–1984
	President	Pratibha Patil	2007–2012
	President	Droupadi Murmu	2022–present
Indonesia	President	Megawati Sukarnoputri	2001–2004
Myanmar	State counselor	Aung San Suu Kyi	2016–2021
Nepal	President	Bidhya Devi Bhandari	2015–present
Pakistan	Prime minister	Benazir Bhutto	1988–1990
			1993–1996
Philippines	President	Corazon Aquino	1986–1992
		Gloria Macapagal Arroyo	2001–2010
Singapore	President	Halimah Yacob	2017–present
Sri Lanka	Prime minister	Sirimavo Bandaranaike	1960–1965
			1970–1977
			1994–2000
		Chandrika Kumaratunga	1994–1994
	President	Chandrika Kumaratunga	1994–2005
Thailand	Prime minister	Yingluck Shinawatra	2011–2014
Vietnam	Acting president	Dang Thi Ngoc Thinh	2018–2018

Sources: Cole (2018); Montecinos (2017); Rodan (2018); Skard (2015); Farida Jalalzai (private data collection).

SIRIMAVO RATWATTE DIAS BANDARANAIKE

Sirimavo Ratwatte Dias Bandaranaike (1916–2000) was the first woman prime minister of Sri Lanka (formally Ceylon) and, notably, the world. Upon her 1960 election, she became politically involved in this role and numerous others, including minister of defense and minister of foreign affairs, planning, economic affairs, and plan implementation. Supported by the Sri Lanka Freedom Party, she became party leader after her husband, S. W. R. D. Bandaranaike, then prime minister, was assassinated in 1959. Encouraged by her support of her husband's politics, she was elected as prime minister in the general elections the following year, when the party won 75 out of 151 House of Representative seats. Bandaranaike pro-

Sirimavo Bandaranaike (1916–2000) of Sri Lanka, the first elected woman prime minister of Sri Lanka and the world. (Embassy of Sri Lanka)

moted socialist economic policies, encouraged Buddhism and the Sinhalese language (instead of colonial-era mandated English), and maintained a foreign policy of neutrality that would continue after her administration. Her politics became more radical in 1970; she nationalized industries, further reduced economic inequality through socialist policies, and turned the former Ceylon into a republic, which we now know as Sri Lanka. In 1977, she lost her seat as prime minister due to ethnic conflict and some being unhappy with her economic efforts. After running unsuccessfully for president in 1988, in 1989, she became opposition leader. Encouraged by her mother's political activeness, her daughter, Chandrika Bandaranaike Kumaratunga, became prime minister in 1994 (Kinnear 2011).

traditional views on gender may actually help women politicians, as voters may see them as more honest, religious, moral, or compassionate than men (Derichs, Fleschenberg, and Hüstebeck 2006). In addition, ties to prominent politicians who were widely revered or seen as heroes of the nation's past may help imbue their women relatives with similar feelings of reverence and respect.

For example, the first woman president of the Philippines, Corazon Aquino, was elected immediately after the overthrow of Ferdinand Marcos, a violent and repressive dictator who was also responsible for assassinating her husband, Ninoy Aquino. Similarly, Aung San Suu Kyi became a symbol of the 1988 revolution not only because she helped found a political party, the National League for Democracy (NLD), to challenge the military government but also because she had blood ties to a popular founding hero of Myanmar. Though Aung San Suu Kyi faced years of house arrest, the NLD eventually prevailed, which led to the military government stepping down in 2011 and partially democratizing the country. Aung San Suu Kyi was viewed as such a threat to the military government that Myanmar's constitution explicitly prohibits her from becoming president. However, in 2015, she became the state counselor, which is one of the highest political offices in the country (Minoletti 2019).

Not all women leaders in South and Southeast Asia have dynastic ties, however. Some women in India, like Sushma Swaraj, who has held multiple high governmental positions, simply rose through party hierarchy over a long and devoted political career that began in the 1970s (Jensenius 2019). In another example, Jayaram Jayalalithaa, who served as chief minister for the South Indian state of Tamil Nadu, first gained fame as a movie star in over a hundred movies before she turned to politics and took over leadership of the All India Anna Dravida Munnetra Kazhagam (AIADMK) party, founded by her costar (Keating 2001). The current president of Nepal, Bidya Devi Bhandari, also boasts no notable dynastic ties and yet became the first woman in her country's history to hold this executive leadership position (Ostermann 2017).

Beyond the highly prominent roles of president and prime minister, cabinet minister is another important executive leadership role to examine to get a more complete sense of the status of women in politics in this region. Though there has been less scholarly attention paid to the subject of women cabinet members in South and Southeast Asia, a few general trends are worth noting. First, women generally make up only a small

MARIA CORAZON SUMULONG COJUANGCO AQUINO

Maria Corazon Sumulong Cojuangco Aquino (1933–2009), more commonly referred to as Corazon or simply "Cory," was the first woman president of the Philippines. She is most renowned for her leadership of the 1986 People Power Revolution, a massive nonviolent civil disobedience campaign that ended the twenty-one-year dictatorship of Ferdinand Marcos. Prior to her presidency, Aquino had never held elected office. Her entry into the political sphere began when her husband, Senator Benigno "Ninoy" Aquino Jr., was assassinated for his outspoken criticism of the Marcos regime. In the wake of her husband's assassination, Corazon Aquino became a symbol of the mounting opposition to his dictatorship. Sensing his hold on the country was slipping, Marcos declared a snap election would be held in 1986 as a gambit to reclaim his legitimacy as a leader. Corazon Aquino ran against him with widespread support. Though Marcos was proclaimed the winner, few believed that the electoral process or outcome were legitimate.

Riding the wave of popular support for her campaign and growing opposition to the Marcos dictatorship, Corazon Aquino called upon the Filipino people to wage a nonviolent protest movement challenging the results of the election. Over two million people assembled in the country's capital, Manila, for three days, demanding that Marcos step down. This massive show of support prompted the national military, which had become Marcos's primary source of power, to lay down their arms. Marcos was forced to flee the country, and Corazon Aquino was sworn in as president the same day.

portion of cabinet members in the region overall, which suggests that there is still a considerable amount of progress to be made in terms of achieving true gender equality in political representation. Indonesia, the Philippines, India, and the Maldives all stand out for comparatively having the most women cabinet ministers than other countries of the region (Joshi and Goehrung 2018). In contrast, Pakistan, Bangladesh, and Malaysia have had the lowest number of women cabinet ministers in the region (Joshi and Goehrung 2018). Despite these low numbers, women in South Asia do occupy a number of positions in the areas of health, development, and social welfare (Fleschenberg 2011). Some exceptions in Pakistan include notable women ministers like the recent foreign minister Hina Rabbani Khar and the federal minister of human rights Shireen Mazari. This said, most countries fall somewhere in between with a few cabinet ministers in recent history but at a modest level.

Barriers to Political Parity

While women from South and Southeast Asia have set a number of precedents for women in executive roles, these gains do not usually translate into similar levels of participation at other levels of political decision-making (Fleschenberg 2011). Like much of the world, despite regional increases in terms of women's political participation, considerable barriers to parity remain. Scholars of gender and politics have focused a considerable amount of energy on understanding these participation challenges. Some of these barriers are near universal, inhibiting women from successfully running for and winning elected office to some degree in nearly every country in the world. Other barriers are more context specific.

In this section, we review some of the most significant barriers to gender parity in South and Southeast Asia specifically, though many of these are also relevant to other regions of the world. A useful way of thinking about the barriers to gender parity in politics is by examining women's political representation as a process in which there must be both a supply of and demand for women candidates (Norris and Lovenduski 1995).

Having a supply of such candidates means having qualified and willing women with the financial, social, and political support necessary to run for and win political office or otherwise meaningfully engage in politics. At the most basic level, this means ensuring that women and girls are educated at the same level of boys and men and that they have equal employment opportunities. In many countries throughout South and Southeast Asia, as well as other parts of the world, girls often face more barriers to education and to meaningful careers. These are often due to social and cultural factors. For instance, traditional gender norms frequently mean that girls are expected to help more with household chores or caring for younger siblings, often at the expense of attending school (Milazzo and Goldenstein 2019). Similarly, if women and girls are primarily conceived of or valued as wives and mothers, parents may invest less in their daughters' education because, unlike for boys, they may view education as being less important for their futures (Rahayu and Ikayanti 2014). Though educational attainment gaps in South and Southeast Asia have narrowed dramatically in the last several decades, surveys indicate that higher education may still be valued less for women and girls on average. In representative surveys conducted from 2010 to 2014 across eight countries in the South and Southeast Asian region, a third of respondents on average agreed or strongly agreed that university education is more important for a boy than for a girl (Inglehart et al. 2014).

Without equal educational and employment opportunities, women and girls may find it more difficult to gain meaningful work experience, which usually makes it more difficult to successfully run for political office without kinship ties. Like other jobs, candidates for elected office typically need prior experience to convince voters they are qualified. The same types of gender norms that may limit educational attainment for women and girls often prevent women from pursuing political careers. While women's education is important for a country like Bhutan, a lack of education itself is not a barrier in the context of Myanmar (Minoletti 2019). Women in South and Southeast Asia have lower labor force participation rates than men, tend to be disproportionately limited to lower-paid and lower-prestige careers, and in several countries paternalistic policies attempting to protect women from more dangerous but typically higher paid work environments directly exclude women from some occupations (Milazzo and Goldstein 2019; Strachan, Adikaram, and Kailasapathy 2015). Similarly, social and cultural attitudes about men being breadwinners may limit opportunities for women. In a survey on attitudes in eight South and Southeast Asian countries, only 28 percent of respondents disagreed with the belief that when jobs are scarce, men should have more right to a job than women (Inglehart et al. 2014). This said, the newest wave of women's movements in the region is helping to combat these beliefs and to create more space for women and marginalized groups in the public sphere (Nazneen, Hossain, and Chopra 2019; Choi 2019; Alam 2021).

While the history of women chief executives and activists in South and Southeast Asia is clear evidence that women can achieve the highest political offices, evidence suggests that due to patriarchal attitudes, a pervasive belief that men are somehow naturally better political leaders remains. In surveys of social attitudes, more than 50 percent of respondents in all South and Southeast Asian countries surveyed, with the exception of Singapore, agreed or strongly agreed with the statement that men make better political leaders than women (Inglehart et al. 2014). Of the eight countries in the region that were asked this question, the most extreme gender bias was in Pakistan, where 72 percent of respondents agreed that men make better political leaders than women, while Singapore was the only country in the region where a minority of 45.6 percent felt this way (Inglehart et al. 2014). Although this belief is unsubstantiated by evidence, it remains prevalent.

The strength of such gendered beliefs in shaping political representation should not be underestimated. Several studies show that women and girls tend to view themselves as less qualified for political office than their male counterparts and only run for office after receiving encouragement from their family or friends (Schwindt-Bayer 2011; Lawless and Fox 2010). This may be due to the repeated social messaging that politics is culturally seen as men's work and that leadership is a masculine quality. It may also be due to religious beliefs that in some cases enshrine gendered hierarchies in which women must be subservient to men and consigned to private life—emphasizing their roles as wives and mothers. For example, culturally speaking, women in the northern states of both India and Pakistan generally have less autonomy when it comes to political decision-making or movement than their South Indian counterparts (Jejeebhoy and Sathar 2001). Similarly, in Myanmar, beliefs rooted in Buddhist traditions have often meant that women are relegated to support roles in politics rather than becoming political leaders themselves (Loring 2018). In the Philippines, as well as other countries in the region, traditional family structures place men as the head of the household and a notable portion of women in parliament in the Philippines were elected only after their male relatives' term limits expired. As a result, many women are viewed (rightly or not) as stand-ins for men rather than as independent representatives (Choi 2019).

Given such deeply rooted social and cultural beliefs that view women as less equipped for political leadership than men and the structural discrimination against women in education, employment, and politics, to increase women's representation, it is often necessary to adopt policies that explicitly support women's entry into political office. As previously noted, gender quotas are often assumed to be one of the most effective ways of helping to facilitate the entry of more women into politics; however, due to the complex political environments found around the world, quotas are not always impactful and depend on institutional conditions, among other factors (Krook 2010; Dahlerup 2013). A motivation behind gender quota advocacy is the idea that in the long run they will encourage shifts in social and cultural attitudes toward women in politics and that the increased presence of women in legislative bodies will result in more policies supporting gender equality. Though the substantive outcomes of gender quotas are debated, there is some evidence that they are effective in creating these changes. In India, for example, areas where local-level village council gender quotas were introduced saw a greater increase in education levels for girls, increased entrepreneurship of women, increased belief among girls that they could hold political office, and shifts in gender norms such that adolescent girls were less likely to be engaged in household chores compared to similar localities that had not adopted gender quotas (Beaman et al. 2012; Clayton 2018; Ghani, Kerr, and O'Connell 2014).

Financial support by political parties and institutional support for women candidates once they are elected to parliament are also key issues hindering the success of women's campaigns and political careers. In South and Southeast Asia, political pathways continue to largely be limited to women from elite families who have either sufficient wealth to fund their campaigns, politically connected families, or both (Choi 2019; Joshi and Och 2014). Even after entering politics, many women face substantial barriers to successful political careers. The threat of political violence and character assassination for women entering public life is also prevalent and can act as a deterrent in the region (UN Women 2014). Criminalization, corruption, and electoral fraud can challenge newcomers to politics, and there is often a lack of networking and caucus support for women politicians, as is the case in both Bangladesh and Afghanistan (Fleschenberg 2019; Ahmed 2013). Furthermore, legislative and institutional constraints can be unsupportive of women's pathways to politics. Clearly, there are many barriers to political parity for both women in local and national elected offices. This said, recent trends positively indicate that women's political participation at various levels of government is increasingly being supported. We now turn to some suggestions for achieving this political equality and gender parity in representation.

ACHIEVING POLITICAL PARITY—A WAY FORWARD FOR SOUTH AND SOUTHEAST ASIA

The unique legal, political, social, economic, and cultural contexts of South and Southeast Asian states mean that complex solutions are needed to achieve gender parity in politics that take these unique settings into account. Fortunately, norms surrounding women's political participation and leadership are generally improving in the region, and attitudes, especially toward women in local politics, are generally positive (Haug, Aasland, and Aasen 2020). Just like rights of equal access to education and employment are increasingly seen as important for all genders, communities are also questioning their associations between politics and masculinity. However, in terms of political parity, there are numerous constraints hindering women's participation in formal politics.

One way that women can be supported in these political roles is to ensure that women are both recruited and financially supported when they run for office. Therefore, to encourage women's political participation in the region, political parties should prioritize recruiting women candidates and consider the quality of their interparty democracy—perhaps by adopting party-level gender quotas. Another way that political parity can be achieved is by training women candidates so they build political knowledge and skills. Similarly, for many women, running for political office will only be viable if their campaigns are financially supported by political parties. Financial support at the party level can help with constituency building and ensure campaign success and survival. Once political parties show that this support exists, candidates may be encouraged that there is political mobility and the potential to move up the ranks in a party. This political will, however, is prefaced on social and cultural norms that are supportive of women's leadership and gender equality. In certain contexts, like Afghanistan, such support might need to come from influential religious leaders, who typically affiliate themselves with conservative parties (Fleschenberg 2019). Media support of women candidates can also help influence public opinion more positively (Wolbrecht and Campbell 2007). In other contexts, addressing issues of development, like combating illiteracy and poverty rates, can encourage the support of women to such leadership roles. A commitment to gender equality, though not necessarily related to levels of development, generally correlates with smaller gender gaps in politics (Inglehart and Norris 2003).

That said, while party support, financial support, and political skills are all important for women's political parity, some challenges to women's elected office roles come from voters. Voters need to be invested in seeing women candidates and women in officeholding positions. There are gendered differences in political participation and when it comes to support for political parties (Kittilson 2019). Though there is a dearth of research on women's voting behavior in South and Southeast Asia, globally speaking, women tend to vote less than men. This also speaks to the issue of political interests, which are important for political participation at all levels. Recent research supports the examination of electoral institutions and how these institutions play a role in narrowing the gender gap (Kittilson 2019). Clearly, the political participation of women in South and Southeast Asia is not monolithic, and more research is needed to fully explain the gender gaps. Likewise, although women in politics is gaining interest as a field of study, men's electoral behavior also remains understudied in the region and can shed more light on women in politics overall.

REFERENCES

Ahmadi, Belquis. 2018. "Afghan Women Defy Violence and Vote." United States Institute of Peace, November 6, 2018. https://www.usip.org/blog/2018/11/afghan-women-defy-violence-and-vote

Ahmed, Kamal Uddin. 2013. "Women and Politics in Bangladesh." In *Women's Political Participation and Representation in Asia: Obstacles and Challenges*, edited by Kazuki Iwanaga, 276–296. Copenhagen: NIAS Press.

Alam, Zainab. 2021. "Violence against Women in Politics: The Case of Pakistani Women's Activism." *Journal of Language Aggression and Conflict* 9 (1): 21–46. https://doi.org/10.1075/jlac.00052.ala

Ali, Shaheen Sardar. 2000. "Law, Islam and The Women's Movement in Pakistan." In *International Perspectives on Gender and Democratisation*, edited by Shirin M. Rai, 41–63. London: Palgrave Macmillan.

Aljunied, Syed Muhd Khairudin. 2013. "Against Multiple Hegemonies: Radical Malay Women in Colonial Malaya." *Journal of Social History* 47 (1): 153–175.

Alkire, Sabina, Mihika Chatterjee, Adriana Conconi, Suman Seth, and Ana Vaz. 2014. "Global Multidimensional Poverty Index 2014." https://ophi.org.uk/global-multidimensional-poverty-index-2014-8-page/

Altekar, Anant Sadashiv. 1956. *The Position of Women in Hindu Civilization, from Prehistoric Times to the Present Day*. Delhi: Motilal Banarsidass Publ.

Amirell, Stefan. 2015. "Female Rule in the Indian Ocean World (1300–1900)." *Journal of World History* 26 (3): 443–489.

Amnesty International UK. 2022. "Women in Afghanistan: The Back Story." *Amnesty International*, July 27, 2022. https://www.amnesty.org.uk/womens-rights-afghanistan-history

Ballington, Julie, and Drude Dahlerup. 2006. "Gender Quotas in Post-Conflict States: East Timor, Afghanistan and Iraq." In *Women, Quotas and Politics*, edited by Drude Dahlerup. New York: Routledge.

Bari, Farzana. 2010. "Women Parliamentarians: Challenging the Frontiers of Politics in Pakistan." *Gender, Technology and Development* 14 (3): 363–384.

Beaman, Lori, Esther Duflo, Rohini Pande, and Petia Topalova. 2012. "Female Leadership Raises Aspirations and Educational Attainment for Girls: A Policy Experiment in India." *Science* 335 (6068): 582–586.

Bowie, Katherine. 2010. "Women's Suffrage in Thailand: A Southeast Asian Historiographical Challenge." *Comparative Studies in Society and History* 52 (4): 708–741.

Cheema, Ali, Sarah Khan, Shandana Khan Mohmand, Anam Kuraishi, and Asad Liaqat. 2019. "Pakistan's Participation Puzzle: A Look at the Voting Gender Gap." United States Institute of Peace, July 18, 2019. https://www.usip.org/blog/2019/07/pakistans-participation-puzzle -look-voting-gender-gap

Chitnis, Varsha, and Danaya Wright. 2007. "Legacy of Colonialism: Law and Women's Rights in India." *Washington & Lee Law Review* 64: 1315.

Choi, Nankyung. 2019. "Women's Political Pathways in Southeast Asia." *International Feminist Journal of Politics* 21 (2): 224–248. https://doi.org/10.1080/14616742.2018.1523683

Chughtai, Alia. 2020. "Pakistan's Women's March: Shaking Patriarchy 'to Its Core.'" Al Jazeera, March 8, 2020. https://www.aljazeera.com /indepth/features/pakistan-women-march-shaking-patriarchy-core -200308095635489.html

Clayton, Amanda. 2018. "Do Gender Quotas Really Reduce Bias? Evidence from a Policy Experiment in Southern Africa." *Journal of Experimental Political Science* 5 (3): 182–194.

Cole, Brendan. 2018. "Who Is Dang Thi Ngoc Thinh? Vietnam's First Female President Takes Over after Tran Dai Quang Dies at 61." *Newsweek*, September 21, 2018. https://www.newsweek.com/who -dang-thi-ngoc-thinh-vietnams-first-female-president-takes-over -after-tran-1132304

Dahlerup, Drude, ed. 2013. *Women, Quotas and Politics*. New York: Routledge.

deAlwis, Malathi, and Chulani Kodikara. 2019. "Sri Lanka: Struggle for Franchise." In *The Palgrave Handbook of Women's Political Rights*, edited by Susan Franceschet, Mona Lena Krook, and Netina Tan, 349–362. London: Palgrave Macmillan.

Derichs, Claudia, Andrea Fleschenberg, and Momoyo Hüstebeck. 2006. "Gendering Moral Capital: Morality as a Political Asset and Strategy of Top Female Politicians in Asia." *Critical Asian Studies* 38 (3): 245–270.

Eichenwald, Kurt. 2016. "Right-Wing Extremists Are a Bigger Threat to America Than ISIS." *Newsweek*, February 4, 2016. http://www.newsweek.com/2016/02/12/right-wing-extremists-militants-bigger-threat-america-isis-jihadists-422743.html

Fleschenberg, Andrea. 2011. "Women in Executive Power: A Global Overview." In *Routledge Research in Comparative Politics*, edited by Gretchen Bauer and Manon Tremblay, 23–42. Florence: Routledge.

Fleschenberg, Andrea. 2019. "Afghanistan: Uphill Challenges for Women's Political Rights." In *The Palgrave Handbook of Women's Political Rights*, edited by Susan Franceschet, Mona Lena Krook, and Netina Tan, 185–199. London: Palgrave Macmillan.

Ganie, Zahied Rehman, and Shanti Dev Sisodia. 2020. "The Unsung Heroines of India's Freedom Struggle." *American International Journal of Social Science Research* 5 (2): 19–25.

Gautam, Shobha, Amrita Banskota, and Rita Manchanda. 2011. "Where There Are No Men: Women in the Maoist Insurgency in Nepal." In *Perspectives on Modern South Asia: A Reader in Culture, History, and Representation*, edited by Kamala Visweswaran, 340–348. Chichester, West Sussex, UK: Wiley-Blackwell.

Ghani, Ejaz, William R Kerr, and Stephen O'Connell. 2014. "Spatial Determinants of Entrepreneurship in India." *Regional Studies* 48 (6): 1071–1089.

Ghosh, Durba. 2006. *Sex and the Family in Colonial India: The Making of Empire*. Cambridge: Cambridge University Press.

Graham Davies, Sharyn. 2005. "Women in Politics in Indonesia in the Decade Post-Beijing." *International Social Science Journal* 57 (184): 231–242.

Haug, Marit, Aadne Aasland, and Berit Aasen. 2020. "Attitudes towards Women's Participation in Local Politics in South Asia." *Forum for Development Studies* 47 (1): 67–87. https://doi.org/10.1080/08039410.2019.1635525

Hoang, Lan Anh. 2020. "The Vietnam Women's Union and the Contradictions of a Socialist Gender Regime." *Asian Studies Review* 44 (2): 297–314.

Hughes, Melanie M., Pamela Paxton, Amanda B. Clayton, and Pär Zetterberg. 2019. "Global Gender Quota Adoption, Implementation, and Reform." *Comparative Politics* 51 (2): 219–238.

Hurley, Siobhan Lambert. 1998. "Out of India: The Journeys of the Begam of Bhopal, 1901–1930." *Women's Studies International Forum* 21 (3): 263–276. https://doi.org/10.1016/S0277-5395(98)00025-9

Inglehart, R., Christian Haerpfer, Alejandro Moreno, Christian Welzel, Kseniya Kizilova, Jaime Diez-Medrano, Marta Lagos, Pippa Norris, Eduard Ponarin, and Bi Puranen. 2014. *World Values Survey: Round Six—Country-Pooled Datafile.* Madrid: JD Systems Institute. https://www.worldvaluessurvey.org/WVSDocumentationWV6.jsp

Inglehart, Ronald, and Pippa Norris. 2003. *Rising Tide: Gender Equality and Cultural Change around the World.* Cambridge: Cambridge University Press.

IPU (Inter-Parliamentary Union) Parline. 2021. "Historical Data on Women in National Parliaments." https://data.ipu.org/historical-women

IPU Parline. 2022. "Monthly Ranking of Women in National Parliaments as of 1st June 2022." https://data.ipu.org/women-ranking?month=9 &year=2022

Iwanaga, Kazuki, and Marjorie Suriyamongkol. 2008. *Women and Politics in Thailand: Continuity and Change.* Copenhagen: NIAS Press.

Jacobsen, Trudy. 2008. "Beyond Apsara: Women, Tradition and Trajectories." In *Women's Political Participation and Representation in Asia: Obstacles and Challenges,* edited by Kazuki Iwanaga, 149–172. Copenhagen: NIAS Press.

Jayathilake, A. M. K. H. K. 2016. "Women, Politics and Poison: A Comparison of the Julio-Claudian Empire and the Anuradhapura and Polonnaruwa Periods of Sri Lanka." In *Proceedings of the International Conference on the Humanities and the Social Sciences (ICHSS),* 210–214. Peradeniya, Sri Lanka: University of Peradeniya.

Jayawardena, Kumari. 2016. *Feminism and Nationalism in the Third World.* London: Verso Books.

Jejeebhoy, Shireen J., and Zeba A. Sathar. 2001. "Women's Autonomy in India and Pakistan: The Influence of Religion and Region." *Population and Development Review* 27 (4): 687–712.

Jensenius, Francesca R. 2019. "India: A Contradictory Record." In *The Palgrave Handbook of Women's Political Rights,* edited by Susan Franceschet, Mona Lena Krook, and Netina Tan, 673–688. London: Palgrave Macmillan.

Joshi, Devin K., and Ryan Goehrung. 2018. "Conceptualizing and Measuring Women's Political Leadership: From Presence to Balance." *Politics and Gender* 14 (3): 350–375.

Joshi, Devin K., and Malliga Och. 2014. "Talking about My Generation and Class? Unpacking the Descriptive Representation of Women in Asian Parliaments." *Women's Studies International Forum* 47 (Part A): 168–179. https://doi.org/10.1016/j.wsif.2014.06.004

Kamat, A. R. 1976. "Women's Education and Social Change in India." *Social Scientist* 5 (1): 3–27. https://doi.org/10.2307/3516600

Kamdar, Bandari. 2020 "Women in Sri Lanka Make up 56% of Voters, But Only 5% of Legislators." *The Diplomat.* https://thediplomat.com/2020/09/women-in-sri-lanka-make-up-56-of-voters-but-only-5-of-legislators/

Keating, Christine. 2001. "Maneuvering Gendered Nationalisms: Jayalalitha Jayaram and the Politics of Tamil Womanhood." *Women & Politics* 22 (4): 69–88.

Kinnear, Karen L. 2011. *Women in Developing Countries: A Reference Handbook.* Santa Barbara, CA: ABC-CLIO.

Kittilson, Miki Caul. 2019. "Gender and Electoral Behavior." In *The Palgrave Handbook of Women's Political Rights*, edited by Susan Franceschet, Mona Lena Krook, and Netina Tan, 21–32. London: Palgrave Macmillan.

Kodikara, Chulani. 2009. *The Struggle for Equal Political Representation of Women in Sri Lanka: A Stocktaking Report for the Ministry of Child Development and Women's Empowerment and the United Nations Development Programme.* Ministry of Child Development and Women's Empowerment. https://www.academia.edu/35341451/The_Struggle_for_Equal_Political_Representation_of_Women_in_Sri_Lanka

Krook, Mona Lena. 2010. *Quotas for Women in Politics: Gender and Candidate Selection Reform Worldwide.* New York: Oxford University Press.

Labonne, Julien, Sahar Parsa, and Pablo Querubin. 2019. "Political Dynasties, Term Limits and Female Political Empowerment: Evidence from the Philippines." Working Paper 26431, National Bureau of Economic Research.

Lawless, Jennifer L, and Richard L Fox. 2010. *It Still Takes a Candidate: Why Women Don't Run for Office.* Cambridge: Cambridge University Press.

Liu, Shan-Jan Sarah. 2020. "Gender Gaps in Political Participation in Asia." *International Political Science Review* 43 (2): 209–225. https://doi.org/10.1177/0192512120935517

Loring, Nicole. 2018. "Overcoming Barriers: Myanmar's Recent Elections and Women's Political Participation." *Asia Pacific Viewpoint* 59 (1): 74–86.

Milazzo, Annamaria, and Markus Goldstein. 2019. "Governance and Women's Economic and Political Participation: Power Inequalities, Formal Constraints and Norms." *Research Observer* 34 (1): 34–96.

Minoletti, Paul. 2019. "Myanmar: Women's Political Life." In *The Palgrave Handbook of Women's Political Rights*, edited by Susan Franceschet, Mona Lena Krook, and Netina Tan, 657–672. London: Palgrave Macmillan.

Montecinos, Verónica. 2017. *Women Presidents and Prime Ministers in Post-Transition Democracies*. Palgrave Studies in Political Leadership. London: Palgrave Macmillan.

Mulder, Stella. 2019. "WAVE: Women and Political Leadership in Timor Leste—Literature Review." Reviewed by Amanda Scothern and Tracy McDiarmid. Research Report, October 2019. https://www.iwda.org.au/assets/files/Women-and-Political-Leadership-Literature-Review-Timor-Leste_publicPDF3_3_2020.pdf

Mustafa, Mahfudzah binti. 1999. "Women's Political Participation in Malaysia: The Non-Bumiputra's Perspective." *Asian Journal of Women's Studies* 5 (2): 9–46.

Nazneen, Sohela, Naomi Hossain, and Deepta Chopra. 2019. "Introduction: Contentious Women's Empowerment in South Asia." *Contemporary South Asia* 27 (4): 457–470. https://doi.org/10.1080/09584935.2019.1689922

Neher, Clark. 1995. "Democratization in Thailand." *Asian Affairs* 21 (4): 195–209.

Nijat, Aarya, and Jennifer Murtazashvili. 2015. "Women's Leadership Roles in Afghanistan." US Institute of Peace, September 4, 2015. https://www.usip.org/publications/2015/09/womens-leadership-roles-afghanistan

Norris, Pippa, and Joni Lovenduski. 1995. *Political Recruitment: Gender, Race and Class in the British Parliament*. Cambridge: Cambridge University Press.

Ostermann, Susan. 2017. "Nepal in 2016: Nepali Women Rise above a Sea of Instability." *Asian Survey* 57 (1): 60–64.

Paasilinna, Silja. 2016. "Women's Reserved Seats in Bangladesh: A Systemic Analysis of Meaningful Representation." USAID & UKAID. https://www.ifes.org/publications/womens-reserved-seats-bangladesh-systemic-analysis-meaningful-representation

Rahayu, Ruth Indiah, and Adisti Ikayanti. 2014. *The Success and the Barriers to Women's Representation in Southeast Asia: Between State*

Policies, Political Parties and Women's Movement. Jakarta: Kemitraan bagi Pembaruan Tata Pemerintahan.

Rallonza, Ma Lourdes V. 2009. "Women and the Democracy Project: A Feminist Take on Women's Political Participation in the Philippines." *LEAPS: Miriam College Faculty Research Journal* 30 (1). https://ejournals.ph/article.php?id=3449

Rhoads, Elizabeth. 2012. "Women's Political Participation in Indonesia: Decentralisation, Money Politics and Collective Memory in Bali." *Journal of Current Southeast Asian Affairs* 31 (2): 35–56.

Rodan, Garry. 2018. "Singapore's Elected President: A Failed Institution." *Australian Journal of International Affairs* 72 (1): 10–15.

Schwindt-Bayer, Leslie A. 2011. "Women Who Win: Social Backgrounds, Paths to Power, and Political Ambition in Latin American Legislatures." *Politics & Gender* 7 (1): 1–33.

Skard, Torild. 2015. *Women of Power: Half a Century of Female Presidents and Prime Ministers Worldwide.* Bristol, UK: Policy Press.

Strachan, Glenda, Arosha Adikaram, and Pavithra Kailasapathy. 2015. "Gender (In)Equality in South Asia: Problems, Prospects and Pathways." *South Asian Journal of Human Resources Management* 2 (1): 1–11. https://doi.org/10.1177/2322093715580222

Sturman, Rachel. 2012. *The Government of Social Life in Colonial India: Liberalism, Religious Law, and Women's Rights.* Cambridge Studies in Indian History and Society, Series Number 21. Cambridge: Cambridge University Press.

True, Jacqui, Sarah Niner, Swati Parashar, and Nicole George. 2014. *Women's Political Participation in Asia and the Pacific.* Social Science Research Council, October 2014. https://www.ssrc.org/publications /women-s-political-participation-in-asia-and-the-pacific/

UN Women. 2014. *Violence against Women in Politics: A Study Conducted in India, Nepal and Pakistan.* Delhi: United Nations Entity for Gender Equality and Empowerment of Women.

UNDP (United Nations Development Programme). 2019. "2019 Global Multidimensional Poverty Index (MPI): Illuminating Inequalities." https://hdr.undp.org/content/2019-global-multidimensional-poverty-index-mpi

UNESCO. 2018. "Afghanistan." http://uis.unesco.org/country/AF

Uprety, Sudeep. 2018. "What Does Nepal's Recent Elections Reveal about Patriarchy in Politics?" *South Asia@ LSE.* https://blogs.lse.ac.uk

/southasia/2018/01/17/what-does-nepals-recent-elections-tell-us
-about-patriarchy-in-politics/

Wolbrecht, Christina, and David E. Campbell. 2007. "Leading by Example: Female Members of Parliament as Political Role Models."
American Journal of Political Science 51 (4): 921–939.

World Economic Forum. 2020. "Global Gender Gap Report 2020." https://
www.weforum.org/reports/gender-gap-2020-report-100-years-pay
-equality/

Yadav, Punam. 2018. "Women in the Parliament: Changing Gender Dynamics in the Political Sphere in Nepal." In *Women in Governing Institutions in South Asia*, edited by Nizam Ahmed, 79–96. Cham,
Switzerland: Palgrave Macmillan.

EIGHT

Oceania

Elise Howard, Kerryn Baker, and Sonia Palmieri

The Oceania region comprises fourteen independent countries: **Aotearoa** New Zealand, Australia, and the Pacific Islands of Federated States of Micronesia, Fiji, Kiribati, Nauru, Marshall Islands, Palau, Papua New Guinea, Samoa, Solomon Islands, Tonga, Tuvalu, and Vanuatu. The region encompasses countries with some of the highest and lowest rates of women's political representation in the world. Women in New Zealand and Australia were among the first in the world to win the right to vote, while universal suffrage was only introduced in Samoa in 1990. Adoption of gender quotas in the independent states of the region has lagged behind global trends, although such measures have proven remarkably effective in increasing women's representation in some of the nonsovereign territories. On the surface, the region is marked by diversity and stark contrasts, yet a deeper dive into the contexts and histories of each country shows that the true picture is much more nuanced.

Across Oceania, gains in women's representation in national politics have been neither linear nor rapid. As this chapter will show, women share some common barriers to political participation, regardless of the diversity of political statuses, electoral systems, and histories of women's leadership in the region. Progress in increasing the number of women in politics across most countries in the Pacific Islands region has been markedly slow; where women's representation is higher in Australia and New Zealand, women continue to face challenges presented by gendered political institutions and social norms that privilege men's leadership. In Australia, political party recruitment mechanisms are at the heart of women's electoral disadvantage; in New Zealand, changes to electoral arrangements have benefited women, but more subversive barriers to equality remain; and women across the Pacific face multiple formal and informal structural challenges. The chapter demonstrates the importance of taking these complexities into account and shows that long-term and locally led approaches are key to progressing gender equality across Oceania.

WOMEN AS VOTERS

Australia and New Zealand were at the vanguard of women's suffrage reform. New Zealand was the first nation in the world to grant women, including Indigenous women, full suffrage in 1893. In 1894, women in South Australia became the first to have the right to both vote and stand for election; Western Australia followed suit in 1899. In the latter, full suffrage was restricted to white women, although Aboriginal women who owned property could also vote. In 1902, women were given the right to vote and stand for election in the recently established federation of Australia, although the legislation specifically excluded Indigenous people from Australia, Asia, Africa, and the Pacific Islands.

Unlike the more militant suffrage movements of Britain and the United States, suffrage campaigns in Australia and New Zealand largely consisted of peaceful demonstration and persistent political action. Letters were written to newspapers and magazines, public speeches were made, and rallies and marches were held. Suffrage campaigners used petitions to gather signatures and raise awareness and support, traveling around the country to knock on doors. One petition on suffrage presented to the New Zealand Parliament was signed by 31,872 women—including some **Māori** women—and spanned 300 yards. It was described by prominent suffragist Kate Sheppard as a "monster" petition and was the largest on any issue that had ever been presented to Parliament. Successful reform in South Australia was spurred on by a petition with over 11,600 signatures.

In New Zealand, the suffrage movement was spearheaded by the Women's Christian Temperance Union (WCTU), the first national women's association established in New Zealand. The WCTU also played a key role in Australian suffrage campaigns (Grimshaw 1987, 2009). The movements benefited from relatively liberal political cultures and a pervasive idea that places on the margins of the British Empire could be sites of progressive social experimentation (Dalziel 2000). These suffrage campaigns were closely interconnected with international suffrage campaigns (Keating 2020).

Within the WCTU-led suffrage movement in New Zealand, **Pākehā** (European) voices overwhelmingly predominated. That suffrage would apply to both Pākehā and Māori women, however, was taken by many as a given. Suffrage had been extended to all adult Māori men in 1867, twelve years before full suffrage was extended to Pākehā men.[1] Also in 1867, four Māori seats were created. These reforms were an attempt to integrate Māori into the formal political system and quell dissent as the land wars came to an end while still ensuring Māori were underrepresented relative to population. The Māori male members of Parliament, while not generally supportive of suffrage, did make the case that, should it be applied, it should apply equally (Dalziel 2000).

The fight for women's suffrage in the Pākehā Parliament was taking place at the same time as Māori parliamentary movements, including **Te Kotahitanga**.[2] This movement adopted parliamentary governance practices modeled on the Westminster system to seek to gain recognition from the Crown without being assimilated into Pākehā political structures, within which Māori were marginal actors (Bargh 2010). Within the Kotahitanga movement, women activists led by Meri Te Tai Mangakāhia were pushing for women's inclusion in Māori politics.

Yet, as women's suffrage expanded in Australia, the exercise of full political rights remained racialized. While initial suffrage debates in South Australia and other colonies with smaller Indigenous populations were not overly concerned with the effects of full enfranchisement, Queensland and Western Australian delegates at the federal level campaigned strongly against voting rights for **Aboriginal and Torres Strait Islander** women and men. The success of white women in gaining full citizenship rights in Australia must be considered hand in hand with the

---

[1] Men who owned or leased property—either Māori or Pākehā, although given communal landownership structures among Māori, the requirement was harder to fulfill for the former—had been entitled to vote since the first parliamentary elections in 1853.
[2] Another Māori parliament movement was Te Kauhanganui, founded in the late nineteenth century by the Kingitanga movement. The two movements had similar aims—although Te Kotahitanga sought to represent all Māori tribes, while Te Kauhanganui was concentrated in the Waikato-Tainui region—but operated separately, with women also politically active in the latter movement. Te Kauhanganui is still in existence.

MERI TE TAI MANGAKĀHIA

Meri Te Tai Mangakāhia was a prominent advocate for women's political rights within Te Kotahitanga, a movement that sought to establish separate Māori political institutions. She was the wife of Hāmiora Mangakāhia, a Ngati Whanaunga chief who was the first premier of Te Kotahitanga. During the second session of the Kotahitanga Parliament in 1893, the Speaker of the lower house introduced a motion from Mangakāhia on women's suffrage. She was invited to speak to the motion, becoming the first woman to address Parliament.

In making the case for women's suffrage and the right to stand for Te Kotahitanga, Mangakāhia drew on Māori traditions of women landowners as well as European examples of women's leadership, arguing that Māori women might be able to petition Queen Victoria on land disputes more effectively. Her aims were more ambitious than the mainstream suffrage movement; she argued that women should not only have the right to vote but also the right to contest Te Kotahitanga's elections.

Although Mangakāhia's petition was unsuccessful in the 1893 sitting, in 1895, women's participation in Te Kotahitanga was formalized through the incorporation of five women's committees. Women eventually won the right to vote and stand for Te Kotahitanga in 1897. In 1902, Te Kotahitanga was dissolved following the establishment of Māori councils.

Source: Ballara (1993).

exclusion of Aboriginal and Torres Strait Islander women and men from citizenship rights, a democratic injustice that was not rectified until the 1960s.

In the Pacific, women's suffrage was generally not the result of sustained struggle but incorporated into wider decolonization processes in the twentieth century. Tonga is unique in the Pacific Islands region in that it was never officially colonized but negotiated a treaty and was a **British protected state**. Its 1875 constitution, one of the oldest in the world, created a Legislative Assembly that included directly elected people's representatives along with reserved seats for nobles.[3] The franchise was initially restricted to men, but it was expanded to women by Queen Salote in 1951.

---

[3] Constitutional reforms in 2010 increased the number of people's representatives from nine to seventeen, giving them a majority in the Legislative Assembly.

Women were also given the right to stand for election as people's representatives at that time; the first woman elected was Princess Si'ilikutapu in 1975.

In some countries across the Pacific, women were active in independence movements. The women's Mau movement in Samoa had 8,000 members in 1930. Despite criticism from religious leaders of women's involvement in politics, the movement persisted in activity, including rallies, fundraising, and filing petitions to Parliament (Macquoid 1995). In 1929, 2,000 women marched in Apia in protest of the Black Saturday shootings, in which New Zealand police fired into a crowd of Mau members, killing paramount chief Tupua Tamasese Lealofi III and others. Women were leaders in anticolonial and secessionist movements elsewhere, including

JOSEPHINE ABAIJAH

Dame Josephine Abaijah was the first woman elected to national office in Papua New Guinea. First elected to the preindependence House of Assembly in 1972, five years later, Abaijah was elected to the first postindependence Parliament. After losing her seat in 1982, she was reelected to Parliament in 1997. When she was first elected, the results were recounted several times, as the officials could not believe that a woman had been elected. As the first woman in the legislative assembly, Abaijah experienced many challenges, including being spat upon, but she gradually won the respect of her male counterparts (Abaijah and Wright 1991; Kemish, Sinebare, and Ritchie 2015).

Abaijah stated that she avoided campaigning as a "woman's candidate" but rather campaigned on issues that were relevant to men and women across her electorate and took advantage of the strong connections she had built with communities through her work with the health department (Commonwealth Secretariat 1999). She mobilized voters behind the Papua Besena movement as one of the founders and leaders of the secessionist group, which opposed the combining of the territories of Papua and New Guinea into the independent state of Papua New Guinea. Abaijah was outspoken about the rapid withdrawal of the colonial Australian administration and the hurried arrangements for independence, arguing that this would result in marginalization and disadvantage for Papuans.

Abaijah was also a leader in the women's movement. In 1974, she led a protest in Port Moresby that attracted thousands of women. Women marched and protested for two days and stormed government buildings and the airport, "taking police by surprise who did not know how to handle a bunch of unruly women" (Dickson-Waiko 2010, 9).

Hilda Lini in Vanuatu and Josephine Abaijah, the head of the Papua Besena secessionist movement in Papua New Guinea.

Samoa became independent in 1962 with a restricted franchise. Only *matai* (chiefs), who were overwhelmingly men, could vote and stand in parliamentary elections. Universal suffrage was introduced in 1990; this move was not explicitly framed as a gender issue but resulted in the enfranchisement of a huge number of women. The right to stand in elections is still restricted to *matai*, and this means only around one in ten potential parliamentary candidates are women.

Colonization in the Pacific was a gendered process, with Pacific women largely sidelined by colonial administrations: their leadership discounted and their political activity ignored. The establishment of national institutions and decolonization processes were heavily influenced by international standards and frameworks rather than in response to citizen interests. Women in particular were treated as marginal subjects in these processes (Dickson-Waiko 2013). This marginalization has led in the postcolonial era to an unequal citizenship for women, notwithstanding the equal rights enshrined in most regional constitutions. A key indicator of this unequal citizenship is the enduring poor rates of women's political representation across the independent Pacific.

WOMEN'S POLITICAL ENGAGEMENT

While women represent close to or over half of registered voters in the Pacific Island region (Baker 2018b), gender-disaggregated data on voter turnout has not been collected systematically. The ability of women to vote freely, however, can impact voter turnout and choice in some parts of the Pacific. This may take the form of subtle coercion, where family choices dictate voting behavior, or overt intimidation. Women's lack of ability to vote freely and according to their own preferences has been noted in elections across the region (Haley and Zubrinich 2018; Kaviamu 2016; Guttenbeil-Likiliki 2006).

In Australia, compulsory voting was introduced in 1924, resulting in voter turnout rates that have since ranged from 91 percent to 96 percent. Australian women have been marginally more likely to vote than men, although this has not had a significant effect on turnout overall (Hannan-Morrow and Roden 2014, 16–17). In New Zealand, voting is not compulsory, and a long-term downward trend in voter turnout has stabilized somewhat since the mid-2010s. Women were more likely than men to vote in 2017, but there has not always been a significant gender gap in turnout (Curtin and Greaves 2020, 200).

WOMEN AS MEMBERS OF PARLIAMENT

Across Oceania, women occupy vastly different positions in formal politics. New Zealand has a solid recent history of women's executive leadership and 48 percent representation of women in Parliament, while in some parts of Micronesia and Melanesia, women are absent from elected office at the national level. Across the Pacific Islands region, while women lack representation, there are many notable examples of women who have defied the barriers and held important executive positions, including as head of state. In addition, time lags between universal suffrage and the year that women were first elected to office are not as pronounced in some parts of the Pacific as in other parts of the world (see table 8.1 and figure 8.1).

New Zealand has a long tradition and widespread acceptance of women's leadership and political participation (Curtin 2008). Elizabeth McCombs became the first woman parliamentarian in 1933, winning a by-election for her late husband's seat. The first Māori woman to be elected to the New Zealand Parliament was Iriaka Rātana in 1949, who was also the widow of a former member of Parliament (MP). The first woman cabinet minister was Mabel Howard in 1947; in 1972, Whetu Tirikatene-Sullivan became the first Māori woman cabinet minister.

In 1996, New Zealand introduced a **mixed-member proportional** (MMP) system that resulted in an immediate increase in the proportion of women in Parliament from 21.2 percent to 28.3 percent. Party lists have been an important mechanism to increase women's representation, although the proportion of women holding electorate seats has become more equal over time. In the 2020 election, women won two out seven Māori electorate seats (29 percent) and thirty out of sixty-five general electorate seats (46 percent); of the forty-eight list MPs elected, twenty-six (54 percent) were women. MMP has resulted in greater diversity in Parliament: the first Asian woman MP, Pansy Wong, was elected in 1996, and the first Pacific Islander woman MP, Luamanuvao Winnie Laban, in 1999.[4] Both initially entered Parliament through party lists before successfully winning electorate seats. The first openly lesbian parliamentarian, Maryan

---

[4] Wong was the first Asian MP (male or female) elected to the New Zealand Parliament.

Table 8.1 Women's Political Rights across Oceania

	Year Women Granted Right to Vote	Year Women Granted Right to Stand for Election	Year First Woman Elected (E) or Appointed (A)	Total Number of Women Elected (E) or Appointed (A) to National Legislature
New Zealand	1893	1919	1933 (E)	175 (E)
Australia	1902/1962	1902/1962	1943 (E)	237 (E)
Tonga	1951	1951	1975 (E)	6 (E), 4 (A)
Nauru	1951	1951	1986 (E)	4 (E)
Fiji	1963	1963	1966 (E, A)	34 (E), 8 (A)
Papua New Guinea (PNG)	1964	1964	1973 (E)/1951 (A)	7 (E), 2 (A)
Marshall Islands	1965	1965	1987 (E)	6 (E)
Palau	1965	1965	1990 (E)	8 (E)
Micronesia (FSM)	1965	1965	NA	0
Solomon Islands	1967	1967	1965 (E)	7 (E)
Kiribati	1967	1967	1971 (E)	15 (E)
Tuvalu	1967	1967	1989 (E)	3 (E)
Vanuatu	1979	1979	1987 (E)	5 (E)
Samoa	1990	NA	1970 (E)	18 (E), 1 (A)

Source: Based on author research.[1]

[1]Table is current as of March 2021. The year of suffrage and counts of women elected or appointed to national legislatures draw on data from a range of region-specific resources, including parliamentary, academic, and historical media reports. We acknowledge with thanks the assistance of Wendy Hart and Pleasance Purser at the New Zealand Parliament.

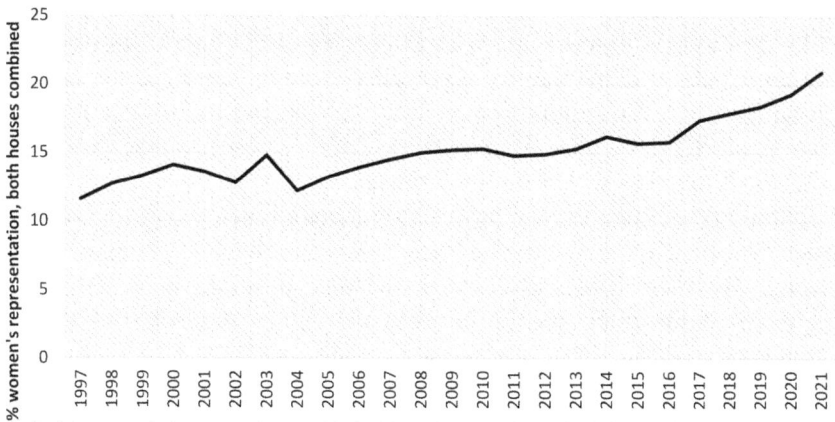

Figure 8.1 Women's Representation in Oceania: Regional Average over Time (Inter-Parliamentary Union: Parline database on national parliaments, July 31, 2021 IPU Parline (2021)).

Street, was elected as a list MP in 2005.[5] New Zealand—and the world's—first openly transgender MP, Georgina Beyer, held the seat of Wairarapa from 1999 to 2005 and was a list MP from 2005 to 2007.

Prior to the Second World War, none of Australia's major political parties had supported women candidates for election to federal parliament. While some women had run independently or through minor parties, none had received sufficient votes to win. Women first entered the federal parliament in 1943: Enid Lyons in the House of Representatives and Dorothy Tagney in the Senate. Lyons ran for Parliament following the death of her husband, a former prime minister. From 1943 to 2020, 236 women have been elected to the Australian Parliament.[6] Penny Wong, elected to the Senate in 2002, was the first woman of Asian descent elected at the federal level and became the first openly lesbian member of the cabinet in 2008. Former senator Lucy Gichuhi, the first federal parliamentarian of Black African descent, was elected in 2017, and Senator Mehreen Faruqi was the first Muslim woman elected to Parliament in 2018. Even accounting for their delayed franchise in 1962, representation of Australia's Aboriginal

[5] Marilyn Waring was outed as a lesbian by a tabloid during her time in Parliament (1975–1984) but did not discuss her sexual orientation publicly until she had left politics.
[6] The seven women who have served in both houses of the parliament are only counted once.

and Torres Strait Islander women in politics has been particularly poor. In 2013, Nova Peris, who identifies as a member of the Kiga, Yawuru, and Muran People, became the first Aboriginal woman elected to the Senate. Linda Burney, a Wiradjuri woman who was elected in 2016, is the first and, as of 2021, the only Aboriginal or Torres Strait Islander woman to hold a seat in the House of Representatives.

In the Pacific Islands, men vastly outnumber women as electoral candidates. When women stand, they are much less likely than men to be elected. Between 2014 and 2016, in the nine elections held across the region, nine out of ten candidates were men. Only 14 percent of women candidates in these elections were successful, compared to 22 percent of men (Baker 2016).

Consequently, women's representation in Parliament is low, historically averaging less than 10 percent across the region (see table 8.2). As of

Table 8.2   Seats Held by Women in Lower or Single House of Parliament

Country	Number (Percent)	
	October 1999	October 2019
New Zealand	35 (29.2)	49 (40.8)
Australia	33 (22.4)	46 (30.5)
Fiji	8 (11.3)	10 (19.6)
Palau	0 (0)	2 (12.5)
Nauru	0 (0)	2 (10.5)
Samoa	2 (4.1)	5 (10)
Marshall Islands	0 (0)	3 (9.1)
Tonga	0 (0)	2 (7.4)
Kiribati	2 (4.9)	3 (6.5)
Tuvalu	1 (8.3)	1 (6.3)
Solomon Islands	1 (2)	2 (4.1)
Micronesia (Federated States of)	0 (0)	0 (0)
Papua New Guinea	2 (1.8)	0 (0)
Vanuatu	0 (0)	0 (0)

Source: Drawing from IPU data (1999, 2019).

March 2021, the region was home to the only three countries globally with no women representatives in their parliaments: Papua New Guinea, Vanuatu, and the Federated States of Micronesia. The independent nations of the Pacific stand in stark contrast to nonsovereign territories: in New Caledonia and French Polynesia, the French parity laws have ensured near equal numbers of women and men in politics, and in 2018, the voters of Guam elected ten women to the fifteen-seat legislature.

WOMEN AS LEADERS

New Zealand has had three women prime ministers. In 1997, Jenny Shipley became the first woman prime minister of New Zealand. Helen Clark succeeded her in the role, serving just under a decade, from 1999 to 2008. In 2017, Jacinda Ardern became New Zealand's youngest woman prime minister at thirty-seven. In July 2020, Judith Collins won the leadership of the National Party and became **leader of the opposition**. The 2020 election was the second in New Zealand's history, after the 1999 election, in which the two major parties were both led by women, and this led to a record 48 percent of parliamentary seats being won by women.

Combining motherhood with political leadership is in many ways a radical act (Curtin 2018). In 2018, Jacinda Ardern made global headlines when she announced she was pregnant with her first child. While Ardern is not the first woman prime minister of New Zealand, nor the first head of government to have a baby while in office, her prime ministership has redefined boundaries of political leadership. As prime minister, Ardern has also faced significant challenges: the 2019 Christchurch mosque shootings, in which fifty-one people died, prompting her government to introduce strict gun control legislation; the 2019 Whaakari/White Island eruption, which killed twenty-one; and the COVID-19 pandemic. In her tenure, she has championed what has been called a "politics of kindness." As a young, progressive leader championing a different style of political leadership, Ardern has made global headlines, appearing in *Vogue* in February 2018 and on the cover of *Time* in February 2020. A February 2020 profile in *Time* noted that "Ardern has infused New Zealand with a new kind of soft power" (Luscombe 2020).

Julia Gillard served as Australia's first woman prime minister from 2010 to 2013, and as of March 2021, she is the only woman to have served as either leader of the government or the opposition at the federal level. Female deputy leaders of both major parties have either been unsuccessful in their quest for leadership (Julie Bishop) or cited family and work-life balance as a reason not to contest (Tanya Plibersek). Women have, however, fared better as leaders of minor parties, including the Greens, One Nation, and the Australian Democrats (in which women actually outnumbered men as federal parliamentary leaders).

In a coincidentally symbolic act of gender equality, Julia Gillard was sworn into office on June 24, 2010, by the first woman governor-general of Australia, Dame Quentin Bryce. Gillard led a minority government that required the support of independents in the House of Representatives to pass legislation. Despite this, she is credited with passing more legislation than any previous Australian prime minister (Evershed 2013), including paid parental leave, a price on carbon emissions, and disability insurance. She famously established a royal commission into institutionalized child sexual abuse in the hours before her term expired. Less often remarked upon, however, is Gillard's "unprecedented historical commitment" to gender equality in the Pacific (*SBS News* 2015). In 2012, Gillard pledged

---

HILDA HEINE

In January 2016, Casten Nemra, the president of the Marshall Islands, was defeated in a no-confidence motion after just one week in office, the shortest tenure in Marshallese history. The following day, more history was made as Dr. Hilda Heine was elected the Marshall Islands' first woman president and the first woman head of government in the independent Pacific Islands. Heine was no stranger to firsts. In 2004, she became the first Marshallese person to be awarded a doctoral degree. Prior to entering politics, Heine had an illustrious public service career in the field of education, including serving as secretary of education and president of the College of the Marshall Islands. She was also a cofounder of a women's rights nongovernmental organization (NGO) Women United Together Marshall Islands. As president, Heine's nickname was "mother of the nation" (Cox, Spark, and Corbett 2020).

As president from 2016 to 2020, Heine gained global prominence as an advocate for climate change action. She was chair of the Climate Vulnerable Forum from 2018 to 2020. In 2019, she cowrote an opinion piece for the *Washington Post* titled "Don't Let Rising Seas Drown the Marshall Islands." As a world leader on environmental issues, she was an outspoken proponent of the inclusion of women in climate change negotiations: "It's important for women to understand the issues and also to be brought to the table too, to help make policies that are relevant to them as a marginalised group" (quoted in Lyons 2019).

over AUD$300 million in support for a program aiming to increase the number of women in leadership and decision-making roles, facilitate women's economic empowerment, and fund violence against women prevention initiatives.

Women have secured key leadership roles in the Pacific region. In 2016, Hilda Heine in the Marshall Islands became the first woman head of state in the region. Other women who have served in executive positions in Pacific politics include Taufa Vakatale, deputy prime minister of Fiji (1997–1999); Sandra Pierantozzi, vice president of Palau (2001–2005); and Teima Onorio, vice president of Kiribati (2003–2016). In 2020, Jerrylyn Uduch Sengebau Senior was elected as the second woman vice president of Palau.

In 2021, Fiamē Naomi Mata'afa became the first woman prime minster of Samoa, having previously served as the country's first woman deputy prime minister. Fiamē led a newly established party to a narrow—and contested—victory over the incumbent government, which had held power for decades. When the outgoing prime minister refused to concede, Samoa faced a constitutional crisis that dragged on for nearly four months before an appeal court ruling formally instated Fiamē as prime minister. Her complicated path to power is indicative of an entrenched resistance to women's leadership in the region; yet her eventual success proved it can be overcome (table 8.3).

In Oceania, women have also been present in politics in cabinet positions. In New Zealand, the election of the Fourth Labour Government of

Table 8.3   Women Heads of Government in Oceania

Name	Country	Assumed Office	Left Office
Jenny Shipley	New Zealand	December 8, 1997	December 10, 1999
Helen Clark	New Zealand	December 10, 1999	November 19, 2008
Julia Gillard	Australia	June 24,2010	June 27, 2013
Hilda Heine	Marshall Islands	January 28, 2016	January 13, 2020
Jacinda Ardern	New Zealand	October 26, 2017	Incumbent
Fiamē Naomi Mata'afa	Samoa	May 24, 2021	Incumbent

Source: Based on author research.

New Zealand in 1999 saw women's representation in the cabinet increase dramatically, from 11 percent to over 30 percent; it remained consistently around 30 percent in the next twenty years, rising to 40 percent following the 2020 election. In Australia, women had been represented across all key ministerial portfolios, bar that of treasurer, as of March 2021. Following the 2019 election, women comprised just over 26 percent of the cabinet. Across the Pacific, thirteen women occupy cabinet positions. Excluding the three countries where there are no women in the national legislature, women's average representation within cabinet sits at 13 percent, ranging from 7 percent in Kiribati through to 25 percent in Samoa.

BARRIERS TO POLITICAL PARITY

Despite the diversity of cultures across the Oceania region, women face a common barrier: leadership, particularly political leadership, continues to be socially constructed as the legitimate prerogative of men. Social norms—the ideas and informal rules that determine appropriate social behavior—tend to ascribe men the characteristics of an ideal leader. In addition, campaigning costs and voter expectations of women candidates are high in comparison to their male counterparts. Finally, the gendered nature of legislative assemblies can mean that while formal rules do not appear overtly discriminatory, less visible and informal rules present real barriers to women's political participation.

Restrictive Social Norms

Social norms that equate leadership with masculine behaviors often result in women being more reluctant to seek, or accept, positions of influence (McLeod 2015). For many women in the region, becoming a political leader provokes an unfair double standard. Women face gendered expectations about their performance and intense scrutiny for any perceived failures. Women leaders across Oceania are more likely than their male counterparts to face criticism and harassment precisely because they have stepped out of a traditional role (Baker 2018b). The scrutiny that women face can be heightened in nations with small populations. Not only do women face enormous pressure, but their actions also reflect on their family's reputation.

Across Pacific Island countries, politics and decision-making are commonly viewed as being conducted in men's spaces (Howard 2019). In some cases, local language names of national parliaments are closely linked to local village decision-making forums, which are historically male dominated (Meleisea et al. 2015), and in Papua New Guinea, the national parliament is designed to resemble the *Haus Tambaran*, a culturally important space that is traditionally restricted to men (Palmieri and Zetlin 2020). Less formally, many women lack power in household decision-making and are not expected to discuss politics. Political discussions and candidate mentoring have tended to take place in spaces that exclude women (Baker 2018b).

There is a commonly expressed view in the region that women voters are responsible for the poor success rates of women candidates. In his inaugural statement as prime minister of Tonga, 'Akilisi Pohiva (2015) highlighted the absence of women MPs as an issue but argued that "the hand that deals the cards in this instance are women voters who represent in fact the majority of voters." Assigning blame in this way obscures the complicated dynamics of voting in the Pacific, where there is a widespread lack of trust in the secrecy of the ballot and where voter intimidation—both overt and subtle—disproportionately affects women voters (Palmieri and Zetlin 2020). Even where women can cast their own ballots freely, there are competing loyalties at play, and women may not necessarily choose to prioritize gender over kinship ties, ideology, reciprocal obligations, or other politically salient factors (Baker 2018b).

Prohibitive Campaign Expectations

Irrespective of where they are run, electoral campaigns cost a significant amount of money. Credible political party backing or other means of harnessing significant resources are critical to women's campaigning effectiveness and reach. Party backing and electoral success often require multiple attempts at preselection or campaigning, compounding the financial burden for women. In addition, in many parts of the Pacific, political parties have limited ideological relevance, and many women and men run as independents, creating implications for resource access. Furthermore, women across the Pacific face greater community expectations to provide service to their local area.

In New Zealand, the burden of campaign costs has eased due to the party list system. Of the 131 women who have entered Parliament since the MMP electoral system was introduced, 92 (70 percent) first entered as list MPs. While this new measure has been effective in increasing the representation of women, the gains come with a caveat: list MPs generally have less secure positions, being dependent on party machinery rather than having an individual profile and support base within an electorate.

In Australia, the significant cost of campaigning has left most women candidates at the mercy of political parties, which have historically regarded them as less likely to win, or deliberately placed them in "unwinnable" positions (Bean and McAllister 1990).[7] A largely unacknowledged preselection hurdle for many women in Australia is that they are expected to make multiple attempts at securing the party's endorsement, often in hostile environments.

Electoral costs across the Pacific region are increasing, in many cases reflecting the rise of vote buying and related forms of money politics. Women often struggle to raise sufficient funds to support a competitive election campaign because they are less engaged in the formal economy; where they do earn cash incomes, women tend to earn less money than men. Women are also less likely to have political party backing or access to networks of wealthy patrons who could fund campaigns (Barbara and Baker 2016). Running in consecutive elections to gain name recognition is a strategy for many male candidates (see Haley 2011). Most women contesting elections in the region, however, tend to be first-time candidates. This perhaps reflects the toll—financial, psychological, and relational—that campaigning in the region can inflict, as numerous accounts from women candidates have attested (Baker 2016; Billy 2002; Kidu and Setae 2002).

Pacific women candidates also face the burden of "service," which is tied to ideas about credible leadership. In Samoa, demonstrating service to your village (*monotaga*) is a formal requirement for candidacy. As women are less likely than men to participate in village governance—and in some villages are in fact barred from sitting on village councils—service presents a gendered obstacle (Baker 2018a). In other parts of the Pacific, the requirement to demonstrate community service is less formalized yet still important. Women's service to the community is often not coded as political in the same way as men's service, reflecting social norms that tend to delegitimize women's political leadership. Where it is recognized, it is often seen as adding political value to the aspirations of a husband or

---

[7] Independent candidates have of course had to resource their own campaigns. Successful independent campaigns tend to be funded either by preexisting personal reserves or an extensive and widely mobilized network of support.

family member rather than the individual woman. It is perhaps no coincidence that a significant number of women elected to parliaments in the Pacific Islands are widows, single, or married to foreign nationals (Baker and Palmieri 2020; Crocombe 2001).

Gendered Political Institutions

In addition to social norms and prohibitive campaign expectations, the gendered institution of parliament also acts as a critical barrier to women in Oceania (Palmieri 2018). Parliaments in the region are among the most masculinized in the world and not just because many include very few women. Some have formal institutional barriers to women's access. In Tonga, seats reserved for nobles in Parliament can only be occupied by men. And in Samoa, candidates must hold a *matai*, or chiefly title, yet only around 10 percent of *matai* are women. Beyond these obstacles, informal institutions create a space that is viewed as unsuitable for women. Cultural rules and taboos that are intended to entrench respect for women can be construed as barriers to women's entry to politics, such as perceptions that politics is too "dirty" for women (Guttenbeil-Likiliki 2006; Tuuau and Howard 2019).

While New Zealand appears the most progressive country in the region in terms of diversity of representation, a deeper look shows that the incorporation of diverse voices into Parliament has often been a means of staving off more radical agendas and ensuring political structures remain dominated by white male interests. In 1867, Māori seats were introduced to grant Māori men guaranteed representation in Parliament; yet Māori were drastically underrepresented in proportion to their population, and Māori MPs were not treated as equals by their Pākehā colleagues. In 1893, women won the right to vote but were not allowed to stand for Parliament until 1919. Despite significant advances, including three women prime ministers, debate over family-friendly practices in the New Zealand Parliament and inquiries into bullying and harassment of staff and women MPs have revealed serious inequities within Parliament, with women and people of color particularly vulnerable, creating a political space hostile to certain identities and viewpoints (Francis 2019; Palmieri and Baker 2020; Wall and Hayes 2019).

Women also face bullying, sexual harassment, and misogynistic attitudes in other parliaments in the region. Former Australian prime minister Julia Gillard is internationally renowned for her "sexism and misogyny

EXCERPT FROM THE "SEXISM AND MISOGYNY" SPEECH BY PM GILLARD

The slogan "ditch the witch" at anti-government rallies across Australia is just one of the examples of the sexism that PM Julia Gillard faced. (Phillip Minnis | Dreamstime.com)

"I say to the Leader of the Opposition I will not be lectured about sexism and misogyny by this man. I will not. And the Government will not be lectured about sexism and misogyny by this man. Not now, not ever.

"I was offended . . . by the sexism, by the misogyny of the Leader of the Opposition catcalling across this table at me as I sit here as Prime Minister, 'If the Prime Minister wants to, politically speaking, make an honest woman of herself . . .,' something that would never have been said to any man sitting in this chair. I was offended when the Leader of the Opposition went outside in the front of Parliament and stood next to a sign that said, 'Ditch the witch.'

"I was offended when the Leader of the Opposition stood next to a sign that described me as a man's b—. I was offended by those things. Misogyny, sexism, every day from this Leader of the Opposition. Every day in every way, across the time the Leader of the Opposition has sat in that chair and I've sat in this chair, that is all we have heard from him."

Source: Julia Gillard, *House of Representatives Debates*, October 10, 2012.

speech" (Gillard 2012), and since then, several women politicians and political staffers across the political spectrum have made public allegations of sexual assault, harassment, and bullying (AHRC 2021). In 2018, Fijian parliamentarian Lynda Tabuya faced extensive criticism for wearing a "body hugging" and "above the knee" dress from colleagues (Bolanavanua 2018). Parliaments in Oceania have yet to take a comprehensive approach to sexism and harassment that acknowledges institutional responsibility for daily occurrences of workplace discrimination and inequality and establishes appropriate mechanisms for redress.

ACHIEVING POLITICAL PARITY—A WAY FORWARD FOR OCEANIA

Gender parity has become a new international norm and a publicly articulated political goal in certain regions around the world, yet the concept is less widely adopted in Oceania. Understood as an equal distribution of power between men and women, or 50/50, gender parity does not usually frame arguments or measures to improve women's political representation in this region. In the Pacific Islands, this reflects the general sentiment that gender equality is a foreign concept and not necessarily applicable to local cultural contexts. Some success in advancing women's representation in decision-making roles has come through less overt strategies and working through local cultural norms.

Fast-Track Measures

Temporary special measures, and specifically electoral gender quotas, have proven to be an effective but highly controversial means of increasing women's political representation in Oceania. The United Nations and other international organizations have strongly promoted these special measures as a method of rapidly increasing the number of women in politics. Yet, despite significant global uptake in the 1990s and 2000s, few states in Oceania have introduced special measures to date. Where quotas have been most transformative has been in nonsovereign states, including the French Pacific territories, where the French "parity law" has resulted in near equal numbers of men and women political representatives.

The most common form of special measures advocated in independent Pacific Island countries has been reserved seats, where a certain number of parliamentary seats must be filled with women representatives.

The advantage of such a system is that it can be grafted onto almost any political system. Reserved seats for women have been introduced in the Bougainville House of Representatives—where advocates drew on local matrilineal traditions to argue for guaranteed seats for women—and at the municipal council level in Vanuatu. Similar systems have also been proposed at the national level in Papua New Guinea, the Solomon Islands, and other countries. Criticisms of existing reserved seats systems in the Pacific are that they have a silo effect, with a majority of women candidates competing against each other rather than against men, and that reserved seats can act as a ceiling on women's representation, leading to a perception that reserved seats are "women's seats" and general seats are therefore "men's seats" (Baker 2019). In both successful and unsuccessful campaigns for special measures in the Pacific region, there has been criticism that it is an externally driven agenda rather than a local initiative.

Other more innovative approaches have been implemented in Oceania. In 2013, Samoa adopted a relatively unusual "safety net" system at the parliamentary level that sets a minimum level of women's representation at five members, or 10 percent, of Parliament. The safety net does not come into effect unless the number of women elected outright in a general election falls beneath this threshold, in which case additional seats for women are instituted. To be eligible for additional seats, women must have been candidates in the general election so that all women entering Parliament are campaigning against men in the same electoral process. The system was first implemented in the 2016 general election, in which four women were elected outright and one woman entered Parliament through the quota mechanism (Baker 2019). In 2021, the declaration of a sixth woman in the immediate postelection period—on the basis that five women elected outright would represent only 9.8 percent of parliamentary members—was seen by some as electoral engineering and by others as a means of securing women's voice and representation. The move has reinvigorated discussion and debate about the quota and its application.

Within parties in New Zealand, particularly the Labour Party, there is a strong tradition of women's organizing, both separate to and mainstreamed within the formal party structures, that has increased women's representation in Parliament and the cabinet and influenced policy and candidate selection (Curtin 2008). Yet, this coexists with a hostility both within parties and more broadly in public opinion toward institutional measures guaranteeing women's representation. In New Zealand, the only party to institute a formal gender quota to date has been the Green Party, with a gender-balanced party list and a coleadership system of one man and one woman leaders. In 2013, a Labour Party proposal to adopt an **all-women shortlist** option for electorate seat candidate selection was labeled a "man ban" by the media and bloggers, and it was suggested that such a quota would be politically toxic, especially for male voters (Vowles, Coffé, and Curtin 2017).

The Australian Labor Party (ALP), one of Australia's two major political parties, has progressively increased its own targets to ensure women's representation. The other major party, the Liberal Party, has resisted calls for mandatory numerical targets, relying instead on awareness-raising campaigns and the mentoring and training of women candidates to improve their numerical presence in Parliament, with marginal success. The ALP first introduced targets in 1994, with the aim that a minimum of 35 percent of ALP candidates for winnable seats would be women by the year 2002. This target gradually increased to 40 percent in 2009 and 50 percent in 2015. The ALP then mandated a party quota that 50 percent of all seats won by the party across the country were to be held by women by 2025. While these measures were fiercely contested when first introduced, widespread acceptance is now evident for both the measures and women's participation in the party more broadly.

A Long-Term Approach

Shifting restrictive social norms that permeate women's leadership in Oceania is a long-term project. In a speech to the New Zealand Parliament to mark the 125th anniversary of women's suffrage, Prime Minister Jacinda Ardern highlighted the need for culture change within Parliament to create a more welcoming and attractive space for women and other marginalized groups (Ardern 2018).

Improving parliaments' gender sensitivity is a new international strategy to reorient the work of parliament—both in terms of its processes and outputs—toward the goal of gender equality (Palmieri and Baker 2020). While there are multiple avenues by which parliaments can address their gender sensitivity, one approach is through the establishment of dedicated gender equality bodies that facilitate the substantive representation of women (Celis, Childs, and Curtin 2016). Displays of legislative collaboration among women have been rare in Australia and New Zealand but, interestingly, have been evidenced in both countries on issues of women's sexual and reproductive health and rights. In 2006, women senators from four different political parties in Australia cosponsored a bill concerning the "abortion pill" RU486 (Sawer 2012). In 2020, in New Zealand, a cross-party group of women MPs not only introduced a joint members' bill to eliminate **female genital mutilation (FGM)** but also persuaded the Speaker to circumvent usual procedures and bring the bill on for debate (Vance 2020). Both of these bills were enacted.

Gender equality bodies aim to create a safe space for women parliamentarians to network and share experiences, particularly considering the increasingly reported incidences of sexual assault, harassment, and bullying against women MPs. In her final parliamentary speech in 2020, New Zealand MP Sarah Dowie (2020) criticized the media for "their conscious peddling of sexism and patriarchy" in their coverage of women politicians. Another retiring MP, Clare Curran, spoke out against the psychological toll of politics, including gendered negative media coverage (Chisholm 2020). When Sarah Hanson-Young raised her experience of sexual harassment in the Australian Senate, she publicly called for a cross-party women's caucus to spearhead a new code of conduct. Yet, in adversarial parliaments with strong party discipline, women's caucuses remain difficult to establish. Shifting existing norms of parliamentary culture and fighting negative public depictions of women politicians will require a long-term approach to institutional change.

Supporting improved gender sensitivity of political institutions in the Pacific is also a long-term project. Development assistance programs in the Pacific Islands that have been focused on fast-track measures such as quotas or that have tried to circumvent strongly held customary and religious views about leadership have been largely ineffective in improving the participation of women in politics. New projects that articulate social norm change as a primary objective are now being developed and implemented (see Gibert 2020), although, importantly, these do not expect transformative change in the short to medium term.

Women across Oceania are politically active, whether it be in the formal realm of national politics or the widespread activity outside of this domain. Yet, despite the pioneering efforts of suffragists in Australia and New Zealand and women's long history in activism across the Pacific, women continue to be outnumbered by men in national politics across the Oceania region. New Zealand's globally renown prime minister is pushing gender boundaries, and the country's history of women in politics appears progressive; yet this reputation is threatened by continued sexism in Parliament and hostility toward measures that would guarantee seats for women. In Australia, years of high performance by key women political figures has not translated into systemic and widespread approaches to ensuring credible party backing or pathways to political party leadership. Aboriginal and Torres Strait Islander women are particularly underrepresented in politics in Australia.

Parliaments in the Pacific are overwhelmingly male dominated, and despite some individual success stories, on the whole, women's political representation is poor. However, it is important not to play into gendered tropes that position women as weak or helpless but instead recognize the key roles that women have played and the agency that women have brought to activism over many years. As elsewhere, women in the parliaments of Oceania are expected to work within gendered institutions, defined in formal and informal rules as well as unspoken, yet powerful, restrictive social norms.

Gendered barriers and social norms equate leadership with men, set up prohibitive campaigning expectations, and market the idea that politics is dirty or bruising. Until systemic efforts are made to address the gendered nature of institutions, and the sexism and harassment that women are expected to contend with, there will be limited progress in women's electoral success. Fast-track measures such as quotas continue to face resistance and have met with mixed success. Locally informed, systemic, and long-term solutions are key to bringing about the change required to promote gender parity in politics across the region.

REFERENCES

Abaijah, Josephine, and Eric Wright. 1991. *A Thousand Coloured Dreams.* Melbourne: Pearson.

AHRC (Australian Human Rights Commission). 2021. *Set the Standard: Report on the Independent Review into Commonwealth Parliamentary Workplaces.* Sydney: AHRC. https://humanrights.gov.au /set-standard-2021

Ardern, Jacinda. 2018. *New Zealand Parliamentary Debates.* September 19, 2018. https://www.parliament.nz/en/pb/hansard-debates/rhr/doc ument/HansS_20180919_053325000/ardern-jacinda

Baker, Kerryn. 2016. "Pawa Blong Meri: Women Candidates in the 2015 Bougainville Election." SSGM Discussion Paper 2015/14. Canberra: State, Society and Governance in Melanesia Program, Australian National University.

Baker, Kerryn. 2018a. "Gender and Candidate Selection in a Weakly Institutionalized Party System: The Case of Samoa." *Australian Journal of Political Science* 53 (1): 57–72.

Baker, Kerryn. 2018b. "Great Expectations: Gender and Political Representation in the Pacific Islands." *Government and Opposition* 53
(3): 542–568.

Baker, Kerryn. 2019. *Pacific Women in Politics: Gender Quota Campaigns in the Pacific Islands*. Honolulu: University of Hawai'i
Press.

Baker, Kerryn, and Sonia Palmieri. 2020. "Widows and Wives in Pacific
Politics: A Reliable Pathway for Women?" *DPA In Brief 2020/1*.
Canberra: Department of Pacific Affairs, Australian National
University.

Ballara, Angela. 1993. "Mangakāhia, Meri Te Tai." *Dictionary of New
Zealand Biography*. Te Ara: The Encyclopedia of New Zealand.
https://teara.govt.nz/en/biographies/2m30/mangakahia-meri-te-tai

Barbara, Julien, and Kerryn Baker. 2016. *Improving the Electoral Chances
of Pacific Women through an Evidence-Based Approach*. Canberra:
Centre for Democratic Institutions and State, Society and Governance in Melanesia Program, Australian National University.

Bargh, Maria. 2010. *Māori and Parliament: Diverse Strategies and Compromises*. Auckland: Huia.

Bean, Clive, and Ian McAllister. 1990. "The Electoral Performance of
Parliamentary Candidates." In *The Greening of Australian Politics: The 1990 Federal Election*, edited by Clive Bean, Ian McAllister, and John Warhurst, 73–91. Melbourne: Longman Cheshire.

Billy, Afu. 2002. "Fighting for a Fair Deal in National Politics." *Development Bulletin* 59: 58–61.

Bolanavanua, Selita. 2018. "My Dress Symbol of Modern Woman: Lynda."
Fiji Sun, November 27, 2018. https://fijisun.com.fj/2018/11/27/my
-dress-symbol-of-modern-woman-lynda/

Celis, Karen, Sarah Childs, and Jennifer Curtin. 2016. "Specialised Parliamentary Bodies and the Quality of Women's Substantive Representation: A Comparative Analysis of Belgium, United Kingdom
and New Zealand." *Parliamentary Affairs* 69 (4): 812–829.

Chisholm, Donna. 2020. "'I Physically Felt Like I Was Going to Die':
Clare Curran Opens Up on Politics, Toxicity and Trauma." The
Spinoff, July 4, 2020. https://thespinoff.co.nz/politics/04-07-2020
/clare-curran-interview-donna-chisholm/

Commonwealth Secretariat. 1999. *Women in Politics: Voices from the Commonwealth*. London: Commonwealth Secretariat.

Cox, John, Ceridwen Spark, and Jack Corbett. 2020. "Being the President: Hilda Heine, Gender and Political Leadership in the Marshall Islands." *Small States and Territories* 3 (2): 339–358.

Crocombe, Ron. 2001. *The South Pacific*. Suva, Fiji: Institute of Pacific Studies.

Curtin, Jennifer. 2008. "Women, Political Leadership and Substantive Representation: The Case of New Zealand." *Parliamentary Affairs* 61 (3): 490–504.

Curtin, Jennifer. 2018. "Jacinda Ardern Makes Motherhood in Politics Normal." *New Zealand Herald*, January 25, 2018. https://www .nzherald.co.nz/nz/news/article.cfm?c_id=1&objectid=11981026

Curtin, Jennifer, and Lara Greaves. 2020. "Gender, Populism and Jacinda Ardern." In *A Populist Exception? The 2017 New Zealand General Election*, edited by Jack Vowles and Jennifer Curtin, 179–212. Canberra: ANU Press.

Dalziel, Raewyn. 2000. "An Experiment in the Social Laboratory? Suffrage, National Identity, and Mythologies of Race in New Zealand in the 1890s." In *Women's Suffrage in the British Empire: Citizenship, Nation and Race*, edited by Ian Christopher Fletcher, Laura E. Nym Mayhall, and Philippa Levine, 87–102. London: Routledge.

Dickson-Waiko, Anne. 2010. *Taking Over, of What and from Whom? Women and Independence, the PNG Experience*. Alfred Deakin Research Institute Working Paper no. 10. Geelong: Deakin University.

Dickson-Waiko, Anne. 2013. "Women, Nation and Decolonisation in Papua New Guinea." *Journal of Pacific History* 48 (2): 177–193.

Dowie, Sarah. 2020. "New Zealand Parliamentary Debates." July 29, 2020. https://www.parliament.nz/en/pb/hansard-debates/rhr/docu ment/HansS_20200729_031320000/dowie-sarah

Evershed, Nick. 2013. "Was Julia Gillard the Most Productive Prime Minister in Australia's History?" *The Guardian*, June 28, 2013.

Francis, Debbie. 2019. *External Independent Review: Bullying and Harassment in the New Zealand Parliamentary Workplace*. Wellington: New Zealand Parliament.

Gibert, Anna. 2020. "Reframing International Development to Respond to COVID-19: Essential Features of Effective Programs in the New Normal." *Developmental Leadership Blog*, June 10, 2020. https:// www.dlprog.org/opinions/reframing-international-development

-to-respond-to-covid-19-essential-features-of-effective-programs
    -in-the-new-normal

Gillard, Julia. 2012. "House of Representatives Debates (C'th)." October,
    9, 2012. https://parlinfo.aph.gov.au/parlInfo/genpdf/chamber/han
    sardr/5a0ebb6b-c6c8-4a92-ac13-219423c2048d/0039/hansard
    _frag.pdf;fileType=application%2Fpdf

Grimshaw, Patricia. 1987. *Women's Suffrage in New Zealand*. Auckland:
    Auckland University Press.

Grimshaw, Patricia. 2009. "Colonialism, Power and Women's Political
    Citizenship in Australia." In *Suffrage, Gender and Citizenship:
    International Perspectives on Parliamentary Reforms*, edited by
    Irma Sulkunen, Seija-Leena Nevala-Nurmi, and Pirjo Markkola,
    34–55. Newcastle upon Tyne: Cambridge Scholars Publishing.

Guttenbeil-Likiliki, Ofa. 2006. "Advancing Women's Representation in
    Tonga." Report 4. In *A Woman's Place Is in the House—The
    House of Parliament: Research to Advance Women's Political
    Representation in Forum Island Countries: A Regional Study Pre-
    sented in Five Reports*, edited by Elise Huffer and Pacific Islands
    Forum Secretariat, 143–208. Suva, Fiji: Pacific Islands Forum
    Secretariat.

Haley, Nicole. 2011. "Results at Any Cost? The Legacy of 2002 in Koroba-
    Lake Kopiago Open Electorate." In *Election 2007: The Shift to
    Limited Preferential Voting in Papua New Guinea*, edited by R. J.
    May, Ray Anere, Nicole Haley, and Katherine Wheen, 347–383.
    Canberra: ANU Press.

Haley, Nicole, and Kerry Zubrinich. 2018. *2017 Papua New Guinea Gen-
    eral Elections: Election Observation Report*. Canberra: Depart-
    ment of Pacific Affairs, Australian National University.

Hannan-Morrow, Samuel, and Michael Roden. 2014. "Gender, Age and
    Generational Effects on Turnout in Australian Federal Elections."
    Australian Political Studies Association Annual Conference, Uni-
    versity of Sydney Paper. http://dx.doi.org/10.2139/ssrn.2440487

Howard, Elise. 2019. "Effective Support for Women's Leadership in the
    Pacific: Lessons from the Evidence." DPA Discussion Paper 2019/1.
    Canberra: Department of Pacific Affairs, Australian National
    University.

IPU (Inter-Parliamentary Union) Parline. 1999. "Archived Data: Women
    in National Parliaments." http://archive.ipu.org/wmn-e/arc/classif
    101199.htm

IPU Parline. 2019. "Archived Data: World and Region Averages." http://archive.ipu.org/wmn-e/world-arc.htm

IPU Parline. 2021. "Global and Regional Averages of Women in National Parliaments." https://data.ipu.org/women-averages

Kaviamu, Mary Jack. 2016. "The Long Journey: Political Acceptance of Women." *Devpolicy Blog*, March 8, 2016. https://devpolicy.org/long-journey-political-acceptance-women-20160308/

Keating, James. 2020. *Distant Sisters: Australasian Women and the International Struggle for the Vote, 1880–1914*. Manchester: Manchester University Press.

Kidu, Carol, and Susan Setae. 2002. "Winning and Losing in Politics: Key Issues in Papua New Guinea." *Development Bulletin* 59: 51–53.

Luscombe, Belinda. 2020. "A Year after Christchurch, Jacinda Ardern Has the World's Attention. How Will She Use It?" *Time*, February 20, 2020.

Lyons, Kate. 2019. "Save Us, Save the World: Pacific Climate Warriors Taking the Fight to the UN." *The Guardian*, September 21, 2019.

Macquoid, Lisa P. 1995. "The Women's Mau: Female Peace Warriors in Western Samoa." Master's thesis, University of Hawai'i. https://scholarspace.manoa.hawaii.edu/server/api/core/bitstreams/57c9ec90-f8e2-4c69-b457-812737507ef4/content

McLeod, Abby. 2015. "Women's Leadership in the Pacific." Developmental Leadership Program, University of Birmingham. https://www.academia.edu/64634791/Women_s_leadership_in_the_Pacific

Meleisea, Leasiolagi Malama, Measina Meredith, Muagututi'a Ioana Chan Mow, Penelope Schoeffel, Semau Ausage Lauano, Hobert Sasa, Ramona Boodoosingh, and Mohammed Sahib. 2015. *Political Representation and Women's Empowerment in Samoa*. Apia: Centre for Samoan Studies, National University of Samoa.

Palmieri, Sonia. 2018. "Gender-Sensitive Parliaments." In *Oxford Research Encyclopedia of Politics*, edited by William Thompson. New York: Oxford University Press.

Palmieri, Sonia, and Kerryn Baker. 2020. "Localising Global Norms: The Case of Family-Friendly Parliaments." *Parliamentary Affairs* 75 (1): 58–75. https://doi.org/10.1093/pa/gsaa050

Palmieri, Sonia, and Diane Zetlin. 2020. "Alternative Strategies to Support Women as Political Actors in the Pacific: Building the House of Peace." *Women's Studies International Forum* 80 (2020). https://doi.org/10.1016/j.wsif.2020.102404

Pohiva, 'Akilisi. 2015. "Inaugural Address of the Prime Minister Hon. Samuela 'Akilisi Pohiva to the Civil Service and the Nation." Nuku'alofa, January 9, 2015.

Sawer, Marian. 2012. "What Makes the Substantive Representation of Women Possible in a Westminster Parliament? The Story of RU486 in Australia." *International Political Science Review* 33 (3): 320–335.

SBS News. 2015. "US Follows Australian Lead on Gender Equality." February 27, 2015. https://www.sbs.com.au/news/us-follows-aust-lead -on-gender-equality

Tuuau, Ali'imalemanu Alofa, and Elise Howard. 2019. "The Long Road to Becoming a Parliamentarian in Samoa: Political Apprenticeship, Learning New Language and Pushing Gender Boundaries." DPA Discussion Paper 2019/04. Canberra: Department of Pacific Affairs, Australian National University.

Vance, Andrea. 2020. "MPs Reach across the House to Ban Female Genital Mutilation." Stuff, July 29, 2020. https://www.stuff.co.nz/national /politics/122286406/mps-reach-across-the-house-to-ban-female -genital-mutilation

Vowles, Jack, Hilda Coffé, and Jennifer Curtin. 2017. *A Bark but No Bite: Inequality and the 2014 New Zealand General Election*. Canberra: ANU Press.

Wall, Louisa, and Jo Hayes. 2019. "Sexism, Harassment and Violence against Women Parliamentarians in New Zealand." *The Parliamentarian* 2: 158–161.

Glossary

A

Aboriginal and Torres Strait Islander peoples—The original peoples or First Nations peoples of mainland Australia and the 274 islands located north of Australia, in the Torres Strait, and their descendants who identify as an Aboriginal or Torres Strait Islander people and are accepted as such by the communities in which they live.

Afrobarometer—a nonprofit company limited by guarantee with head-quarters in Ghana, is a pan-African, nonpartisan survey research network that conducts public attitude surveys on democracy, governance, the economy, and society.

All-women shortlist—An affirmative action policy by which a political party restricts nominations for certain electoral districts to women only.

Aotearoa—The current Māori (Indigenous) name for New Zealand.

Apartheid—South African apartheid refers to a system of institutional segregation on the basis of race in South Africa and now Namibia. This system was in place from 1948 to the early 1990s.

Authoritarianism—Enforcing strict obedience to authority at the expense of personal freedom; refers to nondemocratic regimes without free and fair elections.

Autocratic regimes—Political regimes where supreme political power over all the activities of the state is concentrated in the hands of one person, whose decisions are subject to neither external legal restraints nor regularized mechanisms of popular control (e.g., Egypt, Belarus, Turkey).

Ayatollah—In Shia Islam, a religious title given to those scholars who have demonstrated highly advanced knowledge of Islamic law and religion.

B

Bicameral—A legislature divided into two separate assemblies, chambers, or houses.

Bolsheviks—(From Russian *bolshinstvo*, "majority") Marxist revolutionary faction founded by Vladimir Lenin and Alexander Bogdanov. After forming a party in 1912, the Bolsheviks seized power during the October Revolution of 1917 and subsequently became the only ruling party of the Soviet Union.

Bourgeoisie—The capitalist class in Marxist theory that owns the means of production in a capitalist system.

British protected state—A self-governing country that was placed under the protection of the British government while not becoming an official part of the British Empire.

C

Canton—Member state of the Swiss federation, akin to a state in a federal system.

Ceremonial head of state—Position that is considered a representative of a sovereign nation but most often has very little authority.

Civil rights—Rights of individuals that protect them from discrimination and allow the free exercise of thought, speech, religion, press, movement, and assembly, among others. They also include rights such as owning property, having custody of children, and serving as witness in a trial, all of which at some point excluded women.

Civil society organizations—Citizens that organize for a common goal independently of the state and business. It includes nongovernmental organizations (NGOs), territorial organizations, charities, faith-based organizations, and so on.

Colonizer—The country or empire that settled and established political control over native populations, most notably Great Britain, France, Spain, the Netherlands, and Japan.

Communism—A political and cultural ideology for which goods should be commonly owned and available to those who need them. It often leads to totalitarian systems in which a single party controls state-owned means of production.

Cooperative socialism—A reformist theory that regards cooperation as one of the chief means for the peaceful and gradual transformation of capitalism into socialism. It arose with the development of the cooperative movement and cooperative theories.

Councilor—Elected representative of a municipal ward in Canada.

Coup—A sudden, often violent, illegitimate overthrow of a government (see also *military coup*).

D

Decolonization—The process by which a state becomes independent from its colonizer.

Democratic backsliding—A measured decline in the democratic characteristics of a political system within a state.

Democratic revolution—A revolution in which a democracy is instituted, replacing a previous nondemocratic government, or in which revolutionary change is brought about through democratic means.

Democratic socialism—A political philosophy supporting political democracy within a socially owned economy, with a particular emphasis on economic democracy, workplace democracy, and workers' self-management within a market socialist economy or some form of a decentralized planned socialist economy.

Dictatorship—A form of government with a single or small group of leaders that usually accesses power through nonelectoral means (although an elected leader can turn into a dictator) and where there is little tolerance for political pluralism.

E

Egalitarian culture—A culture in which the equal treatment of men and women is formally recognized and practiced both in laws and attitudes.

European Union (EU)—The political and economic union of twenty-seven states in Europe that was established with the Maastricht Treaty in 1993.

F

Fascism—A political and cultural ideology for which the nation and the race are more important than individuals. Fascism often led to authoritarian regimes through a violent suppression of opposition, most notably Germany's Third Reich, Italy under Mussolini, and Spain under Franco.

Female genital mutilation (FGM)—A nonmedical procedure predominantly conducted in Asia, Africa, and the Middle East during which external female genitalia are fully or partially removed. FGM is usually performed between infancy and age fifteen. FGM can be classified in four different types, depending how much of the clitoral glans, clitoral hood, and the inner and outer labia are removed or sown together. Visit https://www.who.int/news-room/fact-sheets/detail/female-genital-mutilation   for more information.

First minister—See *premier.*

First wave women's movements—The first big process of women's mobilization that took place between the late nineteenth century and early twentieth century, with the main causes being civil rights, access to education, and suffrage.

G

Gender gap—The difference between men and women in levels of electoral participation.

Gender gap (modern)—When women vote for leftist parties more than men; the modern gender gap emerged in the 1970s onward.

Gender gap (traditional)—When women vote for conservative parties more than men. The traditional gender gap can most commonly be observed from enfranchisement until the 1970s.

H

Hegemonic—Ruling or dominant in a political or social context.

House of Assemblies—The legislature or lower house of a bicameral parliament. Historically, in British Crown colonies, as the colony gained more internal responsible government, the House of Assembly superseded the (usually unelected) Legislative Council as the colonial legislature, often becoming the lower house.

I

Identity politics—Organizing politically around an aspect of identity, which may include race, gender, religion, or cultural group, to address shared experiences of historical injustice or oppression.

L

Leader of the opposition—A member of parliament who leads the largest party, or coalition of parties, that is not in government.

M

Māori—The original peoples of Aotearoa New Zealand and their descendants who identify as Māori and are accepted as such by the communities in which they live. Māori also refers to the language spoken by the Māori people.

Military coup—The violent, sudden, and illegitimate overthrow of a government by the military or other branch of the armed forces after taking power by overthrowing a civilian government by force or threat of violence (coup d'état).

Minister—Corresponds to the American position of a cabinet secretary in the rest of the world.

Mixed-member proportional—A system that provides voters with two votes, one for a political party and one for a directly elected representative. Seats in parliament are distributed proportionally in relation to party vote share, with some members entering as directly elected members of parliament and others as party list members of parliament.

Multidimensional poverty—A state of deprivation in not only material wealth but also education, health outcomes, living standards, and economic opportunities.

N

Nation-state—A sovereign country where citizens are alike in regard to religion, culture, language, and so on.

Nongovernmental organization (NGO)—An organization free of government involvement.

O

One-party rule—State system where only one political party forms the government.

P

Pākehā—New Zealanders of European descent.

Partial enfranchisement—The giving of a right or privilege, especially the right to vote, to some sections of the population and excluding others, often through voting requirement laws limiting the right to vote to ethnicity/race, literacy, or marital status.

Patriarch—The male head of the family; also understood more broadly as a male figure exerting authority.

Patronage Politics—Using government resources, appointments, or contracts to reward individual for political loyalty.

Political action committees (PACs)—In the United States, an organization that collects contributions and uses it to campaign for or against political candidates. Different kinds of PACs have different limitations on fundraising and spending.

Populist leader—A leader who uses a polarizing discourse that divides society into a corrupt elite and a virtuous people, where only the leader can truly represent the needs and interests of that people.

Premier—In Canada, the head of government of a province or territory; also known as a first minister.

R

Racialized—To have assigned a minority or a racial status to a person; another way to say person of color.

Revolutionary governments—Governments that reach power through social mobilization and violently overtaking the state, such as Cuba in 1959.

S

Second wave feminism/feminist—A period of feminist activity that began in the United States in the early 1960s and lasted roughly two decades. It quickly spread across the Western world with an aim to increase equality for women by gaining more than just enfranchisement, the focus of first wave feminism. Second wave feminism broadened the debate to include a wider range of issues, such as sexuality, family, the workplace, and reproductive rights.

Semi-presidential system—A political system that is a hybrid of the presidential system and the parliamentary system, with a popularly elected president and a prime minster usually nominated by the president and approved by the parliament.

Sharia—A religious law derived from the Quran and the hadith (a record of the words and actions of Prophet Muhammad).

Socialism—A political and economic theory of social organization that advocates that the means of production, distribution, and exchange should be owned or regulated by the community as a whole.

Socialization—The process through which individuals internalize different norms, values, and habits understood as appropriate to their gender or other social position/identity.

Soviet ("Council")—The legislative body of the Soviet Union that is elected at different levels.

Soviet Union—A socialist state that included eastern Europe and a large part of Asia from 1922 to 1991 under the leadership of Russia, officially known as the Union of Soviet Socialist Republics (USSR).

Speaker of the House—The presiding office over the house. Generally in charge of the bodies proceedings and responsible for the administration of its business.

Sultanate—The hereditary dynasty and lands governed by a Muslim monarch or sultan.

Surrogate proletariat—The Soviet Union's leaders drew parallels between the oppression of the proletariat (working class) under capitalism and the oppression of women under patriarchy, arguing that women are natural allies in the struggle for communism.

Symbolic representation—The representation of a principal, group, or nation-state through an object or figurehead to which meaning is attached.

T

Taliban—A Sunni Islamic fundamental political movement and a military organization mainly operating in Afghanistan and Pakistan. It is strictly against any role of women outside the household.

Te Kotahitanga—An autonomous Māori Parliament active from 1892 until 1902.

Third Reich—Authoritarian/fascist regime in Germany from 1933 until 1945 in which power was held by Adolf Hitler and the Nazi Party.

Third wave of democratization—A term coined by political scientist Samuel Huntington, who identified three global waves of the expansion of democracy. The third wave started in the late 1970s.

U

Universal suffrage—The right to vote and stand for election of all adult citizens, regardless of wealth, income, gender, social status, race, ethnicity, political stance, or any other restriction, subject only to relatively minor exceptions.

W

Weimar Republic—Federal constitutional republic in Germany from 1918 until 1933.

Welfare state—A type of state organization in which the government provides basic economic security and social and medical assistance to its citizens.

Bibliography

ONLINE RESOURCES

Center for American Women in Politics (CAWP)

CAWP is part of the Eagleton Institute of Politics at Rutgers University and is the flagship center for everything related to women and politics in the United States. CAWP maintains an extensive database stretching back years that takes stock of women running and being elected to local, state, and national office. CAWP's website also features a searchable database for research on women in U.S. politics. Key publications include the following:

1. Carroll, Susan J., and Kira Sanbonmatsu. 2013. *More Women Can Run: Gender and Pathways to the State Legislatures.* New York: Oxford University Press.

2. Carroll, Susan J., Richard L. Fox, and Kelly Dittmar. 2021. *Gender and Elections: Shaping the Future of American Politics.* Cambridge: Cambridge University Press.

3. CAWP (Center for American Women and Politics). n.d. "Facts." https://cawp.rutgers.edu/facts

European Institute for Gender Equality (EIGE)

https://eige.europa.eu

An independent body of the European Union, EIGE's mission is to support and contribute to the promotion of gender equality in EU policies. The Gender Equality Index ranks each EU member country based on six core domains: work, money, knowledge, time, power, and health.

The Gender Statistic Database features a wealth of data on all kinds of topics related to gender, including women and men in decision-making.

European Women's Lobby—European des Femmes
https://www.womenlobby.org/Women-in-Decision-Making-454?lang=en
The European Women's Lobby provides a wealth of resources and information on women in decision-making in the European Union, including news, videos, data, and reports.

iKNOW Politics—The International Knowledge Network of Women in Politics
https://www.iknowpolitics.org/en
The iKNOW Politics platform is dedicated to promoting women in politics by sharing knowledge, best practices, and other relevant information on elections, parliaments, representatives, political parties, women's leadership, and advocacy and lobbying. The library includes a wealth of resources, including interviews with key stakeholders, videos, online courses, and webinars—all available for free.

International Institute for Democracy and Electoral Assistance (IDEA)—Gender Equality and Inclusion in Democracy
https://www.idea.int/our-work/what-we-do/gender-democracy
IDEA actively promotes gender inclusion and equality in democracy building around the world. Information and research on women and politics can be accessed through its publications, databases, tools, and portals.
    Key publications include the following:

1. *Atlas of Electoral Gender Quotas*, published in 2014. https://www.idea
    .int/publications/catalogue/atlas-electoral-gender-quotas?lang=en

2. *Designing for Equality*, published in 2007. https://www.idea.int/publi
    cations/catalogue/designing-equality-best-fit-medium-fit-and-non
    -favourable-combinations?lang=en

3. *Women in Parliament: Beyond Numbers*, published in 2005. https://
    www.idea.int/publications/catalogue/women-parliament-beyond-num
    bers-revised-edition?lang=en

Inter-Parliamentary Union (IPU)—Women and Politics Knowledge Hub
https://www.ipu.org/our-impact/gender-equality/women-in-parliament
/ipu-knowledge-hub-women-in-politics
The IPU is one of the most essential sources for women and politics. The IPU website provides research and information on women in

parliaments, women Speakers of parliament, gender-sensitive parliaments, women's parliamentary caucuses, and women's rights. IPU is also the home to the database on women in politics and the global database on gender electoral quotas.

SELECTED MOVIES, TV SERIES, AND DOCUMENTARIES

1. *Madam Secretary* (2014–2019), created by Barbara Hall, produced by CBS Television.
2. *Pray the Devil Back to Hell* (2008), Fork Films, directed by Gini Retiker. https://www.forkfilms.com/pray-the-devil-back-to-hell/#_about
3. *Mrs. President: Women and Political Leadership in Iran* (2002), Films Media Group, produced by Shahla Haeri. https://ffh.films.com /id/4826/Mrs_President_Women_and_Political_Leadership_in_Iran .htm
4. *Why Aren't More Women in Politics?* (2021), DW documentary. https://www.dw.com/en/a-mans-world-why-arent-more-women-in -politics/av-58958915
5. *Chisholm '72: Unbought & Unbossed* (2004), Sundance, directed by Shola Lynch.
6. *Women, War, and Peace* (2011), coproduced by THIRTEEN and Fork Films, created by Abigail E. Disney, Pamela Hogan, and Gini Reticker. https://www.pbs.org/wnet/women-war-and-peace/
7. *Ms Represented with Annabel Crabb* (2021), written and created by Annabel Crabb, produced by IVIEW. https://iview.abc.net.au/show/ms -represented-with-annabel-crabb
8. *Strong Female Lead* (2021), Northern Pictures, directed by Tosca Looby. https://www.strongfemalelead.com.au/

SELECTED PODCASTS

1. *No Second Chances*, produced by Canada 2020, podcast (2020–2022). https://nosecondchances.ca/season-one/the-podcast/
2. *A Podcast of One's Own with Julia Gillard*, produced by Global Institute for Women's Leadership, podcast (2019–current). https://giwl.anu .edu.au/podcast-ones-own-julia-gillard

3. *Merkel's Last Dance*, produced by Deutsche Welle, podcast (2020). https://www.dw.com/en/politics-podcast-merkels-last-dance/a-54872007

4. *Women in Politics in Papua New Guinea*, produced by LOWY Institute, podcast (2022). https://www.lowyinstitute.org/publications/aus-png-network-podcast-series-women-politics-png

5. Hilda Weyne, "Pacific Women in Politics," June 11, 2021, in *Sista's, Let's Talk*, produced by ABC Radio Australia, 30:00, podcast. https://www.abc.net.au/pacific/programs/sistas-lets-talk/sistas,-lets-talk/13375574

6. *Ms Represented*, produced by ABC Radio Australia, podcast (since 2021). https://www.abc.net.au/radio/programs/ms-represented/

7. Annabelle Quince and Keri Phillips, "Samoa—A Bumpy Ride for the First Female Prime Minister," October 31, 2021, in *Rear Vision*, produced by ABC Radio Australia, 29:11, podcast. https://www.abc.net.au/radionational/programs/rearvision/samoa/13603992

8. Annabelle Quince and Keri Phillips, "The Political Swamp—Poisonous for Women," April 4, 2021, in *Rear Vision*, produced by ABC Radio Australia, 29:04, podcast. https://www.abc.net.au/radionational/programs/rearvision/the-political-swamp%E2%80%94poisonous-for-women/13281440

9. *Womanica*, produced by Encyclopedia Womanica, podcast (2022). https://encyclopedia-womannica.simplecast.com

FURTHER READING

Alexander, Amy C., Catherine Bolzendahl, and Farida Jalalzai. 2017. *Measuring Women's Political Empowerment across the Globe: Strategies, Challenges and Future Research*. Cham, Switzerland: Springer.

Alston, Margaret, ed. 2014. *Women, Political Struggles and Gender Equality in South Asia*. Cham, Switzerland: Springer.

Annesley, Claire, Karen Beckwith, and Susan Franceschet. 2019. *Cabinets, Ministers, and Gender*. Oxford: Oxford University Press.

Arriola, Leonardo, Martha Johnson, and Melanie Phillips. 2021. *Women and Power in Africa: Aspiring, Campaigning, and Governing*. Oxford: Oxford University Press.

Baker, Kerryn. 2019. *Pacific Women in Politics: Gender Quota Campaigns in the Pacific Islands*. Honolulu: University of Hawai'i Press.

Banks, Julia. 2021. *Power Play: Breaking through Bias, Barriers and Boy's Clubs*. Melbourne: Hardie Grant Books.

Bjarnegård, E. 2013. *Gender, Informal Institutions and Political Recruitment: Explaining Male Dominance in Parliamentary Representation*. Cham, Switzerland: Springer.

Blackburn, Susan, and Helen Ting, eds. 2013. *Women in Southeast Asian Nationalist Movements*. Singapore: National University of Singapore Press.

Ceridwen, Spark, John Cox, and Jack Corbett. 2018. *Being the First: Women Leaders in the Pacific Islands*. Birmingham, Australia: Developmental Leadership Program.

Clark, Helen. 2018. *Women, Equality, Power: Selected Speeches from a Life of Leadership*. Auckland, NZ: Allen & Unwin.

Dahlerup, Drude. 2017. *Has Democracy Failed Women?* New York: John Wiley & Sons.

Dalton, Emma. 2015. *Women and Politics in Contemporary Japan*. New York: Routledge.

Darhour, Hanane, and Drude Dahlerup, eds. 2019. *Double-Edged Politics on Women's Rights in the MENA Region*. 1st ed. Gender and Politics. Cham, Switzerland: Springer Nature.

Derichs, Claudia, and Mark R. Thompson, eds. 2013. *Dynasties and Female Political Leaders in Asia: Gender, Power and Pedigree*. Berlin: Lit Verlag.

Devasahayam, Theresa, ed. 2019. *Women and Politics in Southeast Asia: Navigating a Man's World*. East Sussex, UK: Sussex Academic Press.

Echle, Christian, and Megha Sarmah, eds. 2020. "Women, Policy and Political Leadership: Regional Perspectives." Singapore: Konrad Adenauer Stiftung.

Ellis, Kate. 2021. *Sex, Lies and Question Time: Why the Success and Struggles of Women in Australia's Parliament Matter to Us All*. Melbourne: Hardie Grant Books.

Escobar-Lemmon, Maria C., and Michelle M. Taylor-Robinson. 2014. *Representation: The Case of Women*. Oxford: Oxford University Press.

Fleschenberg, Andrea, and Claudia Derichs, eds. 2011. *Women and Politics in Asia: A Springboard for Democracy*. Zurich: Lit Verlag.

Franceschet, Susan, Mona Lena Krook, and Jennifer M. Piscopo, eds. 2012. *The Impact of Gender Quotas*. Oxford: Oxford University Press.

Franceschet, Susan, Mona Lena Krook, and Netina Tan, eds. 2019. *The Palgrave Handbook of Women's Political Rights*. London: Palgrave Macmillan UK.

Gillard, Julia. 2014. *My Story*. Sydney: Random House.

Gillard, Julia, and Ngozi Okonjo-Iweala. 2022. *Women and Leadership: Real Lives, Real Lessons*. Cambridge, MA: MIT Press.

Goodyear-Grant, E. 2013. *Gendered News: Media Coverage and Electoral Politics in Canada*. Vancouver, BC: UBC Press.

Henderson, Sarah, and Alana S. Jeydel. 2014. *Women and Politics in a Global World*. Oxford: Oxford University Press.

Hinojosa, Magda. 2012. *Selecting Women, Electing Women: Political Representation and Candidate Selection in Latin America*. Philadelphia: Temple University Press.

Hinojosa, Magda, and Miki Caul Kittilson. 2020. *Seeing Women, Strengthening Democracy: How Women in Politics Foster Connected Citizens*. Oxford: Oxford University Press.

Inglehart, Ronald, and Pippa Norris. 2003. *Rising Tide: Gender Equality and Cultural Change around the World*. Cambridge: Cambridge University Press.

Iwanaga, Kazuki, ed. 2008. *Women's Political Participation and Representation in Asia: Obstacles and Challenges*. Copenhagen: NIAS Press.

Jacobsen, Trudy. 2008. *Lost Goddesses: The Denial of Female Power in Cambodian History*. Copenhagen: Nordic Institute of Asian Studies.

Jalalzai, Farida. 2013. *Shattered, Cracked, or Firmly Intact? Women and the Executive Glass Ceiling Worldwide*. Oxford: Oxford University Press.

Jalalzai, Farida. 2015. *Women Presidents of Latin America: Beyond Family Ties?* New York: Routledge.

Joseph, Suad, and Susan Slyomovics. 2011. *Women and Power in the Middle East*. Philadelphia: University of Pennsylvania Press.

Kamp, Marianne. 2006. *The New Woman in Uzbekistan: Islam, Modernity and Unveiling under Communism*. Seattle and London: Washington University Press.

Koh, Adeline, and Yu-Mei Balasingamchow. 2015. *Women and the Politics of Representation in Southeast Asia: Engendering Discourse in Singapore and Malaysia*. New York: Routledge.

Krook, Mona Lena. 2020. *Violence against Women in Politics.* 1st ed. Oxford: Oxford University Press.

Krook, Mona Lena, and Sarah Childs. 2010. *Women, Gender, and Politics: A Reader.* Oxford: Oxford University Press.

Lanzona, Vina A. 2009. *Amazons of the Huk Rebellion: Gender, Sex, and Revolution in the Philippines.* Madison: University of Wisconsin Press.

Madsen, Diana Højlund. 2020. *Gendered Institutions and Women's Political Representation in Africa.* London: Bloomsbury Publishing.

Och, Malliga, and Shauna L. Shames. 2018. *The Right Women: Republican Party Activists, Candidates, and Legislators.* Santa Barbara, CA: ABC-CLIO.

Osori, Ayisha. 2017. *Love Does Not Win Elections.* Lagos, Nigeria: Narrative Landscape Press.

Paxton, Pamela Marie, Melanie M. Hughes, and Tiffany Barnes. 2020. *Women, Politics, and Power: A Global Perspective.* Lanham, MD: Rowman & Littlefield.

Political Parity. 2015. *Research Inventory.* https://www.politicalparity.org/research/research-inventory/

Political Parity. 2018. *Path to Parity: How Women Run and Win.* https://www.politicalparity.org/research/path-to-parity-how-women-run-and-win/

Rosser-Mims, Dionne, Janet R. McNellis, Juanita Johnson-Bailey, and Chrys Egan. 2020. *Pathways into the Political Arena: The Perspectives of Global Women Leaders.* Charlotte, NC: IAP.

Santos, Pedro A. G. dos, and Farida Jalalzai. 2021. *Women's Empowerment and Disempowerment in Brazil: The Rise and Fall of President Dilma Rousseff.* Philadelphia: Temple University Press.

Sawer, Marian, Lee Ann Banaszak, Jacqui True, and Johanna Kantola, eds. 2022. *Handbook on Feminist Governance.* Cheltenham, UK: Edward Elgar.

Sawer, Marian, Manon Tremblay, and Linda Trimble. 2006. *Representing Women in Parliament: A Comparative Study.* New York: Routledge.

Sirleaf, Ellen Johnson. 2009. *This Child Will Be Great: Memoir of a Remarkable Life by Africa's First Woman President.* New York: HarperCollins.

Tadros, Mariz. 2014. *Women in Politics: Gender, Power and Development.* London: Zed Books Ltd.

Tadros, Mariz. 2016. *Resistance, Revolt, and Gender Justice in Egypt.* Syracuse, NY: Syracuse University Press.

Tolley, E. 2015. *Framed: Media and the Coverage of Race in Canadian Politics.* Vancouver, BC: UBC Press.

Trimble, L. 2018. *Ms. Prime Minister: Gender, Media, and Leadership.* Toronto: University of Toronto Press.

Trimble, L., J. Arscott, and M. Tremblay, eds. 2013. *Stalled: The Representation of Women in Canadian Governments.* Vancouver, BC: UBC Press.

Tripp, Aili Mari. 2015. *Women and Power in Post-Conflict Africa.* Cambridge: Cambridge University Press.

Wängnerud, Lena. 2015. *The Principles of Gender-Sensitive Parliaments.* New York: Routledge.

Waylen, Georgina, Karen Celis, Johanna Kantola, and S. Laurel Weldon. 2013. *The Oxford Handbook of Gender and Politics.* 1st ed. Oxford: Oxford University Press.

Wolbrecht, Christina, and J. Kevin Corder. 2020. *A Century of Votes for Women: American Elections since Suffrage.* Cambridge: Cambridge University Press.

Young, L. 2000. *Feminists and Party Politics.* Vol. 52. Vancouver, BC: UBC Press.

About the Editor and Contributors

THE EDITOR

MALLIGA OCH is an associate professor at Idaho State University, where she teaches classes on European and Asian politics, gender and international relations, and human rights. An expert on women and politics, her research mainly focuses on women in conservative parties. Her work has been published in academic journals such as *Politics & Gender, Parliamentary Affairs,* and *Politics, Groups, and Identities* as well as in media outlets in Germany, Australia, and the United States.

THE CONTRIBUTORS

ZAINAB ALAM is an assistant professor in the Department of Political Science at Howard University. She earned her PhD in political science at Rutgers University in 2021, where she also directed the Douglass Public Leadership Education Network. She holds an MS in Global Affairs from New York University and has local and international work experience in the nonprofit sector. Through a multi-modal approach, including content, text, and critical discourse analysis, participant observation, as well as social media analysis, her current research agenda focuses on participatory democracy and the digital divide in South Asia.

SARELLE AZUELOS is a master's student in gender studies at Memorial University of Newfoundland (MUN). She has a history degree from the University of Calgary and a background in community engagement and advocacy work on social justice issues in Alberta. She is researching the integration of an intersectional gender lens on public policy development using feminist research practices. She is the lab manager for the Gender and Politics Research Lab at MUN.

KERRYN BAKER is a fellow with the Department of Pacific Affairs, the Australian National University. She holds a PhD in political science, and her research on gender, politics and participation has been widely published. She is the author of *Pacific Women in Politics: Gender Quota Campaigns in the Pacific Islands* (2019) and the coeditor (with Marian Sawer) of *Gender Innovation in Political Science: New Norms, New Knowledge* (2019).

AMANDA BITTNER is a professor in the Department of Political Science at Memorial University, where she also founded and directs the Gender and Politics Lab. She studies elections and voting and has published on a wide variety of topics, including voters' evaluations of party leaders and the effects of those evaluations on vote choice, voters' attitudes about women in politics, the role of parenthood in politics, and the measurement of gender in survey research.

ISABEL CASTILLO is an assistant professor in the Faculty of Government, Universidad de Chile and an adjunct researcher at the Center for Social Conflict and Cohesion Studies (COES). She holds a PhD in political science from Northwestern University. Her dissertation on women's suffrage was cowinner of APSA's Women, Gender and Politics Section Best Dissertation Award in 2020. Her current research projects address issues of historical democratization, women in politics, and the role of religious actors in politics, with a focus in Latin America.

MICHELA CELLA is an associate professor of economics at the University of Milano-Bicocca in Italy. She obtained a PhD from the London School of Economics in the United Kingdom. She began her academic career at the University of Essex (UK) and then moved to the University of Oxford and Nuffield College. She returned to Italy in 2005. She has a theoretical background in microeconomics, but in the last few years, her research interests have moved to political economy and gender issues.

RYAN GOEHRUNG is a PhD candidate in political science at the University of Washington. His research centers on diversity, equity, and inclusion in political institutions, with a particular emphasis on gender and representation and a regional specialization in Southeast Asia. He also holds an MA in International Development from the Josef Korbel School of International Studies and continually strives to produce research that is relevant for development policy and practice, particularly on topics related to human trafficking, migration, and global inequality.

MICHAELA GRANČAYOVÁ is a PhD student at the Faculty of Social and Economic Sciences of Comenius University in Bratislava, Slovakia. In 2015, she graduated from the Faculty of Arts of Comenius University in Bratislava, where she studied English and Arabic. During her studies, she took part in study stays in Cairo, Egypt (Ain Shams University), and Qazvin, Iran (Imam Khomeini International University). In her PhD thesis, she focuses on the role of Egyptian women in the democratization processes within the Arab Spring. Her topics of interest include the Arab Spring, Arab feminism, Egypt, Arabic diglossia, modern trends in Islam, radicalism, and Muslim women in European politics.

ELISE HOWARD is a senior research officer and PhD candidate at the Department of Pacific Affairs, the Australian National University. She is undertaking a research agenda in relation to the gendered aspects of women's leadership in the Pacific in the context of contemporary challenges such as politics and climate change. She has published theoretical pieces on women's leadership as well as first-person stories of women and their reflections on their leadership experiences.

CHANG-LING HUANG is a professor of political science at the National Taiwan University. Her research interests are women's political representation and state feminism. Her works have appeared in various Chinese and English journals, including *Developing Economies*, *Politics & Gender*, and *Pacific Affairs*, and she is a contributor to many edited volumes. She has authored chapters for handbooks such as the *Routledge Handbook of Democratization in East Asia* and the *Palgrave Handbook of Women's Political Rights*. She is a recipient of the Radcliffe Fellowship of Harvard University and the Outstanding Teaching Award and Outstanding Social Service Award of the National Taiwan University.

MARTHA C. JOHNSON is a visiting associate professor of government at Dartmouth College and an associate professor of political science at Mills College. She studies women's representation in executive cabinets and local office in sub-Saharan Africa, with a regional focus on Francophone West Africa.

KRYSTOFF KISSOON is a national of Trinidad and Tobago and has a Doctor of Arts in political science from Idaho State University. His research focuses on gender and sexuality in the Caribbean, and he has presented papers at academic conferences such as the Midwest Political Science Association Conference. He was the producer and host of the weekly program *Navigating Diversity* on KISU-FM and won Best Public Affairs Program in the student division of the 2020 Idaho Press Club Awards.

ELENA MANZONI is an assistant professor of economics at the University of Bergamo. She obtained a PhD from the London School of Economics in the United Kingdom. She began her academic career at Bocconi University and moved to the University of Milano-Bicocca in Italy. Her research interests include political economy and gender issues as well as psychological game theory.

SONIA PALMIERI is a gender policy fellow with the Department of Pacific Affairs, The Australian National University. As an academic practitioner, she has worked in both the university sector and development and parliamentary organizations to support women's political leadership and participation. She has driven the international research agenda on gender-sensitive parliaments and has engaged with current and aspiring women in politics in Africa, Asia, the Caribbean, and, most prominently, the Pacific.

MELANIE L. PHILLIPS is a PhD candidate in the Department of Political Science at the University of California, Berkeley. Her research examines how women's political representation in African countries is shaped by the intersection between the rules governing candidate selection and the norms associated with gendered family roles.

ESTHER SOMFALVY, PhD, is a research fellow at the Research Centre for East European Studies at the University of Bremen. Her research interests include comparative authoritarianism, political institutions (e.g., parliaments, elections), and media. She recently published a book titled

Parliamentary Representation in Central Asia: MPs between Representing Their Voters and Serving an Authoritarian Regime (2021).

CATHERINE WINEINGER, PhD, is an assistant professor of political science at Western Washington University. She earned her PhD from Rutgers University, where she was also a graduate research assistant at the Center for American Women and Politics. She is a cowinner of the APSA Women, Gender, and Politics Research Section's 2020 Best Dissertation Award. Her first book, *Gendering the GOP: Intraparty Politics and Republican Women's Representation in Congress*, was published in 2022.

Index

Page numbers followed by *t* indicate tables and *f* indicate figures.

Lightning Source UK Ltd.
Milton Keynes UK
UKHW022009280223
417828UK00006B/90